PINK GUITAR

THE

The Pink Guitar is as much a work of art as a book of feminist criticism. Noted critic and poet Rachel Blau DuPlessis here fuses meditation and passion, an extensive critical understanding of modernism, and the intensive rhythms of art.

DuPlessis is concerned with the depiction of women and the uses to which culture has put the female figure; at the same time she asks how a woman artist can make a place for herself among these gender-intensive representations. She treats the work of William Carlos Williams and Marcel Duchamp as paradigmatic of the most innovative of male modernists, finding their tactics compromised by their gender ideologies, which she explores with nuance.

DuPlessis turns to a number of modern and contemporary women writers (notably H.D. and Virginia Woolf, as well as Susan Howe and Beverly Dahlen) to explore the possibilities of finding a language, and a set of cultural stances, which would rupture the most deeply held assumptions about gender. The whole tradition of the writing of poetry and fiction DuPlessis argues, has colonized female figures, yet women writers have considerable force: the woman writer is a power in her own work, but an artifact in the traditions of meaning on which she draws. Making of representation itself a site of struggle, DuPlessis's own porous, self-questioning text presents itself as an example of the cultural disturbance she evokes.

The Pink Guitar includes the influential and moving essay "For the Etruscans," along with other work on the gendering of writing practices.

RACHEL BLAU DUPLESSIS is Professor of English at Temple University. She is the author of *Writing Beyond the Ending: Narrative Strategies of Twentieth Century Women Writers*, and *H.D.: The Career of That Struggle*.

Contents

ACKNOWLEDGMENTS
vii

FOR THE ETRUSCANS
1

FAMILY, SEXES, PSYCHE:
An essay on H.D. and the
Muse of the Woman Writer
20

PATER-DAUGHTER:
Male Modernists and
Female Readers
41

SUB RROSA:
Marcel Duchamp and the
Female Spectator
68

LANGUAGE ACQUISITION
83

"WHILE THESE LETTERS
WERE A-READING":
An Essay on Beverly Dahlen's
A Reading
110

"WHOWE":
On Susan Howe
123

OTHERHOW
140

THE PINK GUITAR:
157

NOTES
175

INDEX
195

Acknowledgments

Unlike most collectors of their essays, I have chosen to revise a number of the works in this book. I expanded them, mainly in the summer of 1989, and mainly by the addition of related material written contemporaneously with each essay.

I began to write essays, with an abrupt startled need, in 1978; the first was "Psyche, or Wholeness" (*The Massachusetts Review* 20,1; not collected here) in which elements of guarded, yet frank autobiography, textual analysis, and revisionary myth-making suddenly fused into a demanding voice, with a mix of ecstatic power over cultural materials and mourning for the place of the female in culture. The multiple pressures of living out feminist thinking led me again and again to this non-objective, polyvocal prose, whose writing I experienced as the most pleasure when it became most speculative and most uncontainable, most meditative and most passionate. I began to take as talismanic those essays by Robert Duncan, H.D., Virginia Woolf, and Adrienne Rich in an Anglo-American tradition, and Roland Barthes, Hélène Cixous and Luce Irigaray, in a translated tradition, in which I experienced the same analytic passion and emotional commitment to cultural change. In fact, I secretly appropriated for my own Woolf's statement of 1940 calling for "a new critical method," both "colloquial and yet intense," with the swiftness and lightness of a "sketch" but really "a finished work." That's it, I said; that's it.

Essays have always offered space. Far from *belles lettres*, I wanted these essays to claim a larger and angrier space while remaining lambent and evocative works of art: taking a position of positive negation, I would rather see them be *lettres laides*. It would only be a matter of critical courtesy to other positions to call this voice or mode of writing "feminine"; it seems, rather, to tunnel under and criss-cross gender distinctions in part by evoking gender materials so stubbornly. But—the works do play among female, "feminine" and feminist. If the majority of our cultural depictions of women in fiction, poetry, philosophy, visual art, and religious discourse have colonized female figures, yet if women writers have (as they must) some measure of force and agency, this bi-focal subject/object position creates a staggering and fascinating problem for the woman writer, who is a power in her own work, but an artifact in most of the traditions of meaning on which she draws. The essays turn and return to this cultural situation as their ground.

In these works, I often challenged the sustaining fiction of objectivity, distance, and neutrality in critical studies; a writer has to need what s/he writes, and to need it in ways that implicate other people. If not, why bother? Essays offered freedom for speculation, for voices, for innovative structures, for inter-generic, experimentalist modes, all of which were, to me, crucial to the feminist project. For the level of cultural rupture one must seek cuts to the deepest assumptions of plot, of voice, of closure, of meaning, of languages, of authorities in the author and the reader. While content and theme have been sites of cultural change in recent years, where the representations of women are concerned, a naturalized set of language strategies, or nice, normal presentations of material seemed to partake of the same assumptions about gender that they would claim to undermine. So it has seemed crucial for feminist writing to reexamine and claim the innovative writing strategies for which our century is noted, turning collage, heteroglossia, intergenres, and self-reflexivity (to name just some) to our uses. Hence, in these works criticism and representation of thought is itself a site of struggle, and these works were, from their inception, examples of the cultural disturbance I evoked.

Because of the suspicion with which these works were, at certain times, regarded, I am more deeply indebted than I can say to the heterogeneous listeners who provided empathetic and intelligent understandings of this mode. Among these were Beverly Dahlen, Robert Duncan, Lee Edwards, Kathleen Fraser, Susan Stanford Friedman, Margaret Homans, Frances Jaffer, Kathleen Martindale, Adalaide Morris, Alicia Ostriker, Sherman Paul, Elaine Showalter, Catharine Stimpson, Jane Tompkins, and Eliot Weinberger. I am quite grateful as well to Bill Germano for the honor of publication, and for debates over "a" and "the."

"For the Etruscans" is a shortened and revised version of what was said mainly, but not exclusively, by me concerning the possibilities of a "female aesthetic" at Workshop 9 of the Barnard College Scholar and Feminist Conference in 1979, and what was published in *The Future of Difference*, eds. Hester Eisenstein and Alice Jardine (Boston: G. K. Hall, 1980). For this text, I have also drawn on the version written for delivery at SUNY-Buffalo early in 1980. I have avoided the anachronistic temptation to alter opinions or to respond to commentary on the work, though I have updated (1984) some of the notes.

"Family, Sexes, Psyche: An Essay on H.D. and the Muse of the Woman Writer" was originally published in *Montemora* 6 (1979), ed. Eliot Weinberger; its notes were slightly revised (1984) for inclusion in the volume *H.D.: Woman and Poet*, ed. Michael King (Orono: National Poetry Foundation, 1986); the latter version is published here.

"*Pater*-daughter: Male Modernists and Female Readers" was commissioned by Bruce Boone for the New Critical Perspectives issue of *Soup* 4 (1984). It was considerably revised and lengthened in May–June 1989, in part by the addition of materials from my paper for the Modern Language Association Conference of December 1984 called "Modernism: Agendas and Genders."

"Sub Rrosa: Marcel Duchamp and the Female Spectator" appeared in *Sulfur* 21 (Winter 1988), ed. Clayton Eshleman; it was expanded for inclusion here.

"Language Acquisition," written in 1985, was commissioned by Adalaide Morris as guest editor, for the special H.D. Centennial issue of *The Iowa Review* 16, 3 (1987).

"While These Letters Were A-reading: An Essay on Beverly Dahlen's *A Reading*" was requested by Michael Cuddihy for a special section on Dahlen's work in *Ironwood* 27 (Spring 1986); it was revised for inclusion here.

" 'Whowe': On Susan Howe" was reamalgamated, with new observations, from writing on Howe published in *HOW(ever)* 1, 4 (May 1984), ed. Kathleen Fraser, and in *Sulfur* 20 (1987), ed. Clayton Eshleman.

The essays on Dahlen and Howe are meant to signal the innovative work in poetry, essay, fiction, and intergeneric forms by numerous contemporary U.S. women writers; while I feel particularly affected by the two writers whose work I chose here, I could with equal justice have focused upon Kathleen Fraser, Carla Harryman, Lyn Hejinian, Fanny Howe, Bernadette Meyer, Rosmarie Waldrop, Hannah Weiner, and still others, each of whom has a significant oeuvre. And, of slightly earlier writers, an essay on Lorine Niedecker remained unwritten.

"Otherhow" was originally written for a panel in June 1985 at St. Mark's Poetry Project organized by Charles Bernstein. It appeared in *Sulfur* 14 (1985) and was revised by the addition of materials from other public appearances and panels—at the MLA in 1980, at Langton Street, San Francisco in 1985, at Eastern Michigan University 1988, and at St. Mark's again, 1988.

"The Pink Guitar: Writing as Feminist Practice" was written in 1989 for inclusion in this volume.

They said, "You have a blue guitar,
You do not play things as they are."

The man replied, "Things as they are
Are changed upon the blue guitar."

Wallace Stevens,
"The Man with the Blue Guitar"

FOR THE ETRUSCANS

Thinking smugly, "She shouldn't be working on Woolf." 1964. "Doesn't she know that she'd better not work on a woman?" Why was I lucky to know this. What was the threat? Dickinson? Marginality? Nin? I bought Nin's book, I threw it out. What! Didn't want it, might confront

> The great difficulties in understanding the language . . . not . . . from an inability to read the script, every letter of which is now clearly understood. It is as if books were discovered, printed in our own Roman letters, so that one could articulate the words without trouble, but written in an unknown language with no known parallels.[1]

myself. 1979. The general feeling (of the dream) was that I was free of the testers. However, I was entirely obligated to take and pass their test. My relationship to the testers is——? 1965. My big ambition, my hemmed and nervous space. Her uncompromising, oracular poems. Her fluid, decisive writing. Her dream life, surfacing. Not even to read this? to read with contempt? "This is a Blossom of the Brain———/ A small——italic Seed" (Dickinson, no. 945).

What is going on here? 1968. Is the female aesthetic simply an (1978) enabling myth? Fish on one foot, hook on the other, angling for ourselves. Woolf: catching "something about the body."[2] Crash. MOM! WHAT! "You never buy what I like! Only what YOU like! (Fig Newtons.)

A golden bough. The torch is passed on. His son clutches his hand, his crippled father clings to his back, three male generations leave the burning city. The wife, lost. Got lost in burning. No one knows what happened to her, when they became the Romans.

1

She became the Etruscans?

> Even so, there is nothing to prevent those with a special apti-
> tude for cryptography from tackling Etruscan, which is the last
> of the important languages to require translating.[3]

Sheepish, I am sheepish and embarrassed to mention this

that for me it was always the herding. The herding, the bonding, the
way you can speak their language but also have a language or different
needs so hard to say this. Always: I have heard this story from many
sources—they bond and clump outside your door and never "ask you
to lunch" or they talk and be wonderful, lambent, but when you walk
up "they turn away" or "they turn on you, teasing, making sexual
jokes"

all headed in the same direction, herding and glistening, of course some
don't. But it has been difficult for these to separate from the rest.
Probably the reward system?

To translate ourselves from our disguises. The enthralled sexuality, the
knife-edge brilliance, the intellectual dowdiness, evasions, embarrass-
ments, imprecisions, deferments; smug primness with which there is
no dialogue. Combativeness straight into malice. Invisibility, visibility,
crossing the legs, uncrossing them. Knights in shining amour. Daddy
to the rescue. "Imposing" sex on the situation. "Not imposing" "sex"
on the "situation." "Doesn't she know she'd better not work on a
woman?" She'd better now work on a woman. "I bid you take a wisp
from the wool of their precious fleece."[4] The golden fleece. The golden
bough. The female quest?

Frankly, it was *The Golden Notebook* (1966). Which pierced my heart
with its two-headed arrow.

How to be? How to be-have? I remember one preceptor who brought
her little white dog to school and trotted it up and down the fourth
floor of Hamilton Hall. What delightful, charming, adorable girls! The
temptation of Eve was fruit, of Mary, lambs. Thinking that they followed *you* to school.

It is, after all, always the meaning, the reading of difference that matters,
and meaning is culturally engendered and sustained. Not to consider
the body as some absolute (milk, blood, breasts, clitoris) for no "body"

is unmediated. Not body but the "body" of psychosocial fabrications of difference. Or again, of sameness. Or again, of their relation. The contexts of which are formed and reinforced gendered human beings, produced in the family, in institutions of gender development, in the forms of sexual preference, in the division of labor by gender, especially the structure of infant care, in the class and conditions of the families in which we are psychologically born, and in the social maintenance of the sexes through life's stages and in any historical era.[5] And as such, these differing experiences do surely produce (some) different consciousnesses, different cultural expression, different relations to realms of symbols and symbol users. Different "language," metaphorical; different uses of the grammatical and expressive resources of language (verb parts, questions, and intonation, pronouns).

> *Stein says we no longer have the words people used to have so we have to make them new in some way but women haven't had them at all and how can you deconstruct a language you never constructed or it was never constructed by others like you, or with you in mind?*[6]
>
> Frances Jaffer

And therefore there is female aesthetic, but not *a* female aesthetic, not one single constellation of strategies.

I am watering cattle, who are thirsty. A frisky Holstein, pointed face and horns with pink tips, pokes me, playful, calling attention to herself. I must establish that she is not male (1978). I pick up her little curtain. There. Fleshy pink udders, she is pink, black

and white. I have watered the cattle and they have given me a guide.

Etruscan, the last important language.

What holds civilization intact? The presence of apparently voiceless Others, "thoughtless" Others, powerless Others against which the Law, the Main, the Center, even the Diffusions of power are defined.

Throughout the ages the problem of woman has puzzled people of every kind. . . .You too will have pondered this question insofar as you are men. From the women among you that is not to be expected, for you yourselves are the riddle.[7]

A special aptitude for cryptography. The only ones barred from the riddle. Ha ha. His gallantry is hardest to bear. Not to think about the riddle is to remain the riddle. To break with what I have been told I am, and I am able to? am unable disabled disbarred *un sous-développé, comme tu dis, un sous-capable*[8] The Etruscan language can be heard, if one chooses to mouth it, but not comprehended. Pondering is not to be expected, so why bother?

What happens at the historical moment when the voiceless and power-less seek to unravel their riddle? (For Caliban does seize his voice, reject the magician of civilization in Césaire's writing of Shakespeare's *Tempest*.) ANS.: We are cutting into the deep heart, the deepest heart of cultural compacts. They have already lost our allegiance. Something is finished.

Now did I go downstairs, now did I cut up a pear, eight strawberries, now did I add some cottage cheese thinking to get some more or even some ricotta at the Italian Market so that I could make lasagna so that when B. comes back from New York he would have something nice and so I wouldn't have to cook again for days; now did I put some sugar on the fruit and then fill the sugar bowl because it was almost empty; now did I hang two bath mats out on the line, they are only washed once a year and it was today that I washed them; now did I and do I wonder that there are words that repeat in a swaying repetitive motion. Deliberately breaking the flow of thought, when it comes to change, and with food, with dust. With food and dust.

> must here snatch time to remark how discomposing it is for her biographer that this culmination and peroration should be dashed from us on a laugh casually like this; but the truth is that when we write of a woman, everything is out of place— culminations and perorations; the accent never falls where it does with a man.[9]

I dreamed I was an artist; my medium was cottage cheese.

For the woman artist is not privileged or mandated to find her self-in-world except by facing (affronting?) and mounting an enormous struggle with the cultural fictions—myths, narratives, iconographies, languages—which heretofore have delimited the representation of women. And which are culturally and psychically saturating.

To define then. "Female aesthetic": the production of formal, epistemological, and thematic strategies by members of the group Woman, strategies born in struggle with much of already existing culture, and overdetermined by two elements of sexual difference—by women's psychosocial experiences of gender asymmetry and by women's historical status in an (ambiguously) nonhegemonic group.

All the animals, and I knew they were thirsty. They were mine, and were very thirsty. I had to give them

Something I call an emotional texture, a structural expression of mutuality. Writers know their text as a form of intimacy, of personal contact, whether conversations with the reader or with the self. Letters, journals, voices are sources for this element,

> see "no reason why one should not write as one speaks, familiarly, colloquially"[10]

expressing the porousness and nonhierarchic stances of intimate conversation in both structure and function. Like *Orlando*, like Susan Griffin's *Voices*, like *The Golden Notebook*, these may be antiphonal many-voiced works, beguilingly, passionately subjective, seeing emotional commitment as an adventure. (As our form of adventure?)[11]

"What a secret language we talk. Undertones, overtones, nuances, abstractions, symbols. Then we return to Henry with an incandescence which frightens him."[12]

"addressing the reader, making herself and her reader part of the narrative . . . an offhand, conversational manner."[13]

> I find myself more and more attracted to the porous, the statement that permits interpretation (penetration?) rather than positing an absolute. Not vagueness—I want each component to be clear—but a whole that doesn't pretend to be ultimate, academic.[14]

Not positing oneself as the only, sol(e) authority. Sheep of the sun. Meaning, a statement that is open to the reader, not better than the reader, not set apart from; not seeking the authority of the writer. Not even seeking the authority of the writing. (Reader could be writer, writer reader. Listener could be teacher.)

Assuming for the moment. That this description is true? or that we could find these traits and name them. One way of proving that the female aesthetic can exist would be to find reasons for the existence of this poetics in the gender experiences specific to women, in sexual difference. Deena Metzger speaks of a denial of competition and aggression in women, suggesting that these lead to nonhierarchic forms of mutuality.[15] But female competition of course exists (jealous, "she's said it all"; sibling, "she was there first"; smug, "she should know better than choosing to work on a woman"), wherever there are special rewards for some women at the expense of others. Or just because we are no better than anyone else. Jean Baker Miller and Carol Gilligan argue similarly that roles and functions of women engender a different psychological orientation. Shaped by nurturance, women take both donor and recipient roles, using tactics of giving and receiving. Shaped by the interdependent and relational, women are led to "a more contextual mode of judgment and a different moral understanding."[16]

The second trait is both/and vision. This is the end of the either-or, dichotomized universe, proposing monism (is this really the name for what we are proposing? or is it dialectics?) in opposition to dualism, a dualism pernicious because it valorizes one side above another, and makes a hierarchy where there were simply twain.

> a " 'shapeless' shapeliness," said Dorothy Richardson, the "unique gift of the feminine psyche." "Its power to do what the shapely mentalities of men appear incapable of doing for themselves, to act as a focus for divergent points of view. . . . The characteristic . . . of being all over the place and in all camps at once. . . ."[17]

A both/and vision born of shifts, contraries, negations, contradictions; linked to personal vulnerability and need. Essay and sermon. A both/and vision that embraces movement, situational. (I don't mean: opportunistic, slidy.) Structurally, such a writing might say different things, not settle on one, which is final. This is not a condition of "not choosing," since choice exists always in what to represent and in the rhythms of presentation. It is nonacademic; for in order to make a formal presentation, one must have chosen among theses: this is the rhetorical demand. Cannot, in formal argument, say both yes and no, if yes and no are given equal value under the same conditions. Either one or the other has to prevail. But say, in a family argument? where both, where all, are right? generates another model of discourse.

If one does not just rest silent, stuff the mouth with food.

Lessing has built "Dialogue" on an either-or opposition which becomes a both/and vision of the female. He: the tower, is nihilism, the abyss, rigidity, isolation, and control; is courage, reason and a sickness. She: the leaf, a vulval shape. She is infused with an irrational happiness, sensuality, pleasure, and openness to community. Has common sense, does not drive a philosophical position to the end and bind herself to it. This female mode of seeing holds to one side of a polarity (a "feminine" side) yet is simultaneously that force which includes and transcends male nihilism and rationality.[18] A constellated integrative form. This vision contains feminine, transcends masculine, asserts female as synthesis. Makes me very nervous (are we "just" valorizing our idealized selves?). This structure is parallel to the double status of Mrs. Ramsay in Lily's painting (and in Woolf's To the Lighthouse), as one side of the masculine-feminine polarity, fit only to be surpassed; at the same time, as that stroke in the middle, the one unifying lighthouse stroke, which is love and ambition, mother and child, death and pleasure: the female synthesis.

Of the voices of Woolf's essay Three Guineas, one takes the trial tone: rational, legalistic, logical. The other voice discourses loosely, inventive, chatty, exploring every nook and cranny. As for facts—anecdote is authority. But as the Antigone reference ripens, and we talk of women defying the laws of the state, both masculine and feminine are sublated in a heroic, intransigent but unauthoritarian voice which combines reason and emotion, logic and defiance. This is the noncontractual voice of the Outsiders, (ambiguously) nonhegemonic

who speak the last of the important languages to require translating.

A constant alternation between time and its "truth," identity and its loss, history and the timeless, signless, extra-phenomenal things that produce it. An impossible dialectic: a permanent alternation: never the one without the other. It is not certain that anyone here and now is capable of it. A [psycho]an-

alyst conscious of history and politics? A politician tuned into
the unconscious? A woman perhaps . . .[19]

This both/and vision, the contradictory movement between the logi-
cally irreconcilable, must have several causes. Perhaps it is based on the
bisexual oscillation within female psychosexual development. Nancy
Chodorow shows how the Oedipal configuration occurs differently in
girls and boys and that, because of the way the sexes are reproduced in
the family, most women retain men as erotic objects and women as
emotional objects. This oscillation between men and women, father
and mother, pervades her emotional (and thus aesthetic) life. And do
we also value the K-Mart version of this structure: conflict avoidance.
Everybody is right. Feel like a chameleon, taking coloration—

Insider-outsider social status will also help dissolve an either-or dualism. For the woman finds she is irreconcilable things: an outsider by
her gender position, by her relation to power; may be an insider by her
social position, her class. She can be both. Her ontological, her psychic,
her class position all cause doubleness. Doubled consciousness. Doubled understandings. How then could she neglect to invent a form
which produces this incessant, critical, splitting motion. To invent this
form. To invent the theory for this form.

Following, the "female aesthetic" will produce artworks that incorpo-
rate contradiction and nonlinear movement into the heart of the text.

An art object may then be nonhierarchic, showing "an organization of
material in fragments," breaking climactic structures, making an even
display of elements over the surface with no climactic place or moment,
since the materials are "organized into many centers."[20]

Monique Wittig's *Les Guérillères*, a form of verbal quilt. We hear her
lists, her unstressed series, no punctuation even, no pauses, no setting
apart, and so everything joined with no subordination, no ranking. It is
radical parataxis. Something droning. Nothing epitomizes another. If
fruits are mentioned, many are named, for unlike symbolism, where
one stands for the many, here the many stand for the many. Hol-Stein,
one of the thirsty animals.

May also be a form of sexuality, that multifocal female body and its
orgasmic capacity, where orgasms vary startlingly and are multiple.
And how we think about the body.

> She began to think about "climax" and "anticlimax"—what
> these mean to female and male associations.[21] *The language*

of criticism: "lean, dry, terse, powerful, strong, spare, linear, focused, explosive"—god forbid it should be "limp"!! But— "soft, moist, blurred, padded, irregular, going around in cir- cles," and other descriptions of **our** *bodies—the very* **abyss** *of aesthetic judgment, danger, the wasteland for artists!*

Frances Jaffer

Multiclimactic, multiple centers of attention: *Orlando, Between the Acts* where the cows, the rain intervene in art, where the border be- tween life and art is down, is down!

The anti-authoritarian ethics occurs on the level of structure. We call all this "new" ("new form," "new book," "new way of writing," layered and "strudled," Metzger says), that use of the word "new" which, for centuries, has signaled antithesis to dominant values.[22] And which coincides with the thrilling ambition to write a great, encyclopedic, holistic work, the ambition to get everything in, inclusively, reflex- ively, monumentally.

Moreover there looms ahead of me the shadow of some kind of form which a diary might attain to. I might in the course of time learn what it is that one can make of this loose, drifting material of life; finding another use for it than the use I put it to, so much more consciously and scrupulously, in fiction. What sort of diary should I like mine to be? Something loose knit and yet not slovenly, so elastic that it will embrace any- thing, solemn, slight or beautiful that comes into my mind. I should like it to resemble some deep old desk, or capacious hold-all, in which one flings a mass of odds and ends without looking them through.[23]

The form of the desk, the tote bag, the journal. Interesting that for Woolf it was the form of a journal, and for Pound too it began as a "rag bag," a market mess of spilled fish, but became the form of *Analects*, of codes, a great man's laws. *The Cantos*. For Williams, it was the form of antiquarian history, local lore, wonders, layered in the City. *Paterson*. For both the male writers, a geopolitical stance, and this may have happened in a turn from the female, a reassertion of the polarized sexes. For the woman, it is a diary: her bag, her desk.

We intend to find ourselves. In the burning city.

The holistic sense of life without the exclusionary wholeness of art. These holistic forms: inclusion, apparent nonselection, because selection is censorship of the unknown, the between, the data, the germ, the interstitial, the bit of sighting that the writer cannot place. Holistic work: great tonal shifts, from polemic essay to lyric. A self-questioning, the writer built into the center of the work, the questions at the center of the writer, the discourses doubling, retelling the same, differently. And not censored: love, politics, children, dreams, close talk. The first Tampax in world literature. A room where clippings paper the walls.

of course I am describing *The Golden Notebook* again. Again.

The artwork produced with this poetics distinguishes itself by the fact that it claims a social function and puts moral change and emotional vulnerability at the center of the experience for the reader.[24]

A possible definition?   "female aesthetic"   tackling Etruscan   the doubling of doubleness   cottage cheese   the riddle our
riddle   sphinx to sphinx   sexual difference   artistic production   I am hungry—K-Mart   *The Golden Notebook*   (ambiguously) nonhegemonic

Artistic production. The making, the materials the artist faced, collected, resolved. A process of makings, human choice and necessity. Any work is made to meet itself at the crossroads. Any work is a strategy to resolve, transpose, reweight, dilute, arrange, substitute contradictory material from culture, from society, from personal life. And (the) female aesthetic? Various and possibly contradictory strategies of response and invention shared by women in response to gender experiences.

Take Nin. Her diary as form and process is a stratagem to solve a contradiction often present in acute form for women: between the desire to please, making woman an object, and the desire to reveal, making her a subject. The culturally sanctioned relationship to art and artists which Nin continually imagines (ornament, inspiration, sexual and psychic reward) is in conflict with the direct relationship she seeks as artist, colleague, fellow worker. And Nin's diary as fact and artifact transposes these conflicting forces, reveals and protects simultaneously, allowing her to please others (by showing male friends specially prepared sections) while writing to please herself. Double, sometimes duplicitous needs.

These experiences of difference which produce different consciousnesses, different cultural expression, different relation to realms of
symbols and to symbol users.

And therefore, and therefore, there is female aesthetic

> from this [difference in priorities between men and women]
> spring not only marked differences of plot and incident, but
> infinite differences in selection, method and style[25]

as there is male

> It is a commonplace of criticism that only the male myths are
> valid or interesting; a book as fine (and well-structured) as *Jane
> Eyre* fails *even to be seen* by many critics because it grows out
> of experiences—events, fantasies, wishes, fears, daydreams,
> images of self—entirely foreign to their own.[26]

Female aesthetic begins when women take, investigate, the structures
of feeling that are ours. And trying to take them, find also the conflict
between these inchoate feelings (coded as resistances, coded as the
thirsty animals) and patriarchal structures of feeling—romantic thralldom, fear of male anger, and of our own weaknesses of nerve. Essential-
ist? No. We are making a creation, not a discovery.[27]

Yet it is also clear that there would be many reasons not to see female
work as different. Why might someone object?

First, a desire to say that great art is not made by the factoring out of
the sexes, is "androgynous" as Woolf uses the term in the twenties.
The desire to state that greatness is (must be?) universal, that anything
else is special pleading. The fear that to notice gender in any way
becomes destructive to women. Thus the disincentive: if gender categories have always been used so destructively, our use of them, is it not
"playing into their hands"? (There can be no greater proof of differences
in the relative powers of the genders than this argument.)

> Another reason women don't like their art to be seen through
> their bodies is that women have been sex objects all along and

to let your art be seen that way is just falling right back into the same old rut.[28]

Women may then respond with a strategy of self-chosen, proud ghetto-ization (Richardson's "feminine psyche") or may respond as Woolf did. In that (neo-Freudian) context, Woolf's argument for androgyny is a situational triumph, rejecting the ghettos, stating that women's art contains the man, contains the woman, has access to both.

Where then is (the) "female aesthetic"? In both, in all these strategies of response to difference. Even if, even when, contradictory.

Then, there is the desire at all costs to avoid special pleading, anything that looks like women have gotten by because of our sex (ambiguous word: meaning, our gender, meaning, our sexuality). This is a rejection of the stance of the courtesan for the firm-chinned professional, who does not (in dress, in manner, in talk) call attention to her "sex." She has her babies bravely between semesters. She fears being ghettoized. Being patronized. But it happened anyway. Any way. And she did not "control" it.

Another fear: that any aesthetic is bound to be misused, misappropri-ated, and this one is surely extremely vulnerable, with its blurring of all the elements we have firmly regarded as setting art apart: blurring between art and life, blurring between social creativity and "high" art, blurring between one's journal and one's poem, blurring between the artifact and the immersion in experience. Such exact polarities.[29]

I am hungry. I am very very hungry. Have I always been this empty?

I see that the next day I wrote in my journal. I would love someone (me?) to write a wonderful novel using the aesthetics you speak of— that are in my little list—mutuality, porousness, intimacy, recontact-ing a both/and, using both sides of the brain, nonhierarchic, anti- or multiclimactic, wholistic, lacking distance . . . perhaps didactic—but I think this person would have to be a particularly strong and careful artist. I have to tell you that I don't love one single novel that has come out of the 1960–70s women's movement. I don't think there is anyone concerned enough about either language or the real details of daily life. My sense is that everyone has been in a rush. (I feel in this rush too sometimes. Who wants to be a poor nobody at forty?) Sure there are wonderful moments here and there in different pieces of fiction. But no one has been concerned enough about FORM for me.

None of this conflicts with what you said in our workshop. It's just another vantage point. Or perhaps also a corrective, in the sense that I fear too many women can take your aesthetic and churn out crap in three easy lessons. It's really like petit-point to get so close to one's subject, keep it porous, open, multiclimactic, and still keep it art.

Carol Ascher

The possible characteristics of a female aesthetic that you suggested seemed familiar and true certainly of my own work. Therefore I wanted to find out something else and maybe offer something else (if only doubts or impatience with the deterministic limitation of nonhierarchic, layered, "porously intimate," subjective, etc. work) but felt disappointed and thwarted.

Mira Schor

In my essays' psychic and speculative search for contradictions, for wholeness, linear and constellated forms coexist. The work is metonymic (based on juxtaposition) and metaphoric (based on resemblance).[30] It is at once analytic and associative, visceral and intellectual, law and body. The struggle with cultural hegemony, and the dilemmas of that struggle, are articulated in a voice that does not seek authority of tone or stasis of position but rather seeks to express the struggle in which it is immersed.

As for female aesthetic? this essay points to one set of responses. One. Only. One among several possibilities.[31] Of course, for descriptive purposes, the actual traits matter, but more important are the functions I postulate, the functioning of the traits to express, confirm, illuminate, distort, evade, situations that have a gender valence.

But to test whether this is true, whether what you are calling women's themes do appear in women's writing, would you not have to use objective methods, devise objective tests of this knowledge?

Mirra Komarovsky

We have covered the whole range of the anxiety inherent in scientific methodology—from Mirra's comment that the individual scholar must prove her thesis to have validation for more than herself (by the "objective," "scientific" method), to my concern that to define a female aesthetic is to establish, a rigid norm of female creativity, which repeats the patriarchal tyranny of an "objective" absolute way of doing things.

Lou Roberts

Can I prove it? I can prove that different social groups produce differences in cultural expression. I can prove that women are a social group. I can point to examples of differences in our relation to the symbolic order and in our cultural expression.

But I cannot prove that only women, that women only, use this aesthetic. And this failure is actually the strongest proof of all.

Women are (ambiguously) nonhegemonic because as a group, generally, we are outside the dominant systems of meaning, value, and power, as these saturate us, as they are "organized and lived."[32] To talk of society and culture as involving "hegemonic" practices does not mean that a hegemony is a ten-ton stone falling from nowhere to crush you into some shape.

> Hegemony is not to be understood at the level of mere opinion or mere manipulation. It is a whole body of practices and expectations; our assignments of energy, our ordinary understanding of the nature of [people] and of [their] world. It is a set of meanings and values which as they are experienced as practices appear as reciprocally conforming. It thus constitutes a sense of reality for most people in the society . . . but . . . is not, except in the operation of a moment of abstract analysis, in any sense a static system.[33]

A hegemony, as a set of practices, has "continually to be renewed, recreated, defended and modified" as well as "continually resisted, limited, altered, challenged."[34]

Women, in a generally nonhegemonic position, barred from or quota'd into the cultural institutions of renewal, defense, and modification.

> *the "mainstream" of European intellectual history was carried on without us. The clerical status of scholars in the Middle Ages automatically excluded women from the formal training which would fit them for the learned world, and as you know, this situation was not rectified in modern times until very recently. Moreover, self-study was for most women*

virtually impossible because the formal training was carried on in a highly technical Latin (and Greek after the humanist movement), unintelligible even to the ordinary literate lay person.

Yet still (Margery of Kemp, Christine de Pisan)

At least once before in Western history, women did make a substantial contribution to the formation of what might— in the context of our workshop—be called a nonpatriarchal language, the "mother-tongue" which they spoke in contrast to the formal language of scholars.

Jo Ann McNamara

While it is generally asserted and assumed that women belong to the majority, to hegemony, I could suggest that women are virtually always (ambiguously) nonhegemonic. A great number are formed by residual social practices: ethnic, kin-based, male- and child-centered female communities. Some may be emergent, "alternative or oppositional to the dominant elements."[35]

Why are women as a group (ambiguously) nonhegemonic? A woman may be joined to a dominant system of meanings and practices by her race (say, white), yet not by her gender; she may be joined via her class, but not by her gender; joined thru her sexual preference, but not her gender. May be oppositional, with many sources of alternative conditions (working class, black), but still oriented in ideology and consciousness towards hegemonic norms. (June Jordan's poem "If you saw a Negro lady" speaks of this possibility.)

(Ambiguously) nonhegemonic. For women, then, existing in the dominant system of meanings and values that structure culture and society may be a painful, or amusing, double dance, clicking in, clicking out— the divided consciousness. For this, the locus classicus is Woolf.

Again if one is a woman one is often surprised by a sudden splitting off of consciousness, say in walking down Whitehall, when from being the natural inheritor of that civilization, she becomes, on the contrary, outside of it, alien and critical.[36]

That shifting focus, bringing the world into different perspectives, is the ontological situation of women because it is our social situation, our relationship to power, our relationship to language.

What we here have been calling (the) female aesthetic turns out to be a specialized name for any practices available to those groups—nations, genders, sexualities, races, classes—all social practices which wish to criticize, to differentiate from, to overturn the dominant forms of knowing and understanding with which they are saturated.

Nineteenth-century Russian fiction has analogues with women's writing; both are nonhegemonic practices " 'pointless' or 'plotless' narratives stuffed with strange minutiae, and not obeying the accepted laws of dramatic development, lyrical in the wrong places, condensed in the wrong places, overly emotional, obsessed with things we do not understand, perhaps even grotesque."[37]

Négritude has analogues with women's aesthetic practices.

> Consider then the white European standing before an object, before the exterior world, before Nature, before the *Other*. A man of will, a warrior, a bird of prey, a pure act of watching, the white European distinguishes himself from the object. He holds the object at a distance, he immobilizes it, he fixes it. Equipped with his instruments of precision, he dissects it in a cold analysis. Moved by the will to power, he kills the Other and, in a centripetal movement, he makes it a means to use for his own practical ends. He **assimilates** it. . . . The black African is first of all in his colour as if standing in the primordial night. He does not see the object, he **feels** it. He is like one of those worms of the Third Day, a pure sensing field. Subjectively, at the end of his sensing organs, he discovers the Other. . . . So the black African sympathizes with, and identifies with the Other.[18]

For blacks excluded from a Western world of whiteness will affirm a connection to rhythms of earth, sensuality, intuition, subjectivity, and this will sound precisely as some women writers do.

High modernists are the most problematic nonhegemonic group, because they make a conservative, sometimes *fascisante* criticism of bourgeois culture, with "positive" values ascribed to hierarchical social order, sometimes buttressed by religion, but also, astonishingly, linked to peasant-based agriculture (as opposed, of course, to our urban, industrial morass). These writers constitute themselves as a group-against, whose common bond is opposition to the social basis on which their world in fact rested. Modernists show the strength of a politicized culture based on a shared revulsion to World War I, on one hand, and to the Russian Revolution on the other. This set of individuals with residual values (Eliot, Pound, Yeats, Lewis, Lawrence) depends on responses to a once-existing, and somewhat mythologized, social basis in peasantry and patriarch. Aristocrat, head, *il capo*. A revolution from the right.

Literature by women, in its ethical and moral position, has analogues with the equally nonhegemonic modernism in its subversive critique of culture. (Most—Woolf, Lessing, H. D.—are in no way right wing; this more than just an "interesting observation.") In women's writing, as in modernist, there is a didactic element, related to the project of cultural transformation, of establishing values. In women's writing, as in modernist, there is an encyclopedic impulse, in which the writer invents a new and total culture, symbolized by and announced in a long work, like the modern long poem.

And contemporary women have produced just such works, often in the encyclopedic form of essay, compendia, polemic, collage, sacred and critical texts and images: Susan Griffin's *Women and Nature;* Judy Chicago's *The Dinner Party;* Tillie Olsen's *Silences;* Mary Daly's *Gyn/Ecology.*[39]

Then, literature, by women, in its phenomenological position, is associated with postmodernism, and with the democratic tolerance and realism of Williams, or the generative blankness and fecundity of Stevens. A list of the characteristics of postmodernism would be a list of the traits of women's writing: inwardness, illumination in the here and now (Levertov); use of the continuous present (Stein); the foregrounding of consciousness (Woolf); the muted, multiple, or absent *telos;* a fascination with process; a horizontal world; a decentered universe where "man" (indeed) is no longer privileged. But women reject this position as soon as it becomes politically quietistic or shows ancient gender values. For when the phenomenological exploration of self-in-world turns up a world that devalues the female self, when that exploration moves along the tacit boundaries of a social status quo, she cannot just "let it be," but must transform values, rewrite culture, subvert structures.

As my political analysis became more sophisticated [wrote Sara Lennox], *as I became a Marxist shaped by the Frankfurt School and then a feminist, I was able to present a theoretical explanation for my intuitions* (they were mine, and were thirsty). *I understood that, at least for middle-class Americans under late capitalism, the form* (structure, "language") *of the culture is the sustaining force of social domination. But though I was implicated in those forms, I also knew—perhaps because of my somewhat marginal position as a woman, a petite bourgeoise?* (She became the Etruscans?)*—that I recognized these forms to be, not self-evident and natural, but intolerable and changeable, and that occasionally I discovered, and tried to transmit through my teaching and writing* (printed in our Roman letters)*, examples and visions of how things could be other and better. It's been clearer and clearer to me, since I've been a feminist* (some ricotta at the Italian Market) *that we women were never completely integrated into the structures of capitalism* ((ambiguously) nonhegemonic) *and that our difference* (a vulval shape)*, whether only psychosocial or somehow biological as well, has given us a privileged position* (horns with pink tips) *from which to rebel and to envision alternatives. What's difficult, though, is to believe in those glimmers* (entirely obligated to take and pass their test)*, to hold fast to them, even more, to model them out and explore them. And this is the importance to me of women's writing* (her diary, her bag, her desk)*. If it's really the forms, the language, which dominate us, then disrupting them as radically as possible can give us hope and possibilities. What I'd like to try to understand and explain to other people* (you yourselves are the riddle) *is how the form of women's writing is, if ambiguously* (of double, sometimes duplicitous needs) *nonetheless profoundly revolutionary* (as are, in their confusing ways, modernism and postmodernism, also written from positions of marginality to that dominant culture).

But I've also been thinking recently that we need a writer who would be for feminism what Brecht was for modernism—who understands, to put it a little crudely, that literature doesn't change things, people do (a process of making, human choice and necessity)*. Our literature and thinking still seem quietistic to me, in that they require us to understand and respond, but not to act on our understanding, certainly not to act collectively* (a room where clippings paper the walls.) *More-over, I think we haven't even grasped the most radical implications of feminism for a theory which mediates back to practice: that we have a vision which men have barely glimpsed of what dialectical thought is really about—about a total, specific, feeling and thinking subject, present in her interaction with "objective" materials, overcoming the division between thought and action.* (The golden bough. The golden fleece. The female quest?)

I've been angry recently that, while theory proliferates, we have given up on what was compelling about the late sixties and early seventies—

that feeling of infinite possibility which challenged us to think and live differently. So many of those experiments have fallen by the wayside, victim to the economic situation and our own discouragement and exhaustion.

Sara Lennox

Exploration not in service of reconciling self to world, but creating a new world for a new self

given our revolutionary desire (that feeling of infinite possibility) for a nonpatriarchal order, in the symbolic realm and in the realms of productive, personal, and political relations.

for the Etruscans
1979/1984

F A M I L Y,
S E X E S,
P S Y C H E:

An Essay on H.D. and the
Muse of the Woman Writer

*No, my poetry was not dead but it was built on or
around the crater of an extinct volcano. Not* rigor
mortis. *No, No! The vines grow more abundantly on
those volcanic slopes. Ezra would have destroyed
me and the centre they call "Air and Crystal" of my
poetry.*
　　　　　　　　　—H.D., *End to Torment*[1]

At the end of her life, in several kinds of writing, H.D. pondered her
relations with Ezra Pound and with other of her male "attachments":
Richard Aldington, D. H. Lawrence, Lord Dowding.[2] In the memoirs,
novels, and poems that emerged from this musing over the dangerous
power of these attractions is a double story, a knotted structure: "will
the Lion devour me or redeem me—or both?"[3]

The dark volcanic slope is built of ash that once was fire. *End to
Torment* is full of frank and deeply rooted recollections of desire, of
arousal, of frustration. She is enthralled, and she both suffers and studies
her thralldom in the mirror of time, reconstructing the passion, the
rejections, the refusals. But after the lapse of so many years, why would
H.D. choose to recapitulate her sexual and spiritual passion for these
male figures? Why does she re-immerse herself in the intensities of
romantic thralldom? Whatever, as a woman, a poet, could be her
purpose?

This does not need to be seen as a question if one accepts that women
will necessarily and obsessively return to their only sufficient center:
the men around whom they twine. For the poet's concern is all perfectly
complicit with a script for femininity which culture takes for granted,
which traditionally critics of H.D. have viewed without question, and
which, as far as I know, H.D. never questioned theoretically, in essay
or statement. But this fascination with male power and with the male
"lover" is even more startling when one knows that for many years H.D.
lived in closest relation with Winifred Bryher. Despite this attraction to

a woman, that is, despite the solution to her heterosexual thralldom represented in H.D.'s personal life, the poet was nonetheless transfixed by the psycho-cultural system of romantic love, and she was subject to cycles of seduction and reseduction to male figures throughout her life. Lesbianism *per se*—whether platonic or sexually active—was not for H.D. a sufficient strategy of solution to the cultural problem posed by males.

> In that you are myself I love you and am near to you; in that you are a man I am afraid of you and shrink from you.
>   Letter of Olive Schreiner to Havelock Ellis, 1884.[4]

The novel *Bid Me To Live* is H.D.'s double-entry ledger. The heroine there is a poet (*No, my poetry was not dead. . . .*), so she is questioning and affirming her vocation with every tested and detested word.

D. H. Lawrence (in *Bid Me To Live* called Rico): "I don't like the second half of the Orpheus sequence as well as the first. Stick to the woman speaking. How can you know what Orpheus feels? It's your part to be a woman, the woman vibration, Eurydice should be enough. You can't deal with both." His is a theory of separate spheres as rigid and charismatic as any. I'm telling you what to do, now do it!

And, as far as we know, she did precisely this. There is a poem called "Eurydice." It does stick to the woman speaking. And it speaks about having one's own death appropriated. Then it shows how Eurydice becomes reconciled to her fate as a "dead" woman, because she is in fact secretly alive with a glowering, unregenerate light at the buried center of the cavern.

Not rigor mortis. *No, No.!*

Richard Aldington (in *Bid Me To Live* called Rafe): "A bit dramatic. It's Victorian . . . you might boil this one down about one quarter the length and cut the *clichés*."[5] Aldington here wants to shape her production.

"In that you are a man I am afraid of you and shrink from you." Oh, well, just a rough draft. "It doesn't really matter." "only preliminary scribbling." "She felt no Muse."[6] ". . . she was to be used, a little heap of fire-wood, brushwood, to feed the flame of Rico."[7]

> They flee from me, that sometime did me seek,
> With naked foot stalking in my chamber. . . .

Wyatt

"You want to get through a door, doors are Janus-faced. . . ."[8]

The labors of Psyche are the labors of Hercules.

What does a woman do who *will be* a poet? Those from whom you stand to learn the most can also destroy you.

I flee from them.

The first Janus-faced door was the parents. Hermione Gart, or Her, the heroine of one of H.D.'s novels, feels that the forces of mother and father are at war inside her.

> In Hermione Gart, the two never fused and blended. She was both moss-grown, in bedded and at the same time staring with her inner vision on forever tumbled breakers. If she went away [from Pennsylvania and her family], her spirit would break, if she stayed, she would be suffocated.[9]

Enter Ezra. Here called George. The second Janus-faced door is sexuality.

Her wants George to make the decision about leaving home for her, since if he makes the decision, she solves at once the pull between mother and father, between leaving and staying, between breaking and suffocation.

If George takes her with him because he has decided to, then he is responsible. Yet she gets to leave. This is subtle subversion: good girl veneer, bad girl underneath. She plans to use the man to shatter an irreconcilable, unresolvable tension within the family and herself, in the precise way that will minimize her guilt and responsibility.

Passion. The kisses remembered. The arousal. The sexes, and the family. Her desire to be severed from her family. How (girl, 1905, 1906, in the ought years) can one amass the courage and momentum to leave the family house? By passion. And

by marriage. Why then didn't H.D. marry Pound? Why did she painfully take the responsibility, leave on her own, refuse to marry the available lover?

Because the claims of his wishes and his needs would revert everything back to the kind of relationship she was escaping. The family with its patriarchal control *as* the pattern book of heterosexuality. It is a long-standing equivalence. She wanted to be human; George wanted a woman. She wanted to be Greek; he wanted a Roman. She wanted to be companion. He wanted a courtesan. She wanted the pure tree; he the decorative, the pagentry. She wanted him for her poetry; he demanded her as his muse.

H.D. seems to have used Pound as an already open door. He was so sensual, so attractive, so bohemian. But that door brought her back into that very same house. Courtesan. Muse. She found that marriage to him would recapitulate the familial patterns she had to escape or transpose: Solar Brother, Brilliant Father, Gawky or Gorgeous Hilda. Depending on his eyes. "The Lion will devour me."

For his kisses "smudged [her] out."[10] An astonishing sensation. A self dissolved, erased. Surely fearsome if that self wants to crystallize, wants space which can be hers to define: *the centre they call "Air and Crystal" of my poetry* that *Ezra would have destroyed.*

I recurred in dream to the old lover, the male muse. Is he in fact an evil figure? He had a woman with him. He stated categorically, "I have found another poet." Meaning, to inspire. Instead of me. But it was clear that he was *not* inspiring this courtesan. Simple. For she wasn't a poet. She stared at me (screenplay from the 40s) with the sultry mocking glance of new mistress to ex-mistress. The male muse, it appears, desires the subservient poet. Secretly, the male muse wishes to be a poet. To control the woman poet. To make a courtesan from a poet. Can this be true?

At one stage H.D. had to reject these men, in order to survive, and then later she had to remember them, to glory in that male attention, the male sun gleaming and brilliant. It gives, certainly, a different structure to one's life than we are used to finding. To live, one must not be with men, must refuse; but later, must remember, relish the essence of their power. Sounds programmatic. Rigid. Frigid. Uncompromising virgo. Virago. On her own terms. On her own island. From Leuké, white world egg, Helen calls the encoded names of men from H.D.'s past.

> Achilles? Odysseus? Paris?
> but it was from Song, you took the seed,
> the sun-seed from the Sun;
>
> none may turn back
> who know that last inseminating kiss;
> this is your world, *Leuké,*
>
> reality of the white sand,
> the meadow . . .
> *Parthenos.*[11]

Insists that the men are channels for inseminating power—are not themselves the muse, are paths the muse takes. Woman is Parthenos, virgin, men are the means. "It was from Song." From song.

But jack in the box, the men won't stay down. Not a sexual joke, a cultural truth. The truth of the works we revere.

Take "La Belle Dame Sans Merci" by Keats. The woman destroys, tricks, entices, kills with ashen aftermath of sexual joy. This too is thralldom—of male to female, for it works both ways, this sexual system. But no matter what happens to the knight, he retains cultural control of the story. The knight's paleness and sickly mourning, his compulsive retellings, his projection of the whole landscape as an emblem of his spent power constitute the culturally sanctioned narrative. ("and no birds sing")

So while the sexual system works both ways, the cultural system works in one direction only. To write, the woman must struggle against the weight of both systems, and the center of the struggle is her need to take control of her story. She must de-story the old story, lift the weight of the accustomed tale so she can tell her own. Destroy. Fear, repugnance, terror of doing so. De-story? Destroy? Too hard. Too painful. No one will understand her. Where to put the lever? (and the lover)

This is the central struggle of the woman writer. For every word, each cadence, each posture, the tone, the range of voices, the nature of plot, the rhythm of structures, the things that happen, events excluded, the reasons for writing, the ways she's impeded, the noises around her, vocabularies of feeling, scripts of behavior, choices of wisdom, voices inside her, body divided, image of wonder.

All must be re-made.

At the center of this struggle is the question, what gives her access to the terms of her vocation, what allows her, permits her, bids her to continue?

The traditional muse (always a woman, daughter of memory) is double. She is above, yet below. She is a goddess, beyond you, a contact with a pure force, yet, at the same time is a voiceless, wordless figure who needs you (a male poet) to interpret and articulate what it is that she represents (Beauty, Truth, Nature, Wisdom).

Being a muse, the model, a nude, the voiceless inspiration, the channel for power is a tempting but qualified status for a woman. And even a woman poet, in a group of male artists, will have difficulty not being colonized by the men who desire her as a muse, and who will by their worship, erode her voice. When a woman poet is faced with images of herself as muse, she may become ambivalent about her own Beauty (as was H.D.), may experience a conflict between words and silence that will leave her stuttering, hesitant.

The muse is one of the major emotional institutions of poet and poem-making.

Within the story H.D. called *Her,* the woman finds an alternative love and alternative muse. This is a woman named Fayne (her real name was Frances, and she too is mentioned in *End to Torment*).

A love with cool hands that stroke the neck. Both stroke the throbbing heads, the long necks of the other. A love like a Sphinx with a gnomic way, who riddles and strangles, part in jest, part from repressed desire, part as H.D.'s sign that this love, like the heterosexual, was not unambiguously empowering.

> "Anyhow I love—I love Her, only Her, Her, Her." [meaning Fayne, and herself] And he said "Narcissus in the reeds. Narcissa."[12]

In her love for this woman, the poet also identifies her potential for self-love and self-affirmation. She is torn between being a muse for

George and positing this double, this sister as a muse for herself. She is torn among heterosexual love/marriage and self-love/vocation, and articulated lesbian love. Torn between man and woman. And George names this conflict narcissism. Teasing her: selfish woman, ungiving woman, immature woman. Trying to make her be still.

The female muse of the male tradition can usually be counted on to be stable. Often because she passes through quickly (Dante). Well-trained, does not crave cultural control of her own story. Is silent. Mysterious. What muses are for. When she has wild ravings, wild cravings—stick her outside the gates of the City. (Isn't that what Breton's *Nadja* is about? Muse gets rejected—she's too noisy.)

H.D. must struggle with the materials of failure and the voices of culture to retain control of her story, a narrative, moreover, that is not as yet completely born. Embryonic. Half-formed. Consequently, H.D. is fascinated with psyche images of a particular kind: liminal images of a wavering between stages of development. Where, she asks, is the woman who *will be* a poet.

> you are neither there nor here,
>
> but wavering
> like a Psyche
> with half-dried wings.[13]

The emergent psyche, wavering with half-wet, half-dried wings, sums up a recurrent situation for H.D. as female poet. The nature of sequence is arrested. She is permanently wavering. She wants the lion to devour and redeem. She is muse and she is poet. Two-faced doors. Because the culture into which she is about to step, in which she wants to participate, is the site at which she is negated. She is the anti-body. She steps forward. What will buoy her up? Nothing?

(Pound, via de Gourmont: intelligence is a kind of concentrated seminal fluid in the brain.)

"They flee from me."

And more. The culture which defines her, in which she is saturated, which, if she has a vocation, she has adored, gives knife-bright answers and cogent choices which can sever the tensile thread of her constant, purposeful spinning. So that spinning her own cocoon may be spinning her winding sheet. The culture can break the train of her thought, *en train de,* in the process of

thinking itself. Nowadays my questions never seem to be their questions. I cannot articulate, mine are half-baked, half-

assed. To cite Pound:

> Hen. Miller having done presumably the only book a man cd.
> read for pleasure and if not out Ulyssesing Joyce at least being
> infinitely more part of permanent literature than such ½ masted
> slime as the weakminded, Woolf female, etc.[14]

How then can a woman act who *will be* a writer? What will give her birth? What will nourish her?

———————————

It was the struggle not to be reduced, not to become "poetess."

Choice for the woman: be appropriated ("They flee from me"; "½ masted slime"; "it's your part to be woman"). Or be isolated. So H.D. chooses images of pupae, slugs, worms, snails, the larval bits of undistinguished but fecund matter which crawl and ooze and survive. They seem dumb, dull. Can be overlooked, won't threaten, are negligible.

> that small living grub, that thing that lived in her mind, eating
> into her. Inspiration, they said was a high and vibrant rush of
> wings. It was not. It was a small painful grub that sank deep
> and gnawed into one's forehead and burrowed painfully deeper.
> It must be prodded out like some festering splinter. Inspiration
> was more like a festering splinter than a rush of wings.[15]

This too is herself, the worm that crawls along the terrible ground when all around have wings. The great Grub-to-Psyche poem of *The Walls Do Not Fall* is presented as a summary of her poetic career.

> In me (the worm) clearly
> is no righteousness, but this—
>
> persistence; I escaped spider-snare,
> bird-claw, scavenger bird-beak,
>
> clung to glass-blade,
> the back of a leaf

when storm-wind
tore it from its stem. . . .[16]

She explains her survival by her stubbornness. She persisted "unin-
timidated" until the transformation into psyche is promised in the
final lines. And even then, she retains a visceral longing to revert to
the worm state, to beg forgiveness for having flown. H.D. said to
herself in Freud's voice: "Your psyche, your soul can curl up and
sleep like those white slugs."[17] Butterflies and slugs. Redeems and
devours. Her denial contains assent; she says both yes and no.

It was the struggle not to be reduced, not to become poetess. Enduring
the spider-snare, the bird-claw, cut Orpheus from your poem. This
rough draft is too Victorian. Censorship, orders, "storm-wind."

Allow me, she begs, grant me permission to live. Bid me to live.
Wounded, could barely drag herself away. And the totality of *Bid Me
To Live,* read as a projection of a psycho-cultural structure, suggests
that male poets, complicit with the drives to self-abnegation inscribed
in female poets, could easily help to create poetesses from the raw
material that would have made poets.

---

*No, my poetry was not dead but it was built on or around the crater
of an extinct volcano . . .*

The extinct volcano: the possibility of heterosexual love without phallocratic bondage? The extinct volcano: sexual passion itself? Did sexuality have to be reduced or repressed for H.D. to survive? Did she then
find that the conflicts from the sexual plane recurred on the cultural
plane and had, willy nilly, to be addressed? Did H.D. find that you could
not just jump to the side of patriarchal structures of feeling as out of
the path of a truck? That I am inside the truck. I am the highway of my
own repression.

On my desk, Capulin Mountain rises nearly 1500 feet above the surrounding New Mexican plain. The extinct volcano is rich with bluish
light. Lava tentacles stretch out; the top of the volcano indents in the
sensual tilted slope, the core spurts up flame and molten rock, fluid
burning, a geyser thousands of feet into the sky

subsides,   the mound is black

the lava hardens. Harsh crisp rock, its air bubbles are

the irregular hive of inarticulate bees,
earth's marrow bone,
a gobbet of risen bread.

The fire was spurting. Then stopped. The volcano, extinct, some buried power, the geyser in my dream spurts oil. Oil! Right outside my window.

No, my poetry was not dead
Not rigor mortis. No, No!

It was the struggle not to be reduced, to be neither muse nor poetess.

It is the struggle. The career of the woman poet is the career of that struggle.

Insomnia again.

Rigidity. It makes a surface, impacted and tingling where there was depth. Depth refused, perpetually postponed. Therefore all that possibility, deep corridors of the self and sleep, the elegant tunnelings of dreams erupt silently and maliciously. Harden. Insomnia, as the refusal of exploration, generates symptoms of refusal, like the lump in the throat (neck, breaking point)

divides the body and head. Tired body, quivering with the desire to release the self downward to fall

asleep, fall into the blackness. But the refusal brakes. The fall halts. The head wins, smug, hard. It is divided from the body, from its needs

but, like the Rodin statue ("Thought"), not divided

at the core.

The longing for wholeness is expressed in structure. In rupture. There is a black, sleek bronze, oily with power, and it has two parts. The base is one solid block, and it is nothing. There is no picture *of.* No picture *in.* It is a cube. The earth? The water? The idea? The past? nothing, no name. Coming from this tremendous cube is the giant head of a hooded woman. Her neck on the block, her head so near, so bent it is as if she were searching for reflection in the intransigent matter from which she emerges. With which she is merging.

The woman is pensive, inward, also a block of matter:

This is "Thought."[18]

This essay is about a woman, so there is a rock. She is looking into hewn block, into stone pool, into the one core of earth given for her solid head to come from. To mirror.

Ezra would have destroyed me and the centre they call "Air and Crystal" of my poetry.

Crystal? the crystalline dew drops of Sara Teasdale? Of Elinor Wylie? Is H.D. saying: I was a poetess. Yes. She knows the degree to which she was impeded. She knew the battle. It was her career.

And No. Because for H.D., "crystal" was already—or will become—a code word for something else. It was a word to indicate the concentration of energy, not its dissipation into the pretty, the delicate.

> I grew tired of hearing these [early] poems referred to, as crystalline. Was there no other way of criticizing, of assessing them? But perhaps I did not see, did not dare see any further than my critics. Perhaps my annoyance with them was annoyance with myself. For what is crystal or any gem but the concentrated essence of the rough matrix, or the energy, either of over-intense heat or over-intense cold that projects it? The poems as a whole, and the "Greek" stories I have mentioned, contain that essence or that symbol, symbol of concentration and of stubborn energy.[19]

Stubborn. Concentrated. Rough. Over-intense. The poem: A symbol of that stubborn energy, resolved into light. To fuse the fire with the crystal.

The center is power. The psyche quest occurs to gain access to that power, called "crystal" because formed under pressure, and called air:

to breathe! Had to get into the family, understand the pressure; had to get out of the family to be able to speak.

In *HERmione*, H.D. gives one version of this Ezra/Hilda story—stating that Pound did propose marriage, but that she rejected him. This emphasizes the painful establishment of choice and autonomy which is a theme of the earlier work. But in *End to Torment*, H.D. gives the other version—stating that Pound rejected her although they were nominally and secretly engaged to be married. This version—with its more victimized woman—sets the stage for the move within this work to consummate and control the affair, signaling the end to the torment of female victimization.

Further, two stories occur simultaneously in *End to Torment*, the story of saying no and the story of saying yes. What happened in 1906 or '07 was her decision to refuse. Her refusal of sexuality might, in retrospect, be termed prudishness. This gives one cast to the memoir. Her longing, her desires caught in amber for almost half a century are incandescent. A reader could view the memoir quite simply: she wishes she had slept with Pound, she wishes she had married Pound, she wishes she had borne a child by Pound. Sexual longing, with a nimbus of remorse

> For no "act" afterwards, though biologically fulfilled, had had the significance of the first *demi-vierge* embraces.[20]

But, although true, this view is too simple.

Past. Present. Enter Ezra. Enter Erich. The injection and the injunction. The interrogation. She is both innoculated against and reinfected with—and must have out (she says) again (she says)—the romance that defined her.

So she may define it, define for Erich Heydt (for herself) her position on Ezra Pound (on herself), confined by the memory of him as he too has been confined.

Seems at first to lack authority. Seems compelled by external accidents. (Norman Holmes Pearson's letters, urging, probing, listening.) In this apparent diary, the measures of her shaping seem transparent, crystal, intuitive, natural, casual, simply revelatory. But by her characteristic denial of authority that subversively asserts it, H.D. probes for the fire in the crystal: the shaping, singeing, singing force of flame and she

Figure 1: DIAGRAM OF THE MUSES

MOTHER

"She was a dark lady. She wore a clear-colored robe, yellow or faint-orange. It was wrapped round her as in one piece, like a sari worn as only a high-caste Indian lady could wear it. But she is not Indian, she is Egyptian. She appears at the top of a long staircase; marble steps lead down to a river. She wears no ornament, no circlet or scepter shows her rank, but anyone would know *this is a Princess*. Down, down the steps she comes. She will not turn back, she will not stop, she will not alter the slow rhythm of her pace . . . I, the dreamer, wait at the foot of the steps. I am concerned about something, however. I wait below the lowest step. There, in the water beside me, is a shallow basket or ark or box or boat. There is, of course, a baby nested in it. The Princess must find the baby. I know that she will find this child. I know that the baby will be protected and sheltered by her and that is all that matters."[22]

The thwarted mother. The thwarting mother. The hieratic mother. Vulnerability to the mother. The mother's language is a flame; the mother's singing is repressed. The grandmother is a visionary, the mother has second sight. What gift does the gifted return to these givers?

SISTER

Clytemnestra, sister of Helen, whom H.D. wishes she had incorporated into *Helen in Egypt*. Is this Bryher? The love of woman? Yes. Is this the slim Greek woman running a long relay in *HERmione*? Yes. Is this the dead doubled sisters? Yes. The sister was an absence which she had to fill.

FATHER

Judge. Astronomer. Magus. Doctor. Professor. Master. Wise Man. Healer. God. Freud, the paternal protector of the questing soul. Theseus, in *Helen in Egypt*, both paternal and maternal, gives Helen permission to re-enter a cocoon and reform herself as a psyche.

BROTHER

Pound, Aldington, Lawrence, Macpherson, the attachments: the sexual, solar brothers. They stand with the magnifying glass and the paper bursts into flame. Whenever she is enthralled, she will also record the multiple strategies of response, both to suffer and to control this image. And in the Corfu vision, both man and woman can leap, lift, into the Sun.

CHILD

Necessary. Desperate. Grief over the failure. Finally, Perdita. They both almost die—but they live. "Lost and then found." Being a mother put the muse inside her.

PSYCHE

Image upon image. The dyad throbbing. The psyche quest is the secret plot of the later poetry. A mother surrounds a child; the poet is both mother and child. The madonna of fluidity. Helen in Hellas. Helen in Helen. Brings the self and child to birth in the same moment.

names it. Neither the property of the male, nor the property of the female, but the aura of the child, of art, of Eros.

(of Eros who is the utopian self, the utopian transcendence of frustrations and betrayals in family, and sexes, and psyche)

By her own art, she inseminates herself, completing a missing part of her fictive autobiography: an imaginary pregnancy with Pound (therefore reappropriating, retwisting certain terms of contempt—"imaginary pregnancy," "hysterical pregnancy"). And as she discovers their conceptus, Eros, she also gives birth to Pound, helping, by her imagined projections, participating, in her own gynocentric metaphors, the process by which he is released, by which he is transported.

Sexuality in all its guises (from lust, to "the act," to labors and yearnings, to the child) is a ground of transformations. How dangerous, how healing for a woman to insist upon that by which all women have been taxed. That by which women's creativity has been defined.

So in this memoir, the materials of heterosexuality are rewoven and reassembled—as female (pro) creative power.

At the time of her original refusal of Pound, she also said yes to herself, made an intuitive, painful and inhibiting choice of herself, of her own place & her own pleasure, a choice of a woman, of bi-sexuality. But since the problem of romantic thralldom recurred, this solution was not culturally sufficient. Heterosexual love vs. Quest—let me say it in shorthand—is an opposition written into but not reconciled in such formative cultural texts as *Villette, Middlemarch, The Odd Woman, Portrait of a Lady*. And *Jane Eyre*—depending on how you view it, for it changes like fire. This opposition remained a central and problematic element throughout twentieth-century writing by women who are responding at the same time to the cultural donné of nineteenth-century narratives and to twentieth-century social changes. So in the twentieth century the love and quest plots are visibly isolated, like important "cultures" in an experiment; they are addressed together in one structure, and sometimes reconciled (Woolf's *Night and Day, To the Lighthouse;* Lessing's *The Children of Violence*). And these two plots—love and quest—H.D. herself did finally reconcile in the Pound memoir. By her own chosen, long-retarded act, she delivers herself up to the moment of contact, so that she could, finally, claim both—the brilliance of heterosexual fulfillment, and the importance of the vocation which the two poets shared. The love and quest plots can also be reconciled if one changes the nature and focus of the love. Thus H.D. makes her fusion of the two plots take the shape of a child. And so at the center of *End to Torment* H.D. imagines the child of Pound and herself, a child who is an erotic cupid, described as a baby Pound, radiant with energy and golden hair. He is the child of passion and inspiration, the child of heterosexual desire and poetic vocation finally united. A love child and a quest child at once.[21]

This child is the end of her torment, interpreted as the torment of a separation between heterosexual love and vocation—one torment of the woman writer. And her confinement with their child is the end to the labor of Psyche. For the end to torment is, too, the end to multiple confinements. It is Pound's liberation from his confinement in St. Elizabeths, an event whose day-to-day drama is embedded into her memoir. It is the end to her confinement in her past—her studied amnesia, her "not caring," her hiding, her self-imprisonment.

She had refused him as lover, had refused to be his muse in a cultural structure which would appropriate her; she had refused his likeness in the decisive, brilliant, overpowering Aldington and Lawrence, who wanted to contain her poetry. She refused to be muse, refused to be poetess.

The Pound she accepts and assents to in this memoir she has humanized by making him over from the incandescent lover to—

(associating relation with relation, recalling one tie with another, folding time over time, person over function until she brings to birth her own invention: Pound as the summation of)

—the family that is sufficient to the needs of the female poet, the family which will nourish her. Imagining that she bore Pound's child was not a result of a phallocratic fixation, but was done to reimagine their combined sexual and spiritual force as a family: Mother-Father-Baby. Writing this memoir, she evokes Pound as Father, Brother, Lover, Child; she remembers the woman, Pound's alternate or opposite—Frances, the Sister and Companion. She draws all of the roles together into a family structure.

It is as logical that she would renounce him (*Ezra would have destroyed me*) as that she imagined their child years later from the core of the extinct volcano.

Rodin's "Thought" (Bronze, 1886–89).
Rodin Museum: Gift of Jules E. Mastbaum.

"A woman is about to step out of stone, in the manner of a later Rodin,"
H. D., *Ion*.

It is as logical as the story of the sphinx. Woman stands, locked outside the gates of culture. (Laura Mulvey has a film, she says this.) This woman is the sphinx. The other woman (in that other story) chained to a rock, yearning for immediate rescue, is the heroine. Be either a heroine or a sphinx; this is the opposition with which women writers are confronted. H.D. said both. I will have both, I will suffer both, and, further, I shall keep control of my story. So she was heroine and she was hero. But her control of the story means that, in the final analysis, she is the sphinx. No matter how fervently she tempted herself to be the heroine—returning again and again to relations of thralldom, keeping just enough pain to fire her creative acts—she destroyed the story by controlling it. De-storied it. So she is the sphinx.

And because she is the sphinx, we do not understand her.

In *Riddles of the Sphinx* Laura Mulvey pans in, pans out, back and forth, lens playing on the great lips of the Great Sphinx of Egypt. Loud and piercing music splits my head open. I am listening to the silent mouth which, made of ancient cracking stone, begins to show new shadows, sudden designs, to show

closing in to see another image in the image
closing in on the silent vulval lips

stone vulva

sphynx: to draw tight

A woman outside the gates of culture is called a sphinx, inside called a heroine. Inside is called poetess, outside poet. She feared being poetess (*No, No! my poetry was not dead*); and at the same time, locked in conflict, feared the exile demanded of the woman poet. As riddling sphinx.

For the male muse is only part of the structure, part of the story of how a woman *will be* a poet. The Pound memoir could suggest this equation only:

male muse for female poet = female muse for male poet

Simple reciprocity? No. Wrong valence. Unbalanced equation. For everywhere the grave social and cultural asymmetry between the sexes impedes this simplicity. We must understand the context. The male muse does not satisfy the female poet. What then does she choose to sustain her?

The true context in which to place the Pound memoir is this: Pound becomes part of the multiple family muse of the female poet. H.D. recreates this family as a sustaining system. For herself, who *will be* a poet. That is what H.D. saw. And that is what she did.

> father, brother, son, lover,
> sister, husband and child;
>
> beyond all other, the Child,
> the child in the father,
> the child in the mother,
>
> the child-mother, yourself. . . .[23]

The men whom she loved (with the exception of Freud and possibly Erich Heydt) did not understand.[24] If they had been engaged in the fluidity of seeking? They claimed to be seekers. But did not go outside those gates, not to meet the sphinx on her own unsanctified ground. Because the female muse generally suffices for the male poet, such poets see no need to change the satisfying system of muses (courtesans, mistresses) which, for most poets, structures the system of the sexes. They saw themselves as lovers. It was an embarrassment to be asked to be father? brother? mother? child? They could not be or consider these others, therefore did not allow H.D. the human space to interrogate what she was fixed on, committed to, wounded by: the family, the sexes. *The vines grow more abundantly on those volcanic slopes.*

She had alone to invent, from the interlocking blocks of some original family, the sufficient family that would give her support for her vocation without the tribute which the male muse, the lover, inevitably and repeatedly exacted—pain, sexual despair, isolation, poetic losses. *Ezra would have destroyed me.*

So many people cross. It is a knot, umbilical, Gordian as the labyrinth. She is given, by culture, no particular background for understanding what will bind her and how she can survive and transform this. No models. Few, in fact, had made this familial transformation. Woolf does, in *To the Lighthouse.* But anyway, strategies did not then and still do not abound. H.D. used her life and the active drama of her memories as the laboratory for the creation of ways to transform her contending muses into a structure.

For the woman writer, the family is the muse. If it turns nasty, and it can, it is the combined hydra-head of a monster/herself. For she need not have come to terms with the many heads inside her: sister, mother, father, baby, husband, lover, brother. They will teem inside her; team up inside her.

Can't sort them out. What to do. They are flooding me, fighting over me. I used to hear quarreling voices: a high one a low one; maternal worry voice fast talker, never to the point, always apologizing, spinning a 33 at 45. The other, paternal rumble, taking care of everything, under-cutting, explaining away, neutralizing. I could never hear a single word that they were saying, just the buzzing sing-song.

I was once in Freud's house, London. On the first floor, Freud's consult-ing room exactly as it was in Vienna, as H.D. saw it, when the Nazis——

the couch, shorter than I had imagined, covered with a Persian weaving of dark and luminous pattern. The place both dark and light (Oppen: "the small/huge dark"). What becomes visible? Thousands of figures, everywhere, covering every flat surface, the desk, the little tables, book-cases, the large civilization's gods and goddesses in stonework, metal work, bone work, lined up in phalanx five and seven deep, swarming like seeds to be

sorted. The total life, the totemic life of humankind still stands en-crusted in that room, placental stones of blood in which Freud was mothered and fathered

was mother and father.

> O, sleep-walker; is this fleece
> too heavy? here is soft woven wool;
> wrapped in this shawl, my butterfly,
>
> my Psyche, disappear into the web,
> the shell, reintegrate . . .[25]

Theseus who speaks above enables the psyche to be born, to put the mother inside her, to be the mother herself. Helen is gigantic over her babies, Helen is the baby in the arms of Thetis, Helen the chrysalid, Thetis the cocoon, pupa and moth, flower and fruit, crawling and flying the muse of the woman writer is found in the reordering of family, sexes, and psyche.

The great male poets of that generation tried to make a "new and total culture" through myth, politics and history. In the poem they construct the city which is language and culture at once: *The Cantos, Paterson, The Waste Land.*

Despite their reconstruction of culture, the great male poets of that generation repeat tradition where male-female relations are concerned. Pound's idealized eyes, sustaining him, and his polygamy. The *stil novisti* Lady of Eliot and her counterpart, the typist home at teatime. Williams sends love and more love to the virgin/whore from the king self, the satyr-poet. Only Lawrence does any family work—in the novels. But striving women, willful, die. Yeats hated the muse who would not be still, called Maud Gonne an old bellows full of angry wind because she was a politically active woman. As for Yeats' little daughter—she is already the static female muse, even as a baby in her cradle.

And H.D.? She too works on the culture. On the city (*The Walls Do Not Fall*), on religion. Forges a myth (*Tribute to the Angels, The Flowering of the Rod*). Writes *Helen in Egypt*, the great long impossible poem; it was her *Cantos*

But in that poem and others she also faces male-female relations in a quizzical, suffering, intense fashion. She invents a structure into which the devastations of male-female sexuality, the solar brilliance of heterosexual love, the price and prize of the male muse could be all placed. And changed. Seeing, as Freud did also (for their connection is based on this) that family analysis is an essential basis for the understanding of culture, myth and history.

The Thinker sits on a rock and thinks. He can be above his thought if he so desires. Can separate from it. His body is complete. His elbow crooks accurately and speculatively into the surrounding universe which does not seem to exert any pressure to break his hold, to bruise the pensive and even vulnerable angles.

Thought emerges. She emerges or is sinking. She is self and rock. How can I say this without drowning? The rock directly under her chin, head as rock rock as head, the whole mass of the universe weights her and is a magnet.

Volcanic fact that dark Thought looks struck from hardened lava. She is the core of the volcano, oily with earth, heavy with the organization of earth

Woman. Rock. Equal halves of the balance pole, joined by her
neck   the
well
from which a voice may come resisting its power,
buried to the neck,
wounded
in the neck
born up through the glottal inelegant column.

1979/1984

PATER-DAUGHTER

Male Modernists and
Female Readers

> *Tombeau:* the collaboration between two poets, the
> dead and the living, [whose] interests . . . do not nec-
> essarily coincide . . . . The classic *tombeau* ends in a
> draw.[1]

and if she falls into it; there is no behind or in back of. The eye she has
sees as yet no behind or in back of. The mouth sees it eyes-mouths and
wants either to fall full into and eat it or to have it fall into her and eat
her, and the falling is into surface   which is eating or fall so the surface
enters her

either way she holds that the surface conceals eating, and she amazes
that surface by clambering up to the eating

she will be the purest eating. There is no defiance of eating, only
defiance of the behind, of background, interruptions of eating. Wherein
eating surface changes. Something with dots opens. Something with
dots opens the eating. She is the mouth, she thought she opened it. She
moves over into the beyond which flattens at her touch. Even hills
flatten. No hills but eating. No space but entereth with the holy mouth
of mourning the wh wh wh aaaaaaa for the missing of beyond, to will
the beyond closer into the falling   the mouth turns inside out over the
nipple, the nipple inside out is the mouth. The one empties herself out
in front of the other one; the second empties herself into the first.

Reading the radical literature of our time, reading *Spring and All*, see
at the end how the final flower to bloom is a black-eyed susan "rich /
in savagery— / Arab / Indian / dark woman." This, the final statement
of an amazing document of change, of challenge, of difference, of the
new (and Williams so excited and effervescent) returns us to the "savagery" of sameness. Oldness. A conventional vocabulary of race and
gender. It is true that "the white daisy / is not / enough" for the white
"crowds"; it was not even enough for nature, but stereotypical climaxes
of banal symbolism in a primitive key are also inadequate.[2] I am roused

by the work's saucy claims; I tumble back the same hill again, a boulder heaved and lost by some repetitive hero.

Roll my own boulder. At least I'll be honestly crushed.

Reading the radical literature of our time, reading *The Pisan Cantos*, moved by Pound's grief and intransigence, I read who are evoked liturgically as the "makirs" (mentions Yeats, Beardsley, Ford, Williams, Eliot, Joyce, Symonds, Hulme, Lewis, Hemingway, Antheil). Who is missing? D. Marsden, H. Monroe, H. Weaver, M. Moore, A. Lowell, M. Loy, S. Beach, and other women cultural workers whom Pound knew. He mentions none. The loss, the erasure, the missing. Missing in action, their action missing. Their boulders invisible.

I remember "Remember our brothers at Kent State"! I remember going to them, the grieving mourners and saying "but women were killed too." If it took two women two days to drop out of history—of experienced history, events burnt into us—what equation can we extrapolate here?

Pound speaks, however, of H.D. But look! she has lost her name! She is evoked in his code as a generous, lovely, gracious figure. A goddess, a spirit, inhabitant of myth, a presence. A presence half in tears. "Dryad, your eyes are like clouds . . . Dryad, your eyes are like the clouds over Taishan / When some of the rain has fallen / and half remains yet to fall . . . / Dryad, thy peace is like water."[3] The radical claim that the natural object is the only adequate symbol somehow generates, regenerates the commonplaces of iconography.

How do they choose, word by pokey word? Into what levels, into what minute cells of the practice called "writing" are these gender ideologies imbedded? The page is never blank.

Proposition 3. In writings of male modernists, femaleness is as fixed and eternal a category as ever before in Euro-literature. Male modernists do not deeply resist, perhaps cannot make a critique of this place allocated for female figures because their readability depends on such reliable gender narratives. Their radical forms are made relatively accessible—readable—by the familiarity of gender limits, the iconographies they inherit and repropose.

Proposition 3A. And erasure. A corollary—erasure. A scratching out or a scratching over. The constant mythologizing of Woman is an erasure of women. We—speaking women in historical time are faces masked with a static, unhistorical idea of Woman: a fiction, an intersection of discourses repetitive in Western culture, whether religious, scientific, juridical . . .[4] The parallel actions undertaken with "race" and "class."

H.D. is given her youngest "pseudonym" by the old man who needs her spirit, among others, to heal his pain. She is deeply touched, as an old woman reading his work. She marks that page in her copy. For them the circuit is closed; for us, the question is open. Is his nostalgia for her presence enabling? touching? disenfranchising? Is worship always more attractive when its materials lie in the past? When its struggles, resistances to it are smoothed, planed? Men, Pound seems to say, live in a multi-faceted world—the ideal, the material, the historical, the spiritual. Women, Pound seems to say, do not. They lose their facets. Their history. Their contextuality. Their materiality. They become disembodied "eyes in the tent." Hallucinations.[5] This iconizing is a peculiar form of erasure. Perhaps an encoding for purposes of "discretion"? Discretion is another kind of erasure.

Woman as icon, and the man in any particular case is worshipper. And writer. The icon does not write herself. Hence all women in *The Pisan Cantos* are cast in this iconic role even when they were cultural "makirs." They are barred by Pound (unconsciously, in the "political unconscious" of his act of satisfying writing) from appearing in the historical functions they in fact served.[6] Poets. Publishers. Patrons. On what minutest levels of satisfaction and choice does this gender question position itself? To idealize these culturally active women is to transgress upon their particularity—despite Pound's poetics of particularity. How strong must be the interior impulse which would go counter to this strong-willed poet's announced poetics. The use of female figures—contradictory with his announced, professed poetics.

What is Pound's only comment on a named female artist in *The Pisan Cantos*?

> I wonder what Tsu Tsze's calligraphy looked like
> they say she could draw down birds from the trees,
>   that indeed was imperial; but made hell in
> the palace . . .

(*PC*, p. 73)

Bluff little prurient allusions. Coy. Hell in man's home, his castle. O Boy.

The African-American men in the DTC with Pound are memorialized variously in *The Pisan Cantos*. They are art. (*PC*, pp. 96–97): someone's face reminds Pound of a Benin mask he saw in a museum in Frankfurt. One is lazy (*PC*, p. 42), one mocks him genially in German (*PC*, 101), and at least one has "positively less musical talent / than that of any other man of colour / whom I have ever encountered" (*PC*, p. 62), a remark preening with hearty and superior social understandings: blacks "sing well," and here is one that "doesn't." Indeed, Pound says "I like a certain number of shades [African-Americans] in my landscape" possibly because "the sight of a good nigger is cheering / the bad'uns wont look you straight." (*PC*, pp. 62–63) Cato. On and on, even in blackface. And they may "make" and "care"—one made Pound a table, but he has to deny this care, barred from fraternizing with the ambiguous, suspicious Pound: "Doan' tell no one I made you that table." (*PC*, p. 63, also p. 97) They serve. They are picturesque local color. Backdrops for the drama of Pound. They are shades—a metaphor certainly of the underworld, but perhaps an ungainly one here, for they are shades to set off the yearning for whiteness that animates the moral and physical landscapes of Pound: "who will have the succession? / To this whiteness, Tseng said / 'What shall add to this whiteness?' " (*PC*, p. 73)

Proposition 5. Modernist agendas concealed highly conventional metaphors and narratives of gender, views of women as static, immobile, eternal, goddess-like. Until the problematic of women is solved, no writer is truly modern. Modernist agendas conceal highly conventional views of race—African-Americans as primitive, "colorful," picturesque people. Until the problematic of race is solved, no writer is truly modern. These poetic objects are filled with stored human labor, stored human thought, habituations. It is a work, a practice to begin the long social process of dislodging . . .

A symbolic moment. December 1913.

A group of young men of letters, including Allen Upward, Ezra Pound, and Richard Aldington, petitioned the editor Dora Marsden for a name change of the journal in which that circle of artists was regularly appearing. The name to which the men objected was *The New Freewoman*.

They felt that "the present title of the paper causes it to be confounded with organs devoted solely to the advocacy of an unimportant reform in an obsolete political institution."[7] In two words—female suffrage. Which of course had not yet been won. The literary men proposed a change in agenda by limiting the social allusions Marsden's title made.

This political high-handedness appealed to Marsden. She approved, and the journal became *The Egoist* in 1914. Her reasons symbolically mark the equivocal relationship of "high" modernisms to feminisms and to gender issues. Feminism, o that old thing, we hardly need it any more was what Dora Marsden said in 1913. Feminism is only necessary in opposition to "Hominism" and now we can declare that binary moot and enter into a post-feminist, post-gender era together. The battles are won.

How wonderful to be able to editorialize that the debates on gender were over, that women "can be as 'free' now as they have the power to be," that the assertion of freewoman status no longer need happen, that indeed, such assertions were divisive, backward looking, a form of protectionism, and were not modern. For the assertion of Self in Singularity that the new title claimed was a myth of—let us speak in shorthand—false consciousness. It did not ask how "ego" was socially formed, in what conjunctures. It claimed that invention and imagination are "free" of "ideology." It said that those who spoke of social formations were "controversialists."

Now women can forge ahead. The burden of proof is on you. So write, women, write! The position depended upon feminism (on the "awakening" of women) but denied the continuing relevance of gender.

> What women—awakened, emancipated, roused, and whatnot—what they *can* do, is open for them to do; and judgment as unbiased as ever it is likely to be, is ready to abide by the evidence of their work's quality.[8] (Dec. 15, 1913, p. 244)

How chilling to hear Marsden's hopefulness. If this is a symbolic moment it means: women must be suspicious, dubious of declaring that gender asymmetries have ended. For the men of letters in this episode did not, note well, declare that gender asymmetries were over. They said—only—that they did not want to be reminded of feminist struggles. They wanted no allusions to the political force calling banalities of gender into question. And that—in the same way that girl babies may be found nowadays in light blue, but boy babies are scarcely found in light pink—they did not want to appear wearing the "colors" of women.

Stately flying
saw the shadow of this plane—from the plane
fresh vertigos.

Our shadow seems to be lagging.

So close the ground
cars driving to get us on the freeway we
couldn't possibly fall now?

Eaten alive with feelings
136 129 134 144 140 140 135 131 140 145 146 150 145

For "the icon" to write herself?
What kinds of words? what kinds of structures? how end the habituations? how enter the minutest "cells" of writing and shift them? will
you hear her? (will I hear her? Years pass.) what kinds of listening will
you muster? awkwardness in these resistances, these disbursals. will
she give you

pleasure?

Proposition 2. Early analogies for major form in modernist texts were
different from how they ended up. I am thinking about Pound, his three
"pre-Cantos" now dissolved into the opening of the actual work. In
these his agenda for modernism is curiously supple on the issue of
gender and class. The analogies for his form which Pound used are both
more "female" and more popular/populist than the cantos later became.
The artist's "bag of tricks"—like a showman at a "booth" at a fair. The
quilter's "rag-bag" for the modern world "to stuff all its thought in"—
these random choices of color and design, like a crazy quilt, having
depths of local allusiveness. Pound to make the quilt of the world. (and
didn't he, tho? without admitting it.) Finally a "catch" of fishes, "shiny
and silvery / As fresh sardines flapping and slipping on the marginal
cobbles," a fish plentiful, cheap, unprepossessing.[9]

Most of these analogies disappear; one goes underground for fifty years,
reemerges when Pound makes his depressed, disparaging remarks about
his "botch": "I picked out this and that thing that interested me, and
then jumbled them into a bag. But that's not the way to make . . . a
work of art."[10] Whether or not this is accurate to *The Cantos*, the
nature of the metaphor is significant: the "bag" and the "jumble," the
randomized selection via personal interest—these belong to a feminine
code. Pound is saying that the work failed because its strategies were

too feminine. If the cantos were to remain personal, quirky, situational, Pound would have had to solve the issue of authority and of claim he made immediately in those "pre-Cantos." And the question seems to have arrested him, paralyzed him. He is worried that he cannot "say the filmy shell that circumscribes me / Contains the actual sun. . . ."[11]

Never wanting to say: This is how I see it.
Always wanting to say: This is how it is.

"It was "the marginal cobbles" and "filmy shell" versus "the actual sun." Pater-sun.

I read them, dazzled, Pound, Williams, Eliot. They "read" me. Some me, anyway. I am, within their words, dug into habitual gender sites, repositioned from producer to produced, from writer to written, from artist to inspiration. Or to blockage.[12] And the works are difficult enough so that their "mastery" is a challenge, so that separating from their assumptions is difficult; the reader is slid to scholiast, to epigone, to apologist.

Dream: edible twigs. Slight flowers. Is this an adequate dream?

Parcival in the forest of gender. O look at those wounds! Grandfather, what is going on here?

Dream: I found an animal at home. An animal "tired of being cute." With her (so far) this dream comes true: but by a high level of "5 year old" resistance. Which today means "bang bang" and shell whistle gun noises. (How do they "learn" these noises?)

> A mirror greeting
> century of hustle across 20¢
> stamp their letters
> I tear excitedly at the envelope
> the enormity fecund
>
> Loss
> of mirrors, they
> thin (so thick to thin!)

mercuric lining, the black flat background, the reflector substance
wears thru to glass, what it was

made of
I see what

it was mounted

on, o see.

"Indeed, nothing is more Baudelairean than woman as mirror or as
reflector, the latter causing multiplicity of lights to sparkle or shimmer;
lights of which, if she is not the source, she is at least the present center
of diffusion. In Baudelaire there is always a radiating *luce di femina*, or
a strictly feminine luminosity which, like the illumination of cities at
night, splits into an infinite number of fires."[13]

STRICTLY. If I lose their mirror, do I lose myself? What is true, Moon?

If the male modern is the flaneur, the female modern is—the glass or
blind carafe? the mirror? the vitrine? the present center of diffuseness.
The bride stripped bare by her bachelors, even.

One can appreciate with what intelligent ironies Mina Loy made up
her contemporaneous title: *Lunar Baedeker:* Guidebook to or of the
Moon.

Moony loony how does the "icon" write herself? I mean, one must give
up, wedge up, extirpate the icon, the desire to be the icon, the deep-
rooted assimilation of iconicity, the luscious Green Addresses we have
lived in, the Beauties, and

make other beauties. Make them ugly. Brave words. "Marginal
cobbles."

Cobbler, bunglar. How dare I, etc.

Metaphors: of "cobbling" as "cobbling together." Of moony- looniness.

The cultural production and reproduction of "Woman" is central to
many of the linked chain of major long poems of modernism, poems
intertextual, inter-influenced, mutually read. *The Waste Land, Paterson, The Pisan Cantos.* All want to construct a ritual site in which
(hetero)sexuality is returned to its spiritual or primary ("primitive")

meanings, and the fertile conjuncture of man and woman is affirmed. This may well be a generalized response to specific angsts which feminism provokes. And to the lesbian possibilities of the new free woman. Williams records, in his autobiography, the angry man, raging because he saw lesbians dance together, and thereupon shaking his penis in public. Q: "Have you never seen one of these?"[14]

Another chapter. From *Paterson*. The climax of various addresses and allusions to T. S. Eliot throughout is the rivalry between an "effete" lesbian poet, obviously Eliot combined with other representatives of a symbolist aesthetic, and Paterson himself (Williams) for the attentions of a little New Jersey chippie, tough as nails. A real narrative. A real allegory. A real drag. Williams must think (or behave as if he thinks) that sexuality itself is coterminus with heterosexuality. Any other kind is a misguided and pitiable form of impotence, leading directly without stops, to disability in writing. (A theory of the relationship of sexualities and gender to writing practice.) This section of *Paterson* is, conversely, a slander. That lesbians try to trap heterosexual women. That gays can't write. Figure it out. He has fixed a whole analysis of the blockages in American culture, the prevention of an emerging American poetry on T. S. Eliot, so therefore (*therefore*) the second worst epithet of the 50's is inferentially applied: QUEER.

Heterosexuality is a key to linguistic adequacy. Deracinated language is linked to "perversity" and to manipulative sexuality. By which he means lesbianism, and not (q.v.) rape.

Take Eliot's *Waste Land*, and its shadow poem, the draft to which Pound was "midwife." The poet tries to learn how to handle desire and its failure, given a sense of wasted life and historical doom related not only to World War I, but also to the Russian Revolution—those teeming hordes overrunning from the East—for the apocalyptic class questions. And to the Woman Question—female cunning, female power, and "the good old hearty female stench" (a cut phrase) are promiscuously mingled together. Much, though not all, of the waste land situation is ascribed to women and men who are complicit with painful failures and distortions of sexuality: prostitution (cut from the opening), rape, disgust, various forms of impotence and sexual resistance. Rape, for women, seems to be defined as what they suffer in the absence of arousal—no more, no less. It is the blankness of sex endured without feeling. Rape seems to be something that men, also, suffer—a kind of spiritual rape by the rapacious sexual urges of women. Tiresias c'est nous. But Tiresias' question was about pleasure. Who gets more pleasure. Eliot's seems to be who gets less. Least. Grandfather, what is going on here?

Another cut from the shadow *Waste Land*: Fresca—a fresh tarty modern free woman, her "doorstep dunged by every dog in town" might, in another age, have been "a meek and weeping Magdalene." But in a reductive analysis, female autonomy is the same as female desire— "the same eternal and consuming itch / Can make a martyr, or plain simple bitch." Hey, waddya gonna do? This Fresca is a new intellectual, a poet in fact, but of course deplorably so. In her intellectual role she grows "dull" and loses "the mother wit of natural trull." Yet by the same token, a "natural trull" is none too valued in her frankness of function, whether defecating or suggestively fondling an egg.[15] The cultural abuses of the aggressive female extend from the destruction of sincerity to the "dunging" of sexuality, from the cheapening of emotions to the writing of inadequate poetry. Is there any adequate poetry with a female signature? One hardly knows what the woman is being criticized for—a kaleidoscope of contradictory flaws is set swirling. Is there a way to win this game? Is there a "good" woman? Eliot sums "Woman" up: "For varying forms, one definition's right / Unreal emotions, and real appetite." So the answer is no. What was the question?

> Punk in the orfice (maws)
> junk virus here and there
> fungus under
> phlegm-sinus:
> what kind of topos, what topoi
> oi
> weh
> Long Island Semite Viennese
>
> "Rachel *née* Rabinovitch"
> tears at the rapes with murderous paws.

Eliot's somber and reflective notes to *The Waste Land* are distinguished by the recalling of Ovid, Dante, Baudelaire, Webster, Verlaine, Spenser, Marvell, Goldsmith, St. Augustine, Gérard de Nerval—among others, who contribute phrases, words, appropriated, material woven. However, not a word is said about the person who contributed the longest section to this poem. Ellen Kellond.

The passage in the pub, the working-class monologue, is " 'pure Ellen Kellond'," a domestic worker employed by the poet and his wife, "who recounted it to them."[16]

"You are much too hyper-sensitive! This happens all the time. One of Picasso's mistresses, I forget which one, painted the horse in Guernica—probably not the face. That's just like a scuola. Jessie Chambers gave Lawrence her diary so he could correct dialogue between 'them' in *Sons and Lovers.* Are you against helpfulness? A friend of mine, a novelist, told a really moving story about her childhood to her (then) husband, a writer; he wrote it down (you see, she wasn't able to, she was really blocked), and he published it. It was his story. She just contributed. You are really over-reacting."

A woman, Ellen Kellond, is a cultural producer, an "author" (story teller, Cockney griot) but in ways that cannot easily be heard or credited by our class segment of the culture, nor permanently available except as her words are appropriated and reshaped (jocularly, without her authorship ascribed except in genial, accidental memory years later).

Certainly not "noted," not a Baudelaire.

When Fresca is erased, Alexander Pope is not erased. But when "Lil" is published, Ellen Kellond is erased.

Ellen Kellond may even have intended something quite different with this story than Eliot makes of it. "O now you are really over-doing it; how are you ever going to discuss the 'intention' of an 'erased' woman." In her story, there is a horney husband, a resistant wife, a fresher younger woman, five kids, and an abortion. Is this a deformation of femaleness and sexuality? No more than usual.

Of course there is an abortion.

An abortion!
Just some "strong female tabules" which "remove all obstructions and restore regularity."[17] Is this the secret sin, the secret festering guilt at the center of the poem? A choice. Female choice. Is chosen; happens. Which women choose. Has never stopped happening (in various forms, with varying degrees of success).

An abortion! A female choice. Is this the secret sin, the secret festering at the center? The autonomy of women? An aborted fetus? with whom the poet identifies? Strange thought: to the tune of a woman's hair, "bats with baby faces . . . crawled head downward down a blackened wall." Lines so bad it's a wonder neither Eliot nor Pound cut them.

Dream: I dreamt that my mother was studying the sinus.

Sinus: bend, curve, fold, hollow.

Losing Ellen Kellond is regular, it removes all obstructions and restores authority.

The desire for a massive critique of gender relations in language, in writing, yet the indication that the character, the propositions, however numbered, of plots, of conventions, of recognizable beauty, of reward systems, of myth, and of memory impede and prevent this critique from occurring.[18]

If this is so, better stop writing. An impasse. Hegemonic relations, habituations, though contradictory, will never be broken. Besides, as a woman writing, there is a proportionately greater chance of my work being, eventually, erased. Obliterated.

Proposition 4. Here is the gender system of asymmetry around female-ness, as all cultural history to date tells us. A woman's work will (work with a female signature will)

    a) be less able to be written
    b) be less able to be consumed, read, received, thought about, no-
        ticed, understood
    c) have strange explanations attached to its success[19]
    d) author will endure personal insults for professional activities[20]
    e) be less able to be assimilated either to the mainstream or to the
        margins of our culture
    f) be more easily excluded from anthologies or any institutions of
        record
    g) be more "naturally" forgotten.

I say this neutrally, in a kind of rabid grief.

Mainly, our culture has, sooner or later, divested itself of the impact of any woman writing or producing art works within it. To say "I hope this has now changed" is to drape a Pollyana-ish skirt over a constant struggle within the politics of culture. We can say it if you want. "I hope this has now changed."

Where, how do they break? What is "deep enough"; where is the "level" or which are the "modes" through which one can enter and transform?

Let the discourses crash against each other, for the opposite of cleansing the words of all connotations ("cleansing" is a word which Williams will typically use), the opposite of purifying the language of the tribe (the phrase typical to Eliot) would be to let the connotations and the discourses—the appropriate, the inappropriate, the intelligent, the silly—swirl, coagulate. The social meanings imbedded. The words "the new free woman" in the resonance of their implications. The words "restore regularity." The word "glass." But but but but—if the discourses slide and crash, doesn't this just make an exotic decorative texture in the work? They will say I cannot control my argument. They will say how I am growing fat. They will say that this rhythm is impossible, it is jumpy, it flickers like something whose technology is imperfect or has gone awry. And besides, is collage really a tactic adequate to what I must get from it, to where I must get?

reckless impetuous gesture,   where is "the life"   o a thunderstorm, a social worker, the dog angled on the floor, a boy arrested, old blue sugar bowl on the window sill, a careless love (for the language), filled with potpourri, means rotten flowers. Stir it. A pink dust rises. Sneeze.

From this dust you will remake the rose? (Yiddish accent)

Do you really want to? is this just a convenient question? Is it "a rose" you want, or "an end—of roses" (S&A, p. 108). Grandfather, I don't even know my question! Nor whether I want your help.

All the "levels" of destruction to proceed simultaneously. Line break. Gender break, Dish break. Center break. Plot break. Sound break. Destroy worship and worshippers. Let the fragments roar, the dust blow like snuff, annoying, in pertinacity and pressure. And grief. If you can.

silver leaf
o a jay blue shine
crude cry

o blue blue leaf shit on these leaves. Who cares about this? or about someone or other's guitar?

What are you doing, listening, to a cry cry cry—she's hungry? she's frustrated (no quality of that word for the emotions of a certain kind of toddler—anguished might be closer, anguished without language, and without certain skills, without certain power). She wants to walk she wants to talk, she wants to make marks, empties, spills, shakes, her whole body shakes

What is mommy doing? Is mommy washing her hair? Why am I talking in questions? Why do I call myself "Mommy" and not "I"? Hi, baboo, aren't you cute in your pretty blue sundress, aren't you "a cute little girl."

> to speak the unspoken?
> cannot rest there, more
> than the unspoken, there
> is the spoken

I create gender.

Gender creates me. Again and again. I am clay in its hands. She is in mine. Us in his. Theirs. These shifters. Have they really shifted very far?

As an "idea"—like many "ideas"—the feminine is contradictory. The "beautiful illusion"   the decoration   a certain kind of loveliness have clearly been banalized. "Beauty" must be separated from this sugared loveliness, and brought to "a state in which reality plays a part" (S&A, p. 117).

> The imagination, freed from the handcuffs of "art," takes the lead! Her feet are bare and not too delicate. In fact those who come behind her have much to think of. Hm. Let it pass.
> (S&A, p. 97).

Populist, in the fray, like Liberty leading the People, this "imagination," gendered female is a figure on whom the male artist makes explicitly sexual propriatary claims. Wink wink. Coming behind her. She may lead him, but he can think penetrating thoughts about her. Like Paterson's sexual fantasy about fertilizing many women: that only in sexual conjuncture is born VOICE. In these meditations of Williams, considerable energy is devoted to separating a "female" power of dynamic presence from a "feminine" of banality, commonplaces, cliches, decoration. The banal "rose is obsolete" (S&A, p. 107). But if "to engage roses becomes a geometry," if roses can be "copper roses / steel roses" (S&A, p. 108), then powers of science and technology are grafted to the rose. The sotto voce gender narrative in Williams will offer the banal feminine back as the property of the despised female artist. (He asks, in The

Great American Novel, parodically what is good poetry made of, what is bad poetry made of. Answers: "Of rats and snails and puppy dog's tails" for the good kind, and for bad poetry? "Of sugar and spice and everything nice / That is what bad poetry is made of." No kidding.) He will offer the banal feminine back, and take hold of, claim, the female of power grafted to masculine codes.[21]

This is satisfactory, very, for a male writer, because it makes him boundless, inclusive, central and marginal at once. An embodied man has achieved the privileges of male gender—education, travel rights, free speech, life support services of food preparation, cleared time, financial independence or at least right to earn, some autonomy, father-hood of benevolence and distance—and then has also reached out to claim those undeniable marginalities which by form and analogy are gendered female. How could he not be complete?

What "parallel" formulation for an embodied woman? How does she integrate the privileges of femaleness with the powers of maleness? How, did you say? I didn't hear you.

Thus Williams can state, "It is the woman in us [in men] / That makes us write," claiming the complexities of a subject position that incorpo-rates both genders; he can solemnize his poetics in the figure of Mme. Curie; and he can appropriate and transpose the "hysterical" effusions of a woman writer, blocking her unlovely attempt to claim powers—powers, powers, of autonomous art.[22] (I'm talking about Cress's letters, in *Paterson.*)

They have a most curious position, those letters of desire and failed desire—Ginsberg's letters about a literary career, the funny letters dis-gusted with the sexual activities of a dog, letters from Dahlberg, from Sorrentino, letters from an African-American domestic, and finally from the pseudononymous Cress.[23] These letters are generally real folk writing, real "writing": all are local, situated, processual, even drowned in minutiae (Ginsberg touchingly characterizes his vacillating behavior after a Williams poetry reading). The letters in general seem to ask: can "the language" come forth here, from this rich, generative ground. And Cress is, therefore, in a pivotal role—as a letter writer, as a female writer. Williams, indeed, makes an enlarged and privileged place for Cress. Her voice is singularly powerful. And she is probably the most unsettling place for the female
reader/writer to find

her mirror, her site
in reading these words.

The themes to which Cress addresses herself—a denial of and saturation in thralldom, a desire for recognition, an ambition, inferences about and bafflement with the cultural paralysis of women—we know her well. The voice complains, overexplains, justifies vapidly, accuses, seems daft, sly, paranoid. The tones are an embarrassment. Borderless tones, shifting, shiftless. In which she wants the other, wants to be the other, wants the other to want her, wants wants wants wants. Bottomless maw. Wanting Dr. Paterson is a way of wanting herself, wanting her own career as a writer. Her blockages are almost fecal, for cloacal metaphors characterize these letters; the writing does not seem to "remove obstruction" but, with surpassing irony, to create it. Her eloquent, manipulative self-division is personalized with panache. She accuses Dr. P of causing some troubles, exacerbating others, despite his help. A conspiratorial tone. A martyrdom.

(Correction—which she partly knows too—and who wants to hear it? gender relations, gender ideology, gender positionality have caused them.)

Cress has, she says, no personal identity (yet she seems to overwhelm the very text in which her words are appropriated!). Hence she has no language, no sense of the meaningfulness of her thoughts. She is unable to write the poems she desires. For Williams, she is a consummate avatar of a central issue in America and in his diagnostic poem: divorced, unrooted, and therefore voiceless. For a woman writer, she is a pre- or proto-feminist mirror (how did they survive? those women of the 40's, of the 50's?).[24] She is a mirror of one's female self—starved, and over-full at once. Grappling

for the questions and the answers, resisting both
everything out of order, no logic, the nail in the shoe, the backache, the bad haircut, the bad education, the digestive problems, the editor who might have but didn't, the misunderstood meeting, the confusions of personal and impersonal, the impossibility of getting or keeping a job, the unstrategic choices

(I am inventing, I am inventing from memory—of the work? of my life?)

the embarrassing run in a stocking, the embarrassing remark said under pressure, the giggle in the voice, the inability to stop talking once started, to start talking once stopped

(I am inventing, I am inventing from memory—of what?)

no sense of proportion, no priorities, emphasis skewed. All Wrong! (Woolf: "the accent never falls where it does with a man")

"completely in exile socially." Cress knows it. (*P*, p. 110). Internal exile. Arrest. Yet would it be possible to breathe this, it is so awful: that Nardi's letters, rewritten slightly and selected by Williams, are her most striking works?

This is, then, a very ornery muse, a muse-protest. A muse-resister. And filled with a particularity, an eloquent malice that can make a critical statement upon the poem's losses, the perpetual escape of the fresh thing beyond the poet. A position, however, perfectly consistent with Williams' poetics.[25] So however resistant, a "muse" Cress is, insofar as "muse" is that cultural position of not being able to hear and build on one's own words but having them inspire a (male) writer. Exactly the situation to which she herself points. And Williams is an excited appropriator, staking a claim to all her letters to him, even (at one point) wanting to use them throughout his poem. And these letters perfectly present two of the central conventional meanings ascribed to the figure Woman: excess but wasted fecundity. And lack.

One might well say about Cress what Stephen Heath says about a film by Mulvey-Wollen called *Riddles of the Sphinx* (1977): these letters are an apparent "point of resistance" because they are such an intrepid fleyting of Williams. However, this point of resistance "seems nevertheless to repeat, in its very terms, the relations of women made within patriarchy."[26]

He does? does not? dwell on her case as the problem of organizing the female subject. She does? does not? dwell on her case as the problem of organizing the female subject.

What does she want? How can she write the unheard self, the discredited self, the self-divided, self-rejected self, the self uncompaniable with other women. Is this problem solved by a feminist practice?

Well, Cress wants herself, but she has him on her mind, his position, his centrality (which she may poignantly, comically, willfully, therefore contemptibly exaggerate: our sympathy is with Williams). She is complaining, but complicit. She assumes her cultural position as Other within his text by virtue of her use of / by virtue of his use of the brilliant, strident, demanding, aggressive, unreasonable letters, Have I, saying this, given her no way out? Is there no way to escape the power of Williams' appropriative gesture?

Mme. Curie. Her procedure is correct, for it is his. Or his is hers. To collect several tons of material, letters, reports, newspaper accounts, sermonizing, local writing, and distill it by selection and juxtaposition, so that it boils down, so a spark of the unifying themes can be discerned as the material crosses and recrosses. Mme. Curie, persistent, indefatigable, first sighter of radium . . .

Cress and Curie, Curie and Cress. These giant women. Curious. Curie stirs the sludge, pregnant, noting some chemical dissonance, in despair at having found "nothing" returns one night, led back, to find her drop of distilled matter *Luminous.* The climactic moment. Williams, saying it in just this way incidentally registers (appropriates? overwrites?) Mina Loy's early tribute to Gertrude Stein: "Curie / of the laboratory / of vocabulary / she crushed / the tonnage / of consciousness / congealed to phrases / to extract / a radium of the word[.]"[27]

She, the woman, the cook/scientist, the central actor in this distillation of a "radiant gist" which is a key to his poetics—this central figure of his poetics is female (although her mind is "neutral")[28]

yet   she   never   speaks   one   single   word.

her discovery paradigmatic
her discovery "luminous"

she says nothing! nothing! nothing!

In the contradistinction to Cress the garrulous. What an equation. What a proposition: named, known, historical figure, Curie is effectual, but without speech, voice, or word within Williams' poem, while unknown, actual, but occluded figure, Nardi, is highly ineffectual but possesses wild, effusive speech and voice. The successful woman is "coincidentally" to her patent success without voice. The unsuccessful woman is "coincidentally" to her failure highly voiced with hysterical complaint. A study in the representation of woman. For Cress the accumulator, Curie the refiner—together can be inside him, each offering her peculiar kind of stubborn effort. And so he can have words, effective, luminous words.

Men can swallow women.
Can women swallow men?
What monsters come forth
then?

Sinus: "a fistula or channel to a suppurating cavity."

The great moments in *Paterson* occur when Williams releases his poem to pass beyond gendered limits into contradictory and swarming meanings. That is, the great moments follow *Kora in Hell* (1918), *Spring and All* (1923), *The Great American Novel* (1923), *A Novelette* (1932). The writing in motion, a rhythm, a pulse, desire always and desire shifting, its object car, flower, cloud, woman, birth, rusted metal; its object skunk cabbage, vase, light lines, machinery, pregnancy; its object glass shattered, asphalt, a sore, the tire; its object heterogeneous, persistent, pulsing ahead of itself, its momentum dazzling, its stop and starts precious data. "Neither poem nor novel but polylogue, both pulverizing and multiplying unity through rhythm. . . ."[29]

This pulse of meaning and no-meaning, the heteroglossic possibilities of writing, of writing as practice. Polyloquacious. (without his hopelessly limiting ejaculatory endings)

If, in a binary economy, "his speech requires her silence," one must declare by intensities of fiat, every which way, the end of binaries, the end of complicity in binaries, "pulverizing and multiplying" I cannot say what, I cannot, either, say "unity."[30]

There are words. One must use them! writing into pleasure from a position like the scraping of an eyeball, pain, staying up into tepid nights, lonely and driven, into the exhaustion of grasp, endless hunger and touching, grappling with hunger so that the eating eye, the poet's eye, can be filled. So that category be "shifted"; so that objects be risked into accidentals; so that relationships enter "the disjointing process."[31]

For all this, Williams' metaphor is the falls: bounty, plurality, force, confusion, heterogeneous speech-sound roaring. Is *Paterson*, then, a feminine discourse neutralized and undone by certain masculine subject stances of the author-narrator mythically done up as Priapus, as the Satyr: phallic sexuality, homophobia, and rape? Surely after such a poetics, such an avalanche of drive and of necessity, to enter, on principle and with triumph, into the banalities of gender is an insult.

> Saturday June 22nd, 1940. I wish I could invent a new critical method—something swifter and lighter and more colloquial and yet intense: more to the point and less composed: more fluid and following the flight; than my C.R. essays. The old problem: how to keep the flight of the mind, yet be exact. All the difference between the sketch and the finished work. And now dinner to cook. A role. Nightly raids in the east and south coast. 6, 3, 22 people killed nightly.[32]

If I were to be where I am, where would I be?

There is hardly one answer. Hardly one place.

I dreamt my mother was "working on the sinus"—which was also the topic of another woman who was writing a book on—Heady Coincidence!—"The Sinus." "The sinus," she had said at a meeting, "is a very primitive form. Did you know that all of its chambers are connected?" My mother had built, inside her apartment, a person-sized model sinus. A series of doors. When she went in, you could never predict which door she would come out of.

And what does one do with the intermittent conviction that every single word to date has been wrong, mismanaged, imprecise? I could hear him talking about myth yet. Easy enough to descend into the other side of the library. How then to descend into some "other sides" of language, remaining intelligible (enough). Which is in itself a value. A limit? is it a limit? a limiting value? The humbling awareness of how many authors there have already been in the recanting of language. Its negation. How can we "deconstruct" a language we "never" possessed before? Or is saying this, the most miasmic sentimentality? Of course we possess the language—yet what does it mean to have language, but few of its social instruments (of authority, of dissemination)? How can it be said that women talk both "too much" and "too little." How can we be both garrulous and silenced?

We have languages, are bifocal in language, are "bilingual" in a subtle way. "Few" of its "social instruments"? We speak "Woman," we may speak and mainly listen to "Man" and we speak "feminine" and we have a passable comprehension of "masculine," we are fluent in "female" and have a reading knowledge of "male." This certainly sounds funny. (For one thing, it does not speak about class languages intersecting with gender, and thus not about multi-linguality in social determinants.) But where do I go for my words?[33]

This pink guitar, this pinked guitar.

Do you think this is easy? I suppose the measure of success is the illusion that the author has no resistances. The words "pour onto" the page. (Well, all the doors are connected.) Perhaps the resistances are part of the design of the work, a revelation of its devices, a waylaying of reader in her desire for a truth rather than a making. A work in which the resistances are not part of the design? An impeded writer. And by whom is "impeded" defined? And how? If I define "impeded" as characterized by a banal view of gender, who will hear me. Who, in hearing, will not shrug, o that again. Can't we finally be done with the tendentious. Yeah.

The sweater "sets," "the matches," "dyed to match," "mix and match." You can see that the issue was once uniformity. Pink flats for pink dresses. "I've heard that this is a really terrible poem." "I've heard that this is a really naive writer." Already known knowledge. Formatted. Verif-eyed. The measure of my excellent education was, in 1963, a resistance to *Paterson* and to Williams. Until I read it, the great confrontative entry into accumulation, discontinuity, fissure, rift. . . . Eyed as we were, eyed, we arch girl sophisticates. No poetry from these. Terrible girls, cultural (fleas) positionalities.

enabled by his enabling
disenfranchised by my position in his enabling
wobble wobble wobble

And I am forever in his debt. He opened writing. Writing as writing. Writing as praxis. Ongoing. Curious. Situated. Rapid. Rabid. Marked with one's markings. Not uniform. An exposure. Incomplete. Unsafe. Even deplorable.

It is as Alice Notley said: "It's because of Williams that you can include every thing that's things—& maybe everything that's words—is that going too far?—if you are only up to noticing everything that your life does include. Which is hard. Too many people have always already been telling you for years what your life includes."[34]

Including Williams.

Chapter: Williams made a critique of representation, but there was something else to criticize.

They were all, all revolutionaries except for one idea, one feature, one substance. The writing they perfected, the eloquent emptiness, drawn to the burble, the midden, sheer rhythm, a dance and not a mirror, an electricity

was deflected from the contemporaneous revolution in, and of, gender.

This plenitude and mysterious fecundity in *Paterson* will narrow into a figure, a theme, an idea. How could one leave the generative material otherwise (formless, inchoate, excessive), and not make it ground for a triumphant figure, the tune to which the male subject forever dances when, phallopotent, some unicorn stands in the green(y) millefleur ground hoof deep in flowers.

"Keep your pecker up," he instructs himself, "whatever the detail!" (*P*, p. 273). Is this stagey? yes. It is also honest. To him. But here, as in the earlier panicked assertion "[the sea] is NOT our home!" (*P*, p. 236) gender scripts act to limit Williams' scope and address, reduce his achievement. Reduce his "writing." By virtue of his major unexamined ground. Gender.

Yet he thought he had answered how writing is engendered. The world, it is a woman. The poet, he is a man. Writing is a sexualized drama. Terms that recur in *Paterson* for culture and writing: marriage, divorce, love. Terms of importance: pecker, brothel, pregnant, fertile, virgin, whore. Terms that define, even if they do not appear: rape, queer.

Text is made, radiance is found, the center (gist) is luminous by (hetero)-sexuality. Somewhat counterfactual in this model—but not completely—is the woman writer. She is counterfactual when she is angry, furious, livid; she can be absorbed and accounted for when she enters (as Sappho does) the propulsive economy of sexual desire.

The sexual, for Williams, occurs in the critical fusion of virgin and whore—ideal figure and degraded figure—the fusion claiming that these are one, that they are the same, and that they represent the female. He has taken binaries and fused these polarized categories without altering the traditional terms. He reproposes the power of these terms by exaggeration.

There is a Beautiful Thing [sic] at the very center of the poem (P, pp. 123, 128–29, 144–54). A "thing" powerful. So powerful that recognition of her can burn the library down. She is a radical figure against the easy pleasures of consumable culture. She is a Black woman, a domestic worker. And she has been raped. Gang raped. Williams has been called onto her case.

She is examined by the doctor (the poet)
She is rescued by the poet (the doctor) as he is rescued by her from staleness, from the library, from habitual culture
She is revered by the poet (given back her "real" self, called beautiful)
She is "raped" by the bluntness and brutality of the poet. (This is a metaphor.)
He makes this radical probe a form of searing desire. Of seeing desire. Seizing.
He replicates the gang rape in a professional guise (a professional ruse), possessed with the desire that caused it, for

  black plush, a dark flame (P, p. 154)

he is the doctor   the poet   the rapist   these
are all identities he claims
the rapist is the consummate subject position
He wants it the most
it alone is adequate

to what he $\begin{cases} \text{feels.} \\ \text{sees.} \end{cases}$

$\begin{cases} \text{In him?} \\ \text{In her?} \end{cases}$

One critic talks about Williams' progress through *Paterson* as a release from the desire for mastery, an acceptance of all experience as it comes.[35] For this, it is claimed, his trope is rape, which is an extreme form of the Keatsean negative capability. (Rape is something to accept as it comes?) But depiction, however bold, is not identification. The raped "girl" is voiceless. Williams is not "in her point of view." As they say. And Williams does identify with the battering men—"TAKE OFF

YOUR CLOTHES," he shouts, shaking with desire and anger (*P*, p. 128).
At least the poet is more honest than the critic.

Does one affirm female power by damaging it? while claiming it is far
ahead of oneself in capacity? by "making it" do one's own most hidden
and shocking desire?

By which I mean: burn the library down.

Chapter 2

What do I want? What is it I want?

Chapter 1

The poet knows the multiplicity of the world: symbolically as the
multiplicity of women, allegorically as the pursuit of women, metaphorically as a field of flowers (of women), metaphysically as (his)
desire. All things are powerful, fecund, dynamic, swarming, quickening
around him. He is excited! He can barely keep up! Vision, vision, who
would begrudge him!

Chapter 2

How do women achieve the "chora," the fecund voicing emptiness
before the "Law" enters, who have been taxed with emptiness, form-
lessness. How find our kind of semiotic babble, how propose it without
being colonized by the symbolic function of already written language.
How allow the social heteroglossias of language women might recognize: workplace, friendships, sex, baby talk, and of languages-for-profit
addressed to us. How make our conjuctures heard, and not only as
the temporarily exotic, the bow (cordial, dismissive, bitter, resentful,
chivalric) in our direction. How to lay bare the device of gender when
we are immersed in its symptoms; I mean systems. How to write?

What allows the female subject to constitute "it" self? What kind of
desire or possession?
what metaphors of desire
is it staying as far away as possible from all metaphors of rape?
And how can we, when from Graeco-Roman myth to *Clarissa* (the book
that Fresca reads) and *The Waste Land*, Euro-culture is built on rapine
conjunctures. And when every daily paper will have this story: He
killed her "because" 'she said she didn't want me any more.'

Kora in Hell.

The subject positions for a woman? are they not the deepest plumbing of that unstable and contradictory mixture—not "male/female" but female/feminine/feminist. When those tricky and challenging combinations are fully explored, then there will be power, there will be authority, there will be joy. I am no one's Other. And then I can with ease and pleasure, possibly, construct some of myself, as, say, "a little boy"—although that very thought seems bizarre.[36] Not andro-gyny but hetero-gyneity. Poly-gyny.

That other chapter

"I could have raped them all!" said Williams, wildly happy, reminiscing to a woman interviewer about reading at Wellesley College (a women's college), about the clamor of the female audience, and his joy at their reception of his work.[37]

It is clear that it is absolutely necessary for him to say this. It seems clear that he is speaking about desiring himself. And the tragedy of his view of gender is that he must penetrate, and "take" the Other in order to express his unbounded eros of the self in and for the world. "Raped" then means constituted-my-ego-in-joy, it means orgasmic pleasure releasing writing's pleasure in being heard. It means possessing a sense of his completeness, by possessing a mythical potency for infiniation of pleasure. All! Them All! Sex is the hymen between deadness (of language, of feeling) and living transformation. He will rupture, he will imagine rupturing that virginal space over and over. Imagine "whoring it." (Imagine "whoring" as the metaphor for sex!) by "raped" he may even ("simply") mean another even more direct, but taboo word. Fucked. Fucked them all.

Whereas to be raped is different. Murder is next, and, if you are unlucky, thereupon occurs. To be raped, taking another point of view, is to have nightmares for years after, to have one's sexual responses compromised, sullied, confused, burdened, mutilated for a long time. To remember and replay minutes in which "choices" were made—as with any tragedy, minutes elongate and time is frozen. Raped! Raped! to rape them all, read darkly, dourly, means to compromise their ability to have and express pleasure. And—in his terms—to compromise their ability to make writing.

I cannot gainsay his joy.
But his innocence?
seems perverse.

The Final Chapter

Will you assume that I have entered a level or a mode of representation "below" or "beyond" the construction (constriction) of my voice within the patriarchal. Is that so easy? It isn't. And I didn't do it, nor would I claim it. I entered a complex, ongoing, everlasting and unstable negotiation with the patriarchal, some border-crossing mix of "symbolic" and second-term "semiotic"—for "semiotic" is always inflected with its passage through the oedipal and then "back" in an imaginative trek to the pre-oedipal.[38] I have engaged in some trek through poly-present languages. Heterogeneous and self-questioning, judgmental and polyvalent, craving and craven—this is the practice. The pleasures of a doing, an on-goingness, a finding, a coming to, a beginning again and again. The sense of totality is gone, the swing to climax deflected. Swerve from the end as end. The practice is trying to articulate critical leverage in form or language, to cite and transpose, to encircle and enter wedge-wide, to parody, to exaggerate, to slow up, to offer gesture inappropriate to genre, and genre riddled with its own gestures.

By some cunning and articulate exile from that to which we are asked to be attached. It is not so much seductions

by the canonical as suspicions

not the speaking of a clean pure lyric line, a clean pure polemical line, a clean pure logic, a real identity, a real origin, the real story

but its interruption, its doubling, the presentation of other manifolds, other centers

so that it becomes impossible to seek a unitary reading, so that one is elaborately gorged

with an ironizing beyond irony for it lacks the sense of norm, of agreement.

Dream: a cakey red lipstick mouth, pouty and intense
The lips part
out of which the protrubering shape of a "form"

a gel in a packet, the representation of a breast to balance things
post-mastectomy.
It pokes from the mouth volcanic
the breast eerie without nipple without aureole
surrounded at its base by the bright red aureole
the mouth
open   the breast volcanic.

What am I doing? What are these desirous "wounds" these great
gapings?

What is that big red mouth?

Proposition 1. Write it, shameless cobbler, driven cob-in-web.

I want writing.
Writing, as feminist practice.

> Summer 1984
> when stamps were 20¢ and
> baby was not 1

> revised June 1989
> when stamps were 25¢
> and "baby" was 5

SUB RROSA

Marcel Duchamp and
the Female Spectator

Sub Rrosa n° 1. A description of *Etant Donnés: l^e la chute d'eau, 2e le gaz d'éclairage* by Marcel Duchamp.

This is an assemblage constructed in a clandestine, second studio by Marcel Duchamp over the 20 years (1946–66), when it was claimed implicitly and explicitly that he was no longer engaged in the making of artworks. The existence of the work was known primarily to Duchamp's wife and assistant for the work, Teeny; much later (1968) to a friend who helped negotiate its purchase; and, after his death in 1968, to the museum officials who, from Duchamp's own meticulous plans, diagrams, and photographs installed *Etant Donnés . . .* in the Arensberg Collection of the Philadelphia Museum.[1] Sub rosa he made it, and sub rosa we view it.

To the side of the bright room in the Arensberg Collection, containing *The Bride Stripped Bare by her Bachelors, Even* and some other notable Duchamps and Duchamp-kits, there is a dark, odd room which contains nothing. At the far end of this cul de sac, in a wall, is built a heavy barn door framed in bricks. This is "real," a door which is or was a door.[2] Its hinges, however, are absent. Until the publication of the facsimile notebook containing Duchamp's diagrams and photographic aids to reassembling this "approximation démontable," there was a fifteen-year ban on the reproduction of the interior tableau, an interdiction now apparently lifted.[3] The temporary play with the inviolable interior was perversely appropriate, as people have felt that the interior is one of the most violable nudes in the history of art. But I am getting ahead of a body of statement.

> on the side   a thickening a bird's
> egg plum down   sidling sidelong along
> fear   THRUSHt down in the word

Walked in to a dark side room, and therein (darkly) up to a rustic door, in which, among the thick nails, there are two eyeholes. Peeped in, curious, saw an oval blast through brick (coded: explosion/explosive;

68

coded: a cinematic fade-thru piercing solids). And through that frame a succinct diorama, as lush and pretty, as filled with an atmospheric stagey light as the best Museums of Natural History provide for the animals and tribal folk, so "naturally" posed.

The feeling is crystalline, blue with puff clouds; the trees evoking all four seasons (pink, green, rust, frosty), and painterly creams of colors stage-lit. Thoroughly "retinal," thoroughly sentimental, one adds, filled with rage and méchante-ness, for the méchance of being a contradiction? an estrangement? a sucker? a puppet, a toy toyed with: *the marked marker*[4] Who is as rebuffed by the work as sucked into it, who may be it, who is "not it." Hide and seek. One can never get close enough to this to "really see" it, for Duchamp prescribes the distance and the level of discomfort you feel (mouth and nose to wood, pushing the door) in the position of consumed consumer. Consumed with curiosity, desire, rage, shame, powerlessness.[5]

Cul de sac. Bottom of the bag. Dead end. Mea cul-pa.

In the museum, we graze among representations, pretend possessors, possessive pretenders, the very conventions of display (anthology, supermarket, store window) in a nonfunctional setting (not a real kitchen for the artifacts, not a real temple for the altar, not a real room for the painting) compelling us to be flaneurs engaged in a sensational practice, culling our version of the rare. In some complicit critique of the museum—playing the museum against itself, playing with the secret, the hidden in this cornucopia of openness, and playing out the museum's social postures of possessor, collector, connoisseur—Duchamp has engineered a mandatory posture for the viewing of this piece, uncharacteristic for the museum's mobile, park-like qualities. This posture of peeking, peering into a secret space evokes overlays of an erotic sort (peepshows, pornographic bookstores) admixed with early 20th century childhood pleasures (of 3-D shows on the stereopticon, of folk parades with floats of giants). Duchamp plays with sex and the museum, putting visual conventions of pornography and sexual display at the core of the collection, and creating some frank oscillation between art appreciation and "ard" titillation, between the arousal to visual pleasure and the arousal to sexual pleasure.[6] So walk up to the door curious; walk away having been made a voyeur.

The main content of this diorama is a life-sized, foreshortened, somewhat disproportionate and cut waxy-looking object which does rather resemble a naked pink woman. "Woman": a lump of female matter, the botanical markers of sex (one breast, open legs) loosely displayed in allusion. This is a post-war piece, mythologizing a supine, sexualized female. There is no head visible, but one sees some long blonde hair. The exact feminine arm (yet a gigantic hand!), holding a lamp (the "gaz d'éclairage" or afflatus of clear purity), a lady of the lamp kind of arm, extending into this picture realistically and ideologically straight from the 19th century. Bringing with it the sweet nobility of "Womanhood" and such cultural icons of enlightenment as Florence Nightingale and the Statue of Liberty. It may even derive from medieval tableaux of the wise virgin who holds her lamp upright. The nobility of the lamp, and the allusions to other of the sentimental tokens of purity like the waterfall and the tender colors are quite confrontative, corny, po(i)sed in our nostalgia. The virginity and intellectual nobility of the lamp shine on the distorted, manipulated ideological and visual hit of sex.

For lamp and waterfall aren't what you "see." What you see, head on, ahead of you, is cunt. Estranged cunt, the cant or can't of cunt. Duchamp has made a twisted, asymmetrical gash—richly labial but curved and wayward—where a vulva "is." Deep, like a S-curved valley, disturbing, uncanny, provocative: (t)his lady has her bottom put on wrong. Like every nude, it is an interpreted depiction of sexual markers, only allusively or by cultural agreement read as "realistic."Like most but not all (male and female) nudes in the history of our art, this figure has no pubic hair, but that deficiency is more than made up by a witty collection of brushwood, or bound faggots with some dead leaves ("bachelors"?), on which this creature is poised as if on the edge of a cliff. Her legs, have I mentioned? are wide open. Her head, her face—have I mentioned?—are absent. In the far background, as if at great airy distance, is a tinkling silvery "faery" waterfall, looks like it was made for desirous consumption of department store windows or popular appreciation of our patronizing understanding of others, as in dioramas dependent upon Western imperialism.[7]

> red round   ocarina
> unspecified brown sweet
> bird whistle thru the rote holes, air
> purple petunia horns blew windsock-stiff.
> Ate rose
> hip jam
> live from the jar
> a door   blue shut   rush
> dims coreopsis bright darks wrinkled rose
> bristle quick rain a reine a wren.

Sub Rrosa n° 2: under what rose?

Held off, attracted—the energies of spectatorship attached to the energies of desire—the distancing barriers imprison the viewer in one spot;
it is a form of visual bondage—the very limits are exciting. The form
is not only implicitly heterosexual (or taken so by commentators, although no partner is present): but also taken as sacrificial (a woman on
a pyre), punitive (the mutilated body) and as self-pleasuring (she holds
the [phallic] lamp autonomously). "The viewer draws back from the
door feeling that mixture of joy and guilt of one who has unearthed a
secret. But what is the secret? What, in fact, has he [**] seen." One of
Octavio Paz's answers, "we see ourselves looking," conceals the further
question "who is looking?"—a puzzle that can no longer be postponed.[8]
Who is "we"? Since some "we" is not a confabulation of "he," how
to see her contribution, her consternation, her con-tribulation, her
conjugation as *the marked marker*?

And yet, she *is* first he. All female readers are first "immasculated"
argues Judith Fetterley; all learn to "read like men."[9] Which means a
female socially constrained to perceive in so-called "genderless" ways
themselves redolent of maleness, the *(marked marker)* constrained
not to seek aspects of female difference, sounding untutored or simplis-
tic if she diverges from the universal-which-is-not-and-never-female. A
woman first or expectedly adopts an "androcentric posture" before
artwork. To read *as* a woman is to rupture this expected practice.

But to read as *what* woman? *A* woman? Is that phrase generic or specific? As any woman reads? or as me, as I read? Is there "a" woman
reader? It seems amazing even to imagine *one,* but to imagine hundreds
is gratifying. So I read as one imagining others. What is subsumed under
the term "woman"—what practices? what formations?[10] Is there a universal humanist woman to counterweight the universal "all-men-are-
created" man? Once, recently, it was bravery to think so. And it's
an irony to attack that presumptive universalized woman of liberal
feminism without trying to puncture the balloon of universal man, or
even harder, the universal man nuanced with, draped in contextuality
and the situational. That "universal"—harder to catch or trap, since it is
made of privilege—geographical, economic, political, epistemological.
Me, Western, and whitish, can find buoyant the same balloon I want,
from my gender perspective, to puncture.

I look down into my pants and see my tag.
Made in Indonesia. Made in Korea. Made in Sri Lanka. And they were
plenty cheap, too.

Perhaps only a clumsy awkward hopelessly an-aesthetic phrase could
begin to signal some social forces as I experience them:

> as "a person mainly gendered female."
> amid my multiple determinants like a Penelope,
> loyal enough to some, but sometimes
> not even sure which way I'm(e) weaving,
> or woven.

Sub Rrosa n° 3: The maze of the gaze

What is that thing behind the door?
What is that thing in front of the door?

> a picture   a nude
>   a pigskin
>   A WOMAN
> a viewer   a casual visitor
>   an eyeball

paranoias of the Bluebeard myth, for the wife: what is that thing behind
the door? Or Pandora, what is that thing, the hand reaching to open?

Duchamp has made everyone OPEN IT.

Duchamp's work here does not beg us to differ from the normal posture
of immasculated looking; in many ways its siting and its dramatic
situation (one peeps at a naked woman) reinforce an androcentric posture even as it is complicit with male powerlessness by registering the
humiliating and vulnerable stance in some male seeking: an eye at the
keyhole peering at a woman is not unambiguously coded as powerful.
And complicit with female powerlessness (this male eye, despite humil-
iations, claims power over an Other). That peeking eye needs an initia-
tion or a pleasure which is always belated, to which it may be impotent.
The voyeur is distanced from pleasures sought precisely in the maintenance of distance. The consistency of this position with completely
naturalized ideologies of romantic longing is startling. Is the work then
a direct re-enactment of such pleasures, or, in ways parallel to its
grotesque segue over mimetic painting, is it a grotesque or ironic torsion

of Romantic ideology? Spectatorship is impotence? And then what of the museum's multiplied insistence of spectatorship, of Duchamp's binding of the gaze? A send-up of the museum in the museum, a bringing of art institutions to their knees. Not uncharacteristic.

Irony directed to art products. Irony directed at museums as cultural institutions. Irony to Art, capital "A." Irony about the nude. Irony towards the way spectators look at a nude, to prurient interest. Irony about what kinds of things are conventionally in one's head afterwards. Irony about implicating the spectator in a performance whose topic is "looking at *Etant Donnés . . .*" Irony about the solemn distinction between much hegemonic art and pornography, solemnities which he would unsettle and, even, undo.

Duplicities of duplication (his little kits, the valises with miniatures or toys of such works as *Nude Descending a Staircase*). A work of art in the age of mechanical

> diminution

> abduction
> over-
> production

Duchamp signifyin(g) on the museum—over my dead body. Over the "dead body" of some pigskin propped on angled joists, gendered female.[11] Can I claim these privileges of duplicity? As John Berger has pointedly suggested, every woman is in a double relation of voyeur, she looks at herself being looked at and is powerless over the refracted gazing; here I look at myself looked at by Duchamp, reobserved by female me, and I am confused between my impotent distance as male voyeur and impotent identification as female voyeur.[12]

So I am the female reader, I am the *marked marker* I am she inside the outside the dividing barrier, I am the penising eye, and the missing I, bit of wiggy blond hair just visible to mark the missing head. I am the one who looks, I am she who cannot gaze, in reciprocity, back. In the situation here, he-is-me, and she-is-me. I am the subject speaking of all this and I am the object for the voyeur. How many mobile places can I be, a feminist tinker bell, marked by conventions of depiction that center me as "cunt" (why one is in front of me right now!). Yet if I read in too intransigent resistance, I risk blocking the very process of assimilation of such images, and may block, in bulk, understanding the discourses of "my" culture, and Duchamp's address to them.

Propose, with Mary Ann Doane, an oscillatory structure for the female spectator. Who can have "a 'narcissistic' identification with the female figure as spectacle, and a 'transvestite' identification with the active male hero in his mastery."[13] But if I want "transvestite"—I might want some other kind of male figure into whom I can cross-dress. Not the "active male hero"—who anyway? Some dandy perhaps. And—I feel transvestite identification with the female. So even the success of this formulation (whose back and forths I even feel here, in this structure) does not mask its indebtedness to binaries. How can gender be freed when we are so marked with it? (I don't want to oscillate among fixed positions with predictable gender content—although I have been marked by them.)

Is the female spectator possible? Is she always finally subsumed under the more interesting male, via transvestite strategies? Can one not say active without saying male? This "she" for whom I search (this "person mainly gendered female") seems possible only if she is drawn to look from as many analytic and personal positions as she can muster. A polymorphous, polyauditory scrutiny. And still an "over reading"; for never to forget the making of the woman, the gendering of the reader and the read thing, being over-written with being constructed female, "the political constructions of gender."[14] Forget decorum. Follow down these tricks and paths. Now fetish, now masturbator, now incendiary, now fire-fighter: always an interested party.

Again. If she is me, sub rosa, what do I feel and what do I see? I feel violée, volée, voilée—violated and robbed by the very veil of knowing unknowing which Duchamp places before an eye he has (apparently) assumed male. Le viol(in) d'anger. Then, faced by the fetish, my first holy response to "Art" makes me fragment and disenfranchise my anger. My second response of anger mixed with protective pity overrides the immasculated reading eye. Thereupon I feel pity, for myself de-picted, for my strained and impotent anger. I feel pity for the image, a compassion, an identification, a happy sorrow, and an arousal—of wonder? Wherefore this crystalline scene surrounding this piggish pink mass? Is she sleeping? is she hurt? is she wounded? is she coming? has she come? What or who has put her there? What has come from her? The distance—of the neo-nate. A scene—of birth? the birth of the eye? for the eye has been expelled, and the little pupil, forever distanced, returns bleating, lascivious, distorted with unfillable desires to the door of the mother. Is this what I want to produce: a reading saying: I am the female reader and I do not see the privileging of the "phallic" in this work. My eye is the eye of a similar; I refuse (can I refuse?) the position of voyeur; I identify; this figure is not the Other.

The pity—my sorrow and pity for the figure cast out, since inside has become outside. This figure is not in a boudoir, but outside in nature. When we look inside (the door) we blast through walls (there is no house, no room, no coded inside) until we are outside. We think (by the turn of the door) that we are looking IN something, but we are really looking from a room (in a museum) into exposure, into outside. It is laid away in a manger, one of those open front scenes staged with choice figurines, camels, kings, and cows, mother and imaginary father. Here all figurines are missing except the "babe." One imagines Duchamp musing the icons: a female nude? or some aspect of the Christ? In a secular age, where the female nude has become Christ—victimized, crucified, resurrected, restoring Eden with transfigured flesh—Christ Himself could not have been sufficiently Other. So he chose a Girl made Flesh. But iconic bits of manger scenes steal into this image: the barn door, the magical light of the spiritual lamp, the halo of waterfall, the rough "hay." Beyond the initial (question—does it really have priority?) immasculation, or in the struggle with it, the culturally unaccounted, unacknowledged fact of female spectators (*marked markers*) even watching the idealization or destruction of women has the power to disturb all elements of an art work, throwing established system of consumption, spectatorship, and interpretation into the must fruitful heterogeneity.

Sub Rrosa n° 4: nu?   de   Q

This is a piece just representational enough to remind us of the sensuous convention of robust pink-meaty nudes of innocence (Renoir, Rubens); puzzling enough to recall the refined challenges of intellectually/sensually knowing nudes (Goya, Manet); shocking enough to recall the torsion of almost unacceptable eroticism (Bronzino, Ingres). So it is a pattern book of nudes, an excess of intertextual alliances is part of the shock of the work: one looks at its excrescent self and knows the whole museum falling on one's head.

That which has accidentally occurred to (say) the Venus de Milo has deliberately been enacted here, a strained coupage not less irrevocable from being in the eye of the beholder (dependent on the mandatory limited position of the eye): does she have feet which are out of view?

or no feet at all, no second arm, no face? The filmic "cut"; the "cut of physical coupure"; and the realized "gash" are in metonymic relation to each other. But this frightening text is conjoined with another banal, though erotic and gustatory set of discourses: the nude is "pretty as a picture" (as!); she "looks good enough to eat." She is also "flat as a pancake" resembling a cake or a sugar-coated almond. Again, these discourses of sexual mutilation and gustatory pleasure are contradictory, though one is placed before that place where the contradictions are fused, impacted: that place is the cultural site Woman.

We know Duchamp for his willingness to engage analytically but also furtively with cultural icons and with the systems of value and representation that stand behind him. He stands on the edge of enfolding systems and critical systems—between complicity and critique. This sincere duplicity may be (pace *La Belle Halaine*, Rrose Sélavy and other transvestite moments in Duchamp) his most female gesture, his most feminine "dress." He draws a moustache and beard on the Mona Lisa in a boy-naughty gesture of defacement. The transposition of a man's beard onto a woman's face toys with androgyny; the placement of a punning emblem of her pubic bottom on her face mocks the sacred icon by gloating over woman as perpetually sexualized. It also transposes the face of the painting into a male leer at the recognition which Duchamp's title proposes: a French anagram, written as if as commonplace as INRI: *L.H.O.O.Q.* = elle a chaud au cul = she has hot pants. The iconoclasm occurs at the expense of the female image, but while it is easy to dislodge Mona Lisa as a sacred cow, it is harder to dislodge woman as sacred cow while also constructing an altar. The new, hot title disembowels the duplicities of the visual gesture (towards androgyny and towards questioning the icons) with a masculinist reductiveness. The overall impact can be summarized with Sandra Harding's feminist distrust of androgyny in men: it is a skimming off of the feminine which leaves the social conditions of gender unchanged.[15] But notice, nonetheless, how Duchamp swirls among gender stances, stirring up the dust.

Now critics have noted that the erotic content of *Etant Donnés* . . . is "immediately apparent"[16] but by that they seem to mean only that the image is explicitly sexualized by genital exposure. One does not know, by looking, the nature of the eroticism, which lies in contextual realms of interpretation: is it arousing, disturbing, aphrodisiac, anaphrodisiac, teasing, violent, brutalizing, awe-inspiring? Nor from whence eroticism emanates: simply from the open genitals read as sexual availability? from the mystery of exposed, inexplicably placed nakedness? from the spectator's distance? from the strange torsion? in the relations among this nude and the pulsing perpetual power of gas and water? in suggestions of defiling, raping, protecting, possessing, never possessing? Far from being assured, one might with greater justice say: this work shows us we have no idea at all how we feel, know, understand eroticism, nor who "we" are when we comprehend it. One can only say: the artist has evoked sexuality and mystery simultaneously, and has written over, cut his trace into, an icon of the female, a manipulation, it suddenly becomes clear, that we agree to call art. Is "art" the defiling, arousing, iconizing of a female nude? Eroticism, as Duchamp said with an opaque elegance, was an important aesthetic "-ism."[17]

> anagrams of C.N.T.
> .R.L.L. cuntroll
>
> or C.N.D.R.L.L. Cinderella
> where the fit in the slipper
> issues: blood bumps
> the dim swoops
> of love-breathing (bird)
> dim sum, doughy pork balls
> yum
> sweet fix the shiny threads by tone
> I fit my clitty slit into my own slipper slot

Sub Rrosa n° 5. What are the "givens"?

Some people are fairly clear about what they see when they see it: "she opens her legs out towards the spectator with no false prurience or sense of shame."[18] Not only does the critic tell us how he feels, he remarkably tells us how "she" feels. She! that headless wonder with crazy-quilt quim, that praline construction of the ironic erotic becomes some critic's little woman-person. With real feelings. No "false prurience" here, o no—as opposed, of course, to "true" prurience, that itch, obsession, or fascination with "improper matters, especially sexual." (Is this piece, my piece, however, however, the "true prurience" of such a critic's projections?) (The erotic *is* an important aesthetic -ism.) Then another phrase, another critic: "the pudenda of the violated female figure"[19] suggests that what we witness is the aftermath of rape, while others suggest what we see is the throes of orgasm, but transposed to spiritual illumination.[20] Is it more like a doll, or a mannequin (if a mannequin could have a sex), one of those back page, small ad, life-sized dolls for masturbatory discharge. But it is, overall, more delicate than that.[21] And yet—it is a dreadful, even revolting, delicacy.

The degree to which this genital material is taken as a transparent, realistic portrayal is one of the curiosities of Duchamp criticism—a point at which ideologies of gender and sex, acting to colonize (mostly male) spectators, override even what they know about Duchamp. To wit: that he is a career-long, tricky overwriter and graffiti-ologist, from the beard and mustache on Mona Lisa, to the hat and make-up on himself in drag, to the mock make-over and reversal of his 58 (years) into 85, to the re-lettered paint sign, adding his mark to a brand name (*Apolinère Enameled*, 1916–17), and in addling a simple ad added an impossible reflection of the back of a little girl's head. So one gets Baruchello and Martin in *Why Duchamp?*: "Duchamp just converted himself to realistic models of female sexual organs. He converted himself to explicitness."[22]

Realistic? Of "what"?

It is important not to flinch from this spot, to try to see the way these genitals "look."[23] And they are wayward: a fact reflected in the criticism only with projective words like rape or orgasm or shame. What do I mean, wayward? Just a patent element: this genitalia looks very strange, long, crooked, visually extended. That spot, made up in order from the abdomen down, is made of three distinct elements. First, there is a curved, long, empty fluvial slash asymmetrically placed in relation to a monstrous right thigh. Second, there is a puckered pink space, bowl shaped. Third, there is a little pink protuberance just visible behind one twig (a parodic envisioning of the total but coy coverage of a fig leaf). Duchamp has made a new kind of collage of genital materials. Each part of this collage alludes to body parts; each calls forth specific readings.

parentheses   ( )

peepholes   ∘ ∘   eye ⊙   pupil from pupilla
                                         little orphan girl
                                         analog. Gk: koré
cunt-mark   (∘)   girl, pupil of the eye

The slashed S-curve is the most harrowing. It looks as if her bottom had been bitten through. Bitten as if the woman has been "castrated."

Is *Etant Donnés* . . . the literalization of the (male) oedipal punishment visited upon a (female) image of (bisexual) oedipal desire for the mother? The work a symbolic map (du champ) of oedipalization? This train of thought gains some confirmation in relation to Duchamp's demonic version of "amor loin" or the sexual paradox of the Keats "Ode"— cannot touch, cannot consummate—this being more powerful than consummation because it holds desire at its purest moment of yearning. But demonic because the lax, post-orgasmic position of Miss Données (miss given   miss taken) suggests that before our penetrating gaze entered this strange little space, someone (now absent) already "had sex" with this nude. This impression is even somewhat necrophiliac, somewhat galatea-ic—sex with this "dead woman," with this "statue." And so the nude could sum up a major crossroads of sexual desire: the rebuff, the perpetual oedipal belatedness of any child (female or male) from any mother. Frustration, rebuff, belatedness—these the "delay in flesh" that make her (plausible? implausible?) satisfaction, or at least her sexual connivance have always already occurred. The piece is about the spectator's "delay."

This important genital consideration can be set in relation to one of the small works of sculpture ("Erotic Objects") contemporaneous with the assemblage. *Objet-dard* (1951): a snake, a penis, a soft but long bone, the pun on "hard on"/"art work" (thus " 'Art on")/"dart, javelin" again offering the reflective play between the museum/the collection and sex and aggression. A conceptual word "d'ard" is made of the interspace among them. The Duchamp pudenda, seen in strained memory, can be imagined as the molded surface onto which this snaky Objet-dard could fit lengthwise. Duchamp invents a variant copulation, not by penetration, but by cogitation, figuring out all the different ways things could fit, could "be read."

The second allusion is contained in the little puckered spot—not visibly open, not at all like the vaginal opening. Indeed, the puckered anal opening is strongly suggested, and yet the spot is as pink and new as the anus of an infant. Thus the pastoral anus—bringing with it a whole set of utopian associations with the pleasures of artifice and the artifice of pleasures (the witty nerve of this is exactly the nerve of pastoral poems). The spot also strongly suggests the puckered knot of the navel. In one economic icon, Duchamp has summarized non-reproductive and reproductive sexuality.

This third of the "Givens" recalls Duchamp's *Female Fig Leaf* (*Feuille de vigne femelle* [1950]) perhaps the strangest of these little objects—

uniformly read as a cast of the female pudenda: *which it cannot visually be.* It looks to be a miniaturized version of a very small ass (tush, I want to say) with the crack between the buttocks curved and extruded. It looks like a small seat, or, more wildly, a knee rest for the tightly closed knees which are a synecdoche for chastity. If it is true that *"Female Fig Leaf* was modeled against the pudenda of the violated [sic] female figure of the *Etant Donnés . . .,"*[24] Duchamp has substituted back for front in the same kind of tongue-in-cheek (another late Duchamp work) gesture as bearding the Mona Lisa in her den. He has opened the cunt to find the ass: the strategy of reversal, a cast from the back of the erotic crack reapplied to the front, still engages with a binary erotic system of "holes" or "spaces."

> sweet ropes
> fell down in stupor
> slid parts a part
> got clipped
> together in
> part.

The third allusion is the most radical. At the very end of this pudendal train, approximately where a (naturalized) anus would be, is popped an unmistakable protuberance, nonetheless just slightly effaced by the discreet twig in the foreground. It is a clitoris, though presented without its close friends, the labia, thus exposed and shorn of some of its pleasure.

Duchamp has, in this work, opened the vulva of the nude: it is a major critique of traditions of representation. (It may—I am not conversant with 20th century pornography—be an application of certain pornographic conventions to a "high art" piece.) He has opened her so that we can see what has always been missing: by its naturalized absence Duchamp calls attention to the clitoredectomy of all Western depictions of the female nude. For it has been decisively argued by Gayatri Spivak that the effacement of the clitoris is a major aspect of the cultural compacts of gender.[25] In his allusive use of the clitoris, Duchamp indeed puts "into some degree of disarray" the system WOME/AN.[26]

Duchamp shows a Steinean interest in the continuous allusive secession from systems of meaning. "One has to be on guard because, despite oneself, one can become invaded by things of the past. Without wanting to, one puts in some detail. There [in *The Bride*] it was a constant battle to make an exact and complete break."[27] Disfiguring. Disfigured (slashed, deformed, turned back side round, reversed) is one way of saying stop this fiction, stop the figural convention, alter it so that it is no longer useable. But then Duchamp puts *in* some detail, a detail hardly before seen, and produces in this shocking artwork both the visual conventions of sentimentality and mutilation overlayered with a major reinterpretation of the genitals, a series of contradictory stories: castration at one end and clitoral presence at the other, pain and pleasure, non-reproductive and reproductive sexualities, "cruel" exposure and "critical" exploration.[28]

Is this major critique of the cultural conventions of representation compromised by Duchamp's gender position? To some great degree, this piece remains a work of high manipulation, effacing wholeness, the head and other humanistic markers; proposing a spectator-voyeur compelled to a certain kind of gaze. However, it remains provocative (though not to date a part of commentary) that the work stands in a critical relation to a central Western convention of representation, to a central part of the cultural compacts of gender. It does not efface, although it does misplace, the clitoral "detail."[29]

How can one have a language of image, theme, allusion, discourse without participating to that degree in the already given, the "étant donnés" of gender? The feminist question. Duchamp's genius: by bringing up certain discourses of sexuality in a lurid, exaggerated manner, by his fluted, flaunted genital collage, he has succeeded in making uneasy, in destabilizing cultural agreements of female representation. Duchamp's detail is the virtually unspoken, undepicted detail. Etant donnés: the givens for Duchamp seem to exist in a kind of brutalizing contradiction. Etant donnés—This being the case, granted this, Duchamp's having done this and gone this far, *then what follows!*

nude skeleton motor   auto-mat   hot knobs   just say the word

runs to the bushes raspberry gathering "there are so many we even get tired of them, squash them with sugar, dribble them over ice cream we call it raspberry mush"

rose voracity
rose veracity

how can the rose speak? (so to speak)

Erato is one muse, lyric plus eros. I have errata.
I say: here are rosaceous errata, sub rrosa, the extra
excessive   interpolated   r
interrupting the general spell.

So to speak, rewrite the rose.

Sub rrosa

> little bits
> arouse
>
> "infra-mince" changes
> dandle the lost button.

>   1987/1989

L A N G U A G E
A C Q U I S I T I O N

. . . her wavering hieroglyph . . .

H.D., *HERmione*[1]

We suggest that naming, always originating in a place
(the *chora,* space, "topic," subject-predicate), is a *replacement* for what the speaker perceives as an archaic mother—a more or less victorious confrontation, never finished with her.

Julia Kristeva, "Place Names"[2]

1.

This is the task of wildflower honey.
Quiet. Initiate of sound.
Poetry is about—
Is negated. All gestures of writing
Made suspect by writing.
Song leaf of pure and burnished gold
Porous at a random touch, plissé.

Began to forget "writing."

The secrets of enclosure
Set drooping.

What is first? First is voicing? Was it when we called her Renata Tebaldi
and moved the crib into her own room, separating her, because the
concerts came too often through the night.

Or was first kitten, sheep, and animal heartless, heartbreaking bleats
inside the dead of night. At first it sounds hopeless, then soon, when a
response is patterned, it sounds perpetually enraged. Now is never good
enough; satisfaction had already to have happened before.

83

Is first the chuckle, the chortle, the gurgle, that sounds like delight: that this is, that "I" this.

Then there is sentence melody; they sing your language before any "language," any "message," any "content."[3] And for the longest time, there is da da. For a long time there is ba ba (which some translate *baby* and others *bottle*). Sometimes a sound comes in floods, then ebbs, an "l" or an "f/v" which crests and then pulls back, some tide moving far away. There are a few other words like "d–g" or "gie" (the second half of *doggie*). With these few syllables, months and months pass in which they are content. And do not (some do not) say ma ma.

These patterns may have no signifying function, but they are socially assimilated in three ways: by translation (baba means bottle), by mimicry, face close to face, to create a dialogue of la la's, and emotionally (this one will not say ma ma).

This babble, these baby melodies

"This *heterogeneousness*, detected genetically in the first echolalias of infants as rhythms and intonations anterior to the first phonemes, morphemes, lexemes, and sentences; this heterogeneousness, which is later reactivated as rhythms, intonations, glossalalias in psychotic discourse, serving as ultimate support of the speaking subject threatened by the collapse of the signifying function; this heterogeneousness to signification operates through, despite, and in excess of it and produces in poetic language 'musical' but also nonsense effects that destroy not only accepted beliefs and significations, but, in radical experiments, syntax itself. . . . We shall call this disposition *semiotic (le sémiotique)*, meaning, according to the etymology of the Greek *sémeion* (σημεῖον), a distinctive mark, trace, index, the premonitory sign, the proof, engraved mark, imprint—in short, a *distinctiveness* admitting of an uncertain and indeterminate articulation because it does not yet refer (for young children) or no longer refers (in psychotic discourse) to a signified object for a thetic consciousness. . . . Plato's *Timaeus* speaks of a *chora* (χώρα), receptacle (ὑποδοχεῖον), unnamable, improbable, hybrid, anterior to naming, to the One, to the father, and consequently, maternally connoted to such an extent that it merits 'not even the rank of syllable.' . . . It goes without saying that, concerning a *signifying practice*, that is, a socially communicable discourse like poetic language, this semiotic heterogeneity posited by theory is inseparable from what I shall call, to distinguish it from the latter, the *symbolic* function of significance."[4]

The inseparability of the two functions: that while it may sing melodies in all and nothing, we in English hear only its English. Translation and focused location occur to filter the heterogeneousness through the meaning-melody we hear, in speaking English. Yet it will always sing more than we can hear.

The semiotic abounds with signs ("mark, trace, index, premonitory sign, proof engraved mark, imprint" "signet—as from sign, a mark, token, proof; signet—the privy seal, a seal; signet-ring—a ring with a signet or private seal . . ."[5])

What is all of this, and why is it important? Kristeva's location of two developmentally distinct registers of normal language, whose intensity and relationship are heightened in poetic language, offers a powerful picture through which certain elements of gender cruise.

2

thay hey ho, aydee thay yo you

thay dg,

hyyyi, O, hi

This "master place" of analysis—how to be true to it and to me? What can it mean? Certainly the massive bilaterality of the system can both satisfy and distress. There are two sides, one sidelong, allusively called "maternally connoted"; the other comically, named in more absolute terms "the father." Does this mean that the genders are divided into the one that speaks and the other that cannot be intelligible? At times (as in *About Chinese Women*) Kristeva has implied that the only way a woman makes sense is through identification with the father. This is not helpful. And it is a tautology. Makes sense is a way of speaking as sense is given: a way of speaking the dominant discourses.[6]

But the maternally connoted chora is not silent: there is babble and pulse, intonation, mark and sign. There is everything of language in it but specificity and form. It is the place that could be any language (Greek, Egyptian). If this area represents the mother, it is a mother visualized as a font of linguality, as well as a mother (they say) repressed by virtue of the transfer of power and allegiance by means of oedipalization: the learning of gender asymmetry, inequalities, one's place in a gendered order.

The "symbolic order" is thus affiliated with the political and social power of dominant discourses. The "semiotic" with the marginal, and with subversion, critique, weakening of the permutations of dominance.[7] Both are social.

One speaks, the other {speaks unheard, from margins
has spoken
will speak

Yet the inseparability of the two functions. When this theory does its dance of naming, we are called into chora, tempted into claiming its dramas. Language in its thickness, layered, can also peel back and become a map of levels, with space behind space.[8]

The interplay of these two sides in H.D. has a particular name: palimpsest. Meaning what it conventionally does in ancient scribal practice: an over-written page, a script under which is shadowed another script, another text. As H.D. defines this as epigraph to her novel called by that very name: one text "erased" but "imperfectly" to make "room for another" writing. Thematically, morally, textually in H.D. the erasure of the signs (mark, trace, index, imprint) of the "mother"—the text made marginal, by the signs of the "father"—the text of dominance. But imperfect erasure. Can see both writings. Can see them as interactive. Could pick and valorize one (as opposed to the other); could say lower one is original, therefore right. Could say recent one by virtue of that place closer to now, to our sense of progress towards us, is therefore right. Or, could as well place them together as the situation of writing. Could say, this palimpsest is the visual image of the situation of writing. Palimpsest is the feel of writing within the consciousness of the producer of poetic language.

So reading (whether choosing one side as the primary though almost eradicated source, or whether mingling both texts by reading all the layers of intercalations) is the key to H.D.'s relation to the "semiotic." And this—although reading or interpreting is, in Kristeva's terms, the precise component missing, absent from the semiotic. Reading would be, definitionally, a function of the "side" of the symbolic. The maternally connoted side would produce only UNreadable marks.

The act of reading must be slid across to the mother.

3.

Kristeva visualizes all people who write as "filial." That is, they are the children of, a second generation with regard to a maternally connoted semiotic and a father-filled symbolic order. Any person who writes (who uses poetic language) is *ipso facto*, in the system, a site of a synthetic act of access negotiating between the pre-Oedipal thesis and the Oedipal antithesis. All poetic writing is a negotiation, after the fact, after a necessary passage (called the "thetic stage") into signification.

Therefore Kristeva calls this a " 'second degree thetic,' a resumption of the functioning characteristic of the semiotic *chora* within the signifying device of language. This is precisely what artistic practices, and notably poetic language, demonstrate."[9]

No pure semiotic; (except in psychosis) no pure semiotic. Exile. That is, mediation. Access to this area is mediated. But what is it that— when reentered—offers itself (in/as language, rhythm, space) as if it were unmediated? As if it were a return? What is IT writing? What are the historical tricks desire plays? Among them the denial of mediation. The filial-parental metaphor somewhat compromises (enriches) the theory of positions in relation to marginality and dominance.

4.

It is a peculiarity of Kristeva's analysis that she is so ungiving, so unsuggestive on the subject of women writers. For if all who write are filial, they are for her, more specifically, the sons. In *Desire in Language* all examples of poetic stances and poetic careers engage only with male writers, even though a most profound, elegant and boldest woman is herself writing. It is odd to read of things "maternally connoted" or to hear that we may "call the moment of rupture and negativity which conditions and underlies the novelty of any praxis 'feminine,' " when this still leaves a little in the air what the specific relations of a woman writer to the semiotic register could be.[10] What is the relation of the woman writer to chora, when she can be that "maternally connoted" area by being/having/wanting mother? Is the chora safe for women? Or do "women tend to move immediately to the other side—the side of symbolic power"?[11]

Then, what if the writer is not a "son" but a "daughter"? Even if one's pre-Oedipal is the "same" no matter what gender, the fact that our return is mediated through gender must make (could make?) some marked difference in language.

Why (asks Kristeva) does Virginia Woolf "not dissect language as Joyce does"?[12] A question which makes me immediately defensive can be translated into a series of other questions that makes this language a question. Why must Kristeva affirm that Woolf does not dissect language as Joyce does? Why does Virginia Woolf not choose to "dissect language as Joyce does"? Why must Joyce be the standard for such activities in language, Woolf not up to that norm? What is the precise level and kind of rupturing practices that must occur for it to be said that "language is dissected"? Would Stein's be "too much"? What is the place of Woman, static, iconic Woman in Joyce's writing practice? How might that Woman function by virtue of her iconic Otherness? What happens when the writer is Other in systems of discourse? How does Otherness own, write its Otherness when it is not only otherness? How can I (a woman) read my our their his her semiotic? What is a woman writer's negotiation with the semiotic to produce poetic language?

For H.D., on the evidence of *Tribute to Freud*, the semiotic is safest when it can be interwoven with a symbolic (interpretive) function so fluid and polyvalent that it almost annexes itself to the semiotic; the semiotic is therefore safest, most satisfying when it is not glossalalia, not syntactic rupture, not invective/obscenity (Céline-Pound), but when it is expressed as signs.

5.

What is it I have also come here to tell you? That I wish they had met? That I wish they had read each other, visibly; some fantasy of intertextual appreciation or influence. But did not. Although H.D.'s daughter, Perdita Schaffner, says that H.D. read all of Woolf's books, we are left simply with a desire, and death. In 1941, Woolf committed suicide. H.D. wrote *The Gift* after, she wrote it also for Woolf. Woolf was her mother. She wrote it out of grief. I am making this up.

Amid the bombs, H.D. instructs May Sarton to write to Robert Herring to find out if H.D. herself or Elizabeth Bowen has been killed in an air raid, or "of any literary gossip or—I do not like to add, 'catastrophy', for we do not feel like that. But Virginia W. was a great shock to us all. I am glad you say it seemed 'unnecessary', as that [is] [H.D. wrote *it*] JUST how I felt and feel. The general attitude was 'poor thing—she went through such a lot—' but having been through so much, I myself, did feel stricken to think she got away like that, just when really everything is very exciting and one longs to be able to live to see all the things that will be bound to happen later. . . . [my ellipses] Times were NEVER so exciting—the last war was not. It is simply a sheer mathematical problem of HOW much can the human frame stand and endure—and we seem to get stronger, as far as nerves go, as we go on. . . . [my ellipses] Virginia's body was found—in that river as expected. There was inquest and letter left to her husband, she believed she was going mad again and could not face it. One heard 'poor Ophelia' . . . [H.D.'s ellipses] but, like you, I did not think it the right end somehow, no matter how poetical and traditional."[13]

What could it mean that H.D. said (as far as anyone has yet discovered) nothing about Woolf but several saddened coolish distant evaluative comments upon her manner of death.

A desire and a set of connections palpable, opaque, readable, odd, nourishing: *The Gift,* with its concussion of paternal consciousness, its oblique moment of childhood sexual assault, near assault, its matrilineal desire for connection, for vision, for language. *Moments of Being,* with its blunt impacted hostility to paternal bullying, its explicit moment of childhood sexual assault, its matrilineal desire for connection, for vision, for language. Autobiographies written under German bombing.

HER: its nursling woman artist, its "you are a poem though your poem's naught," its determination to transcend, to encircle this power of judgment (p. 212).

To the Lighthouse: its nursling woman artist, its "Women can't paint, women can't write," its desire to encircle this power of judgment

and maternal eros at the center of both works.

Bid Me to Live: a synchronic layering of motifs from its time of composition, after the Second World War, back through the First, with its hope that the world could, somehow, be different, a new valence, a new spiritual liberation

The Years: a diachronic spread from the 1880s to just before the Second World War, following a multitude of people but centering on those who

will find that the hope for all is the formation of "new combination"—
a spiritual and political understanding

Both feature the Zeppelin air raids over London in World War I as a
prescient knowledge of terror to civilians to which the civilians had to
respond

Both reinvent the essay, both, do you hear me, reinvent the essay, its
epistemology, its tactics of language, its tremendous claims of authority
and its subtle erosion of authority, its grave meditative sensation, like
feeling the imprint of a "soul," its ridiculous quirks and starts, exposed,
caring and uncaring, jaunty. Its poetics of critique. Its poetics of palimpsest.[14] And

the feeling of listening, the intensity with which they listen and leap,
leap into themselves is met by, creates, the intensity of listening in the
reader. Listening listing.

6.

I take the baby in my arms and sing to her a song my mother sang to
me, the "Riddle Song." I sing it over and over (June 17, 1985, at 16
months). "How can there be a cherry that has no stone?" That day, the
baby in my arms pipes up, repeats "nieuw" (a cross between *no*, repeated, and *new*) I sing "How can there be a chicken without a bone?"
Silence from the little dark voice. "How can there be a ring that has no
end?" "nieuw" She has done it again! "How can there be a baby with
no cryin'?" The voice says "mee mee bay bee."

7.

What is it about the little glowy tip, the dome of light, the bee, the
luminous globule that recurs and repeats what is it about the water,
the beach, the jellyfish

Solid water up the beach, shimmering when all the waves were dark
transparent jellies, bits of them, a little wobble and whoops, a touch.
What has grazed me? Aurelia, the East Coast jelly-fish, cast up in broken
bits upon my dotted shore.

The sea. The light. The core.

For Woolf, a splash of water, the breaking of light over the floor: "of feeling the purest ecstasy I can conceive."[15] It is the feeling "as I describe it sometimes to myself, of lying in a grape and seeing through a film of semi-transparent yellow." The child reconstructed in the medium of the mother, looking out as if through an encasing fluid.

"My vision or state of transcendental imagination when I had felt myself surrounded, as it were, with the two halves of the bell-jar." "When I told him of the Scilly Isles experience, the transcendental feeling of the two globes or the two transparent half-globes enclosing me, I said I supposed it was some form of prenatal fantasy. Freud said, 'Yes, obviously; you have found the answer, good—good' " (*TTF*, pp. 182, 168).

When Lily tries to encompass her love for Mrs. Ramsay, and feels she cannot: "How then, she had asked herself, did one know one thing or another thing about people, sealed as they were? Only like a bee, drawn by some sweetness or sharpness in the air intangible to touch or taste, one haunted the dome-shaped hive, ranged the wastes of the air over the countries of the world alone, and then haunted the hives with their murmurs and their stirrings. . . ."[16] The sound of bees, a collective pulse of life in "the shape of a dome." In *The Gift* H.D. speaks of being the last bee in a domed hive of vision.[17]

In H.D., time and time again, a flame or light wobbles on water, a candle is lit, the media of light and water are readied, there is a dome, a multiplicity contained in a dome:

"The sky above her head seemed so thickly sown with innumerable stars that the whole was at once strange and at once hugely comforting. So many and so near, those stars seemed unfamiliar as if the whole of heaven was in some manner raining, dripping down soft and fragrant dust. The whole thing seemed like mist, like rain, to drift, to sift, to drown and smother like any silver twining London fog. Yet the very substance of that mist was vaguely warm, vaguely near. As if looking upward from the heart of that enormous flower, she perceived, above her head, the rayed-out centre of the flower, heavy with pollen, stable, yet sure with the slightest variation of wind or summer breeze to spill its just hovering, just clinging dust."[18]

"I should make a picture that was globular; semi-transparent. I should make a picture of curved petals; of shells; of things that were semi-transparent; I should make curved shapes, showing the light through, but not giving a clear outline. Everything would be large and dim; and what was seen would at the same time be heard; sounds would come through this petal or leaf—sounds indistinguishable from sights."[19]

In this dome, this dome of babble and humming, of radiance, the access to outside is not clear, but also not necessary, seeming to be made of a space where the outside meets the inside, a meniscus of filling to the brim, yet beyond, unspilling, and still being held, complete: the perfect moment of undifferentiated envelopment, pre-natal/-Oedipal? it seems necessary to say, "a more or less victorious confrontation, never finished with her."

>
in the eager angel rain
a space of the gibbus moon's riant irregular shape
waxed wayward over the irises
a "sign"—suspicious word
a sign-suspicious word.
see bits   travel   and   years later

artesian it spouts
lustro   lustro   lustro   (try Esperanto?)

white flowers look like shadows
of their leaves
sea sheen, seen
seeing deeper by seeing white

seeing rains of seeded light
outside in
and inside out

milk page
(no) libation down
this is the task of wildflower

silence.

8.

HER (1927): its maternal power, its ambivalence to maternal power, daughter-mother who bears whom? "A tiny flame burst up; forest worshiper, fire worshiper (Hermione) enclosed as in a ball of glass, bent to revive life. Eugenia's face was pale, tipped at the chin edge by phosphorescent line as the light crept up, little live flame in the midst of water" (*HER*, p. 89). And in the storm, lightning: "chalk of brilliant sizzling

white fire had written insoluble words across the densest blackness"
(HER, p. 90).

To the Lighthouse (1927): its maternal power, its ambivalence to maternal power, daughter-mother who bears whom? An "insoluble language": "tablets bearing sacred inscriptions, which if one could spell
them out would teach one everything, but they would never be offered
openly, never made public. What art was there, known to love or cunning, by which one pressed through into those secret chambers? What
device for becoming, like waters poured into one jar, inextricably the
same, one with the object one adored?" (TTL, p. 82).

How to remain connected within, immersed to the buzzing honey, the
chaunt, the wordless pleasure, how to notate, the space in which one
has being, how to tell the globes of spell, spell without spilling, spoiling,
splaying

how to put rhythm, pulse, humming space into meaning, without
violating the meanings of that space? "one with the object one" "enclosed as in a ball of glass"

It is to have, to bring or to make some unreadable (ever readable, never
terminable) mark.

"With a sudden intensity, as if she saw it clear for a second, she drew
a line there, in the centre" (TTL, p. 319).

9.

There is in fact a plethora of incest in H.D. One of her tasks as a
writer seems to have been to naturalize, normalize that "incest" and to
overwrite the emotional taboo by measured, articulate, lyric considerations of desires within the family: the depiction of Bertie and Hermione
in HER, the depiction of the brothers in Tribute to Freud, the relation
to the father in Tribute to Freud, to the mother, the mother-daughter
dyad in Helen in Egypt

"If it is true that the prohibition of incest constitutes, at the same time,
language as communicative code and women as exchange objects in
order for society to be established, poetic language would be for its
questionable subject-in-process the equivalent of incest. . . ."[20]

What does it mean when you both be it (the woman/the mother) and want it (the mother/the woman)? The desire to be folded over onto herself (thus, for both H.D. and Woolf, the charge of narcissism). The desire to be both parts of the dyad at once (thus, for both Woolf and H.D., the charge of preciousness). What can lubricate this otherwise complete abrasion? What prevents a woman who writes from unreadable envelopment, unwritable envelopment?

Often, it is the sign of a reader. Often, it is a book, a reader. Someone must read or be reading. (Mrs. Ramsay is reading, and to James—yet— a tale about the boundless sea when Lily is at first inspired. Mr. Ramsay reads a book across the boundless sea, when Lily finishes.) The vision holds a book. It is an unwritten book. It is the perfect sign of exit from the engulfment of maternal incest from the perspective of a woman writer. It is a listening reader, the reader whose book is always waiting, the tolerant listener (and sometimes the demanding "Write, write, or die!") It is the vision of a Mary with the empty (always to be filled, always fillable) book. Because interpretation is always interminable. Because writing IS reading. And there is a sacred triangle: writing (saying); listening (eliciting); reading (interpreting is another form of listening). "her wavering hieroglyph" "never finished with her"

10.

or sees an unreadable sign.

If a wall releases writing, pictures called "writing"
if a space brings up (as lighting the cyc, the backdrop, they
pronounce it "psyche"
as in "psyche it out" and it is short for cyclorama, a large curved screen
or curtain
used as a background in stage settings) writing
if a space is readied for the projection of necessities
if a space seems to possible

a hotel room, in a country called Hellas, that landscape of urgency, of longing in a hotel room in the father-and-master country of our (Western) civilization which H.D. entered only to wedge up, prying, a fulcrum, what lever? to see the other side, Hellas, the mother, Helen the mother, Greek myths first learned from a teacher astonishingly named "Miss Helen" (*TTF*, p. 186)

This room H.D. bore 13 years later into Freud's room, his chambers, the room inside his room.

In another key moment of H.D.'s sorting (out) the lesbian/matrisexual erotics of Hermione's identity, the heroine sits at the breakfast table with her mother, trying to recall to her mother the scene in the storm of a liquid intensity in which a flame of language is lit. She (semi-comically, the novel seems as myopic as Dorothy Richardson but it is also like *Pilgrimage* very, very funny) chooses to read to her mother from Swinburne's "Itylus," the poem which, throughout, indicates the passion of Hermione for Fayne (its "swallow" evokes Bryher as well). A specific event has provoked Her's quixotic attempt to unify by her qualified power the two forces which are most obdurately opposed in the novel: maternal and lesbian passion. The event? the flight of a bird. "Things out of the window, across the window seemed to be on the window, against the window, like writing on the wall. Things, a bird skimming across a window, were a sort of writing on a wall" (*HER*, p. 125). Here is an evocation, written by H.D. in 1927, of the "Corfu vision" of 1920 by its "title" which would not be used again until the Freud experience of 1933–34 (*TTF*, the "Advent" section p. 169), and then not again until it was made the title of the Freud memoir in 1944, a title which indicates H.D.'s entitlement. "I see by that birdflight across an apparently black [blank?] surface, that curves of wings meant actual things to Greeks, not just vague symbols but actual hieroglyphics . . . hieroglyphs . . ." (*HER*, p. 125, ellipses in original, of course).

In *HER*, H.D. is clear about the sources of her writing in a reiterated, layered sense of otherness. H.D. postulated a realm of mystery, something beyond, something vitally generative for her writing, a kind of intensity, a sense of presence and power ("Words with Fayne in a room, in any room, became projections of things beyond one." *HER*, p. 146). A generative space sends forth signs, and these signs are called by a name which connotes an artfully deciphered writing, distant, mysterious, cryptic, strange, of a strange culture: the hieroglyphs of ancient

~~EGYPT~~ GREECE!

Of course, the hieroglyphs of Egypt, but here she says that the Greeks read hieroglyphs, as later she said, about the picture-writing on the wall that they are like "Greek vase silhouettes" (*TTF*, p. 169), as later she will have Helen become a hieroglyph that she is, that she reads, reading the maternal name/the self, reading Greece/Egypt, ciphering (encoding the mystery)/deciphering (decoding mystery), entering a boundless space of containment (contentment) as a reader (a writer), a hero/ine (a poet), a mother (a daughter), reading Greece (the father, the brother) as Egypt (the mother). To pick out the signs from this space "a distinctive mark, trace, index, the premonitory sigh, the proof, engraved mark, imprint—in short, a *distinctiveness* admitting of an uncertain and indeterminate articulation. . . ." Coming from the old country, one of those old countries, from the mother country.

the premonitory s̶i̶g̶h̶ sign

Awakened from illness/madness by the "talking cure," Her walks into the snow, "leaving her wavering hieroglyph as upon white parchment" (*HER*, p. 224). And doing so, she sees that the snowy embankment is a "roll from which more parchment [more space for writing] might be shaken." Writing is listening into the list(en)ing space.

11.

Why hieroglyphs? Egyptian "sacred writing" subsumes three kinds of language function. Although popularly they are perceived simply as "picture writing" (ideograms, sense-signs, one picture for one word), in fact they are not only that. Some pictures are a word, or two or three pictures may make a word, or the denotative association may be called for: *sun* may mean *day*. But some of the pictographs are also alphabetic (phonograms, sound-signs). In fact, the Rosetta stone began to be successfully decoded only by a reading of proper names by means of alphabetic (not pictographic) assumptions. "Throughout the entire course of its history that hieroglyphic script remained *a picture-writing eked out by phonetic elements.*"[21] And finally, some of the pictographs are determinative—in a curious space (as far as I can figure it) between grammatical and semantic functions: they tell you how certain sound-signs are to be read. H.D. was familiar enough with this system to call the Niké pictograph, appearing at the end of her Corfu vision, "the last concluding symbol—perhaps that 'determinative' that is used in the actual hieroglyph, the picture that contains the whole series of pictures in itself or helps clarify or explain them" (*TTF*, p. 56). It is Bryher who sees this Niké-into-Helios image, who sees, therefore, the "determinative."

To evoke hieroglyphs is to evoke:

a bright attractiveness of depiction. In bulk, hieroglyphs look like a little world. There are birds, people, feet, there is water, fish, pans, scales, hooks; there are snakes and loaves, twisted rope and baskets.

a metonymic world of association and juxtaposition, sign next to sign more available (by being pictures) than the alphabet for association, visualization. A world forever extensive by (our imposition of) metonymies, yet presumably readable. Thus a recurrent situation in H.D. (in *Palimpsest* as in *Helen in Egypt*): a woman is faced with some hieroglyphs and the question of reading them is fraught with anticipation and fear.

and three—or two plus—streams of reading—not only pictographic, but also alphabetic, and not only alphabetic, but of those certain signs are "determinative"—a plurality of readings, of reading tactics. Which H.D. would later, in *Trilogy*, bring across so as to treat English "hieroglyphically": "Osiris," "O-sire-is" and "zrr-hiss."

To evoke hieroglyphs is to foreground reading that is part of writing, yet also to show a writing which has built inside it a plurality of reading.

If a woman reads as she has been read, she will be limited.

Reading the sign of the woman, reading signs generated around women, reading the presence of the sign, woman, in culture, means reading a situation of being read. A woman writer is never just written, she is read, as a woman. So, as a woman, she needs to originate her own reading. Her own methods.

12.

The chora safe for women. Why have I used the notion of safety except by the assumption that the habits of mind, emotion and gender position of the male subject offer some secondary protection to the descent, via language and form, to the position before meaning. While female habits of mind, emotion and gender position may look with vertigo upon the temptation to engulfment, and loss of ego. Or, with unassimilable desire.

H.D. makes the chora safe by concentration, within the semiotic, on those features most closely allied to the symbolic: (un)readable signs, with a further evocation of figures of the reader, the book, interpretation, reading—but only as the activities undertaken in the understanding that the signs remain mysteries, and wisdom is not in translation or identification but in the dark illumination of mystery, its layerings, its implications, the variety of its traces, its metamorphoses, using the sign as portal, as entrance to the area where not reading, but readings will forever gush. An activity of mind, a condition of desiring.

One is reminded of Virginia Woolf's pique, anger even, at interpretations of the mark at the end of *To the Lighthouse*.[22]

And so H.D. found a key medium when she found (re-founded) the essay (*The Gift, Tribute to Freud, Compassionate Friendship*), because she makes it the medium of endless interpretation, intellectually bold—bolder indeed than "The Cinema and the Classics" (1927) and thicker, richer than the very short and early "Notes on Thought and Vision" (1919). She makes it palimpsest, she makes it plenitude.

And when she writes out her vision of the picture writing in *Tribute to Freud*, notice that, while she evokes and engages with a rare suggestiveness and multiplicity, she leaves these signs ultimately unreadable, her tribute (or gift) to Freud being first the presence-to-be-reckoned-with of this particular permutation of consciousness—her visions, and second the affirmation of (un)readability—that is, the possibility of meditating upon, but never fixing or pinning any sign.

Already, when she went to Freud, she had found to her intense disappointment that she could not use ("use") any of her visions narratively, directly positioning them in a story, as she had tried to do with the Peter Rodeck material in the destroyed novel *Niké*.[23]

(She decided now not to use them, but to let them use her.)

Because in *Tribute to Freud* (despite; no, because of the nuanced intelligence, the cultural range deployed and displayed, the fact that, with such a touch in writing for exfoliation and depiction—such a writer could have done anything), H.D. does not interpret those signs. That is, while she does make local identifications (Jacob's ladder, Delphic tripod, s's like question marks) the better for us to have evoked the resonance of the signs and their impact, H.D. does not narrate any story or prepare any statement that the images make, separately (as static pictures) or together (as cinematic sequence), although the latter portion of the vision even suggests that direction because it is filmic in conception. Nor does she narrate or interpret despite the presence of the "determinative"—which "contains" or "helps clarify or explain" a set of hieroglyphics. She only takes the time to reject one ("Freudian") reading of one of the hieroglyphs in which Niké=Athene without spear-=castrated woman.[24] She later says that Freud's own theory was premised upon the non-allegorical reading of these materials. "There are all these shapes, lines, graphs, the *hieroglyph of the unconscious*, and the Professor had first opened the field to the study of this vast, unexplored region. He himself—at least to me personally—deplored the tendency to *fix* ideas too firmly to set symbols, or to weld them inexorably" (TTF, p. 93).

She says, when Freud moves in onto her Niké, that in offering her his theory of castration, "She has lost her spear," "he might have been talking Greek" (TTF, p. 69). She would rather be talking Egyptian.

13.

What writes *Tribute to Freud?* H.D. said, "I wish to recall the impressions or rather I wish the impressions to recall me" (TTF, p. 14). This no longer sounds like a sentimental reversal, but a bi-directional bridging between symbolic and semiotic. A hushed incipience, (not) already filled. Not notes, not chronology, not the invigilator but the HearD. The shift from active forming to hushed attention will recall the "me" that each memory could make. And H.D. does here seem to shift between the postulate of a stable ego which may be reformulated through the clarities of memory and the postulation of what Kristeva calls a "subject-in- process," a selving (like a duckling) that can be provisionally postulated given this kind of statement, another selving, given another kind of statement, for H.D. enjoys fragmenting herself when and if she can do this by attending to myth (multi-cultural myths and stories) because these old images are a bottom. So if she loses her ego, her stable sense of self, she can still both gather together and disappear into a larger, more voluminous story, a story with many chapters, a story whose combinations will never conclude.

14.

Week of 1–6 July, 17 months. Words: mur mur mur (more); caow; mMMoo; DIRty; WWWride (ride); RRweh (wet); Bluhh (blueberries).

Record of 26 August, 18.5 months. Words: farm, boat, backhoe, blanket (bottue), cow, roll, milk, up, on, shut, open, I do, bye bye, seat, night, motor (mowë=motorcycle), fish, Nijmegen (=map), map, ice, frites, ride, go, out, cookie, ocean, bird, flower (foür; later flowie), apple (appy), hop in, hole, wash (vash), wipe (vipe), mommydaddy, no, uhhuh, move, more, chicken, eat, baba, carry, baby, help, poop, fountain, noo noo (noodles), ei (egg), watch (vatch), OK, key, animal (amal), bug, mouth, hair, eye, ring, table (tebby), write, book, dog, puppy, they speak about an explosion of language.

Sitting in a crummy hotel room, watching the light brown air flicker, watching a nothing a slash of molding, a nailhead hammered but still emerges, how the world is humanly held, a shell of wallboard over crumbling plaster, a room a room inside a room, a baby lying breathless to calm down, a tear, just one grief for two old men, one dead, the other—I had just kissed him. They are not careless.

The dusk grows thicker.

I held her filling up with darkness.

What writes listens. Listening is one of the major social and intellectual skills necessary for signification. (When they sing to themselves the "language in the crib" is it for the pleasure of listening in the dark to their voice (pause) their voice and the difference it makes "shoes on shoes off pants on pants off" 21 months.)

Listening is not pre-signification, in the sense of lower than or prior to; it is the simultaneous *sine qua non*, that without which, there is no signification: no talk without pauses, no dialogue without silence, no translation without the white emptiness into which bubbles parallel statement.

Holding on: that in the semiotic realm, a plethora of "hieroglyphs," of signs, of "signets"—jewels of the unnameable, that in the maternal (and sometimes elsewhere) is incipience and listening, a waiting

the passage between Mamalie and Hilda in *The Gift* in which Hilda feels she protects her grandmother by a benevolent, interested, receptive hush, protects Mamalie from waking up from her trance state; this is what allows information and a way of knowing to pass between the dyad

and thus for women (well, for a woman, for H.D. as a woman writing) the presentation of unreadable signs to herself, the lush evocation of a plurality of possible readings, the reader of hush, are the materials of primary creation.

"I hug a soft shabby doll to my heart, my Muse is an old doll."[25]

15.

In fact, after the elaborate, pensive and solemn accumulation of statement about the pictographs (*TTF* sections 28–41), which replicates, in the prose, the straining and pressure of the appearance of these signs, and which, as I have said, offers some local interpretation, some reading, as well as some set of questions which precisely alters the position of the self from side to side of an evoked story—"Am I looking at the Gorgon head . . . Or am I myself Perseus" (*TTF*, p. 52)—after the reader is awash with signs, H.D., as if it were the most natural thing to do now, simply offers more signs. "Confetti-like tokens" with "mottoes . . . short and bright and to the point" supporting Hitler (*TTF*, p. 58). "Other swastikas" . . . I followed them down Berggasse as if they had been chalked on the pavement especially for my benefit" (*TTF*, p. 59). "Then there were rifles." These were stacked neatly, looked like "an 1860 print" . . . "familiar pictures of our American Civil War" (*TTF*, p. 59). When she astonishingly arrives for her session at the time of the attempted Nazi Putsch it is that day when she notices the waiting room with its "framed photographs," the "diploma" from Clark University, the "bizarre print or engraving" (*TTF*, p. 61). There is the sign of her coming, the sign of the gardenias she wanted to give, and the dream icon of the "snake on a brick" (*TTF*, p. 64) and the finding in reality of the dream icon in a little case of signet rings at the Louvre (*TTF*, p. 65). Signs, readable, unreadable, a plethora of signs, and then, in climax, the hymn to signs, section 50, based, appropriately for issues of reading, interpreting, decoding—or not—on checking "up on the word 'signet' in my Chambers' English Dictionary" (*TTF*, p. 66). Upon which she discovers that her choice of name, her signature, is a "signet" proof of a royal manner, proof of (as Emily Dickinson might have said) an election: to the saturation in, the creation of, the abandonment to "sign again—a word, gesture, symbol, or mark, intended to signify something else" (*TTF*, p. 66). And in this sign, "*in hoc signo*" . . . "*vinces.*" Now certainly there might be ways and ways of reading this (Christian ways, for example), but let us say this way: that the *vinces* is the victory, the Niké, and what Niké signals is then the plethora of signs, and the emotional investment in noticing them, and the intellectual and poetic energy invested in continuing them. Not in stopping, not in saying one thing, one true thing, but in the sheer continuance, the bubbling of sign after sign. Because the very dramatic structure of the writing on the wall section has meaning: its meaning is continuance—will there be energy enough, intensity enough, care and risk enough to continue to see what the signs themselves want: that "the writing continues to write itself or be written" (*TTF*, p. 51).

I know that this is a somewhat tendentious, limited reading. But satisfying to the degree that the H.D. of the essay is, among other things, the H.D. of continuations, of readings, of bright hieroglyphs forever read, forever unreadable: "her wavering hieroglyph" "the *hieroglyph of the unconscious*"

It is the H.D. who, even when an interpretation "might have led us too far afield in a discussion or reconstruction of cause and effect, which might indeed have included priceless treasures, gems, and jewels, among the so-called findings of the unconscious mind revealed by the dream-content or associated thought and memory" might, even thus, "have side-tracked the issue in hand," still even then continues (*TTF*, p. 88).

16.

There are certainly, as in any important writing, several agendas. *Tribute to Freud* is also a pallinode, a defense of the one unassimilable symptom: the writing on the wall. She begins her defense in the very first words, the very first section—its circumstantiality, its facticity: dates, addresses, setting, datebook arrangements. She passes to other "characters" and their place in the world. Then, the maneuver which Freud sanctions, there is the possibility of their place in interior dramas or fantasies. Although H.D. denies that van der Leeuw figured in this way, she obediently elaborates a fictive set of associations, invented on the spot, reveries which she could have had. The strategy of H.D.'s pallinode (one with which we are already familiar in her, in other women writers)—aggressive humility—is to claim that she would not, on her own, without the Professor's covering sanction, have initiated these intricate associations, even though she had been writing novels for five, for eight, for ten, for twelve years which incorporated, and then became based upon densities, palimpsests of associations rebarbaratively articulated.

(Rebarbarative does not appear to be a word. At least the only word right now near it in the small Webster's is rebarbative which does not mean mercilessly repetitive but rather repellent, unattractive, forbidding, grim.)

The relationship between analyst and analysand then presented as an exchange of gifts amounts to H.D.'s choreography of gesture and response precisely about the question of reading: whether, by implication or by direct evidence, the recipient has received the intended message in all its meanings.[26] The question of encoding and decoding is of course part of the analytic agenda: factual gestures, real exchanges, are raised to a second level. Not only do they exist, but they exist to be read, to be sewn, sown into a dramatic ongoing elaboration of readings.

Then she passes to her own dreams and memories, especially of her family. These too are sanctioned by the Freudian system. Notice how slowly, with how measured, how careful a footstep, she moves on into the one kind of thing (gesture? sign? unconscious event? dream? reverie? memory? gift?), this experiences so far unanalyzed (untapped) by the Professor. "For things had happened in my life, pictures, 'real dreams,' actual psychic or occult experiences that were superficially, at least, outside the province of established psychoanalysis" (*TTF*, p. 39). Her ambition? to bring them into the province of established psychoanalysis.

She will bring this gift to the father (the Vater, as the singing soul says at the end); he in exchange will give her (back) her (himself as) (herself as) mother. Mutter.

17.

Dependency? Independence? The yammerer yanks away: No No No No No. (24 mo.) Power-who-is-thwarted holds on (too) hard. They tug. The one unconscious or unheeding of consequences, one way. The blank to cause and effect, the other pulls, or really just stands fast. Larger, the mother. Weightier. Smaller, but cyclonic, the twister.

So the smaller sprains her ~~writ~~. Her wrist.

The I stretches through the tendons
indeed in this language acquisition "I"
goes in two differing directions,
I is un other
I is amother
She is I   she sees me as the I-No, the "I know"; the "no no"
I am the no-I   she says NO; that's her I (she is me?)
when she speaks NO speaks
She is the No of the pair
I am the weeping angry she
("I sprained her wrist!")
My I goes backwards, I want no I
Her I goes forwards, she wants her I
I is not her, her is not I, she is me, I am not me,
I did not want to hurt her, I hurt her, she hurt me

our language acquisition is splitting us (is splitting me)
I want to go back, to go forward
she seems to want to go forward, by beginning to know there is a back.

18.

" 'Why did you think you had to tell me? . . . But you felt you wanted
to tell your mother.'

All this seemed almost too simple at the time. My mother was dead;
things had happened before her death, ordinary as well as incredible
things, that I hadn't told her" (*TTF*, p. 30).[27]

19.

There are so many places to go. There is "In analysis, the person is dead
after the analysis is over.' " And H.D. asked "Which person?" (*TTF*, p.
141). There is H.D.'s desire to establish (as a fact?) the immortality of
the soul and therefore to establish (as a possibility?) the "theoretical"
potential for cross . . . for cross what? There is probably a term for it. I
mean the actual communication between the dead and the living, the
living and the dead (although in Western culture, from the epic trip to
the Underworld on, isn't it true that only the dead speak?). *The Gift* is
dedicated to Helen. Her mother. With the epigraph "L'amitié passe
même le tombeau."

Writing, anyway, is speaking to the dead. As Alice Walker said. Because
they have the most time. To listen.[28]

20.

H.D. wanted to tell their source her hieroglyphs. Missing it, never to
close the circle, was writing. (What writes? what writes? is it this
distance, the ever more necessary distance even within the dyad, at its
core, that one is not the other?)

back to it, back to the same
local clover, white clover, perk pink hard
a silent sort
a signal tone
humming its way up through single patch of ground
into a sinking patch of time.

Mother, language has appeared to me. Mother, signs appear to me,
impishly, upon a wall.   ♪ ⌒ ♫   I sit (Isis) and watch.
                                  ○

21.

iris paper
crisis paper
rice paper
rise poplar
isis papyrus
I-I bye-bye

22.

mee mee bay bee
ai that I that speaks, she speaks
ahh that I spoken
spoken about
"quoth I, me, she who speaks in my place"   Bev

the I that listens, listeth
(the song asked "how can there be a baby") and the baby said
there is a baby
I am a baby
I am that baby
remember! the baby
no metaphor that baby
the literal baby
(sing it sister)
is me herein
mee
don't speak of me, and speak of me
I speak (of) myself her-in
mee mee
glad tidings!
hmmmmmmmmmm

23.

A translation that folds, that enfolds on-self back into the semiotic. H.D.'s "writing on the wall" in her writing as she writes it, as she narrates it, as she interprets it (to release it quickly back to (un)readability) opens a vast space of endless reading. A vast space endlessly accreting. With connected signs and stories, a vast space of the unreadable, which is slightly, glancingly, read before it is back, it goes back, it ebbs back into continuous signing, the never to be fully explained. Never to be fully articulated surplus. The meaning of essay is the forever surplus signings (sighings) of ruminative pleasure and pain, of seeing the unreadable, of reading, only to have more unreadable bubble. There is no final reading the (un)readable. A perpetual (the essay) and enacted resistance to thetic meaning even in the creation of meaning; the encirclement of meaning

and to mark this process, the sign of a reader; to anchor the question, the presence of a (an ironized) master of reading (a certain Freud in *Tribute to Freud*, Kaspar the Mage in *Trilogy*, Durand as writer/judge in "Hermetic Definition" and as well St. John Perse therein, Amen as an early "read" meaning in *Helen in Egypt*). The presence of an empty book, a blank page. The blank page is (like a) gushing spring. The mother in *Trilogy* who does not carry a child/"tome"/tomb, but a "blank" and "unwritten" book.

24.

"I cannot realize it, but it goes on." Not a citation from the Corfu vision, but from Kristeva on the maternal. Becoming a mother has, the process of gestation (outside in and inside out) has so far been accounted for in only two discourses, says Kristeva. Science. And Christian theology (*cum* art). H.D., did she want to invent a third (singlehandedly, as usual, and therefore she had to encrust herself with the bestudded, bestudied armor of myth)? To invent a way of bringing access to the maternal (the baby) body into . . . she said . . .[29]

the writing on the wall is gestation, is being both mother and child.

25.

In a long excursus fictionalizing an account of, offering some interior monologue about early Freud discoveries (section 59 and its surroundings), H.D. insists that Freud was both scientific (methodological) and intuitive. H.D. insists that Freud modified the Socratic (false dialogic) method: so that, instead of being "egged on" to definition and elucidation by a probing, articulate sword fighter: teacher-mentor, instead "the question must be propounded by the protagonist himself, he must dig it out from its buried hiding-place, he himself must find the question before it could be answered" (*TTF*, p. 84).

First, the protagonist must change the pronouns.
Then she must find her question. What is the question? Is it what is the meaning of this writing? Is it what are the meanings of these signs? Is it what is the meaning of the Niké which is the "determinative"? Is it what are the meanings of my hallucinatory experiences? Is it (how) should I read these signs? Is it what does my desire for union with the maternal body, with the baby body, necessitate for me as a woman writer? What writes, when the writer is a woman?

> milk page
> no libation down, the page is wet but
> a cakey ground
> restrains
> an unusual train (of)
>
> thought awakened
> high engines passing and only tunnels of access.

26.

I have tried only to discuss the section. "Writing on the Wall"—the "written" text—in an unsystematic way, although I have cited from "Advent." Each text in itself deserves a complete (what a word, here) and polyphonic commentary which it has gotten only to a certain degree. This commentary needs to take into account the status of the one text as being, H.D. says, "written" (and it was also published, or, as she says, it "appeared"), and "written in London in the autumn of 1944, with no reference to the Vienna notebooks of spring 1933," which were, of course, the source of "Advent." "Advent" is different. It was "taken direct from the old notebooks of 1933": this says to me that the writing, the physical flow of words upon the page as they had come were mainly retained in that order. But H.D. then says that "Advent" was "not assembled until December 1948, Lausanne" (*TTF*, p. xiv). Probably a cutting and possibly (but not likely) a rejuxtaposing process was engaged. The text of "Advent" is dated by day, and within each day, by hour (thus prefiguring in this tactic both "Sagesse" and *End to*

Torment). It is not likely that H.D. would have violated that organizing principle unless a sentence or two extraneous to a certain date/time but pertinent to, illuminating of, really belonging to another date/time had surfaced and become obtrusive. In that rare case (because the very accidents and conjunctions of this text offer an endless field for speculation, not least to their author), it is plausible that H.D.'s "reassembling" would have moved such material. But basically "Advent" wants to present the raw materials of association in an enlivening, startling, silly and even frightening matter.

H.D. describes "Advent" as "the continuation of 'Writing on the Wall,' or its prelude" (*TTF*, p. xiv). These two terms, both alluding to narrative formation, are of exceeding interest. First, the terms allude to very different points or positions in narrative—pre-beginning and after-ending—yet here suggest some equivalence. Both imply that the "finished" status of the Freud memoir (which "appeared in *Life & Letters Today*") has now been self-ruptured ("now" is when this doubled version of *Tribute to Freud* was first allowed by H.D.—1956). That self-rupture is an act which, not to be tedious, could be assimilated to the strategies of "writing beyond the ending"; here as a kind of self-critique, the rewriting by breaking the sequence, postulating (as "prelude" and/or as "continuation") another sequence. One might say that "Advent" was placed with "Writing on the Wall" to make sure it is remembered that what is learned from the careful (non)reading offered in the Freud memoir is precisely the necessity of continuance. Certainly if "Advent" continued (was the sequel to) "Writing on the Wall"—as it was chronologically, the one finished in 1944, the other in 1948—the climactic status of the triumphant and sentimental ending in the Goethe poem might be seriously undercut. (In that poem it is hard—willful—to read mother for father, to say that the presence of Mignonne the baby is the desire for the baby; so it can be known as a paean to the master.) If "Advent" offered a prelude to the other work—as it did in terms of writing process, of language acquisition—it becomes the space of heterogeneousness which can never be fully explored or explained, whose fits and starts never fused with the lyrical and argumentative cunning of "Writing on the Wall"; the presence of "Advent" making us see signs bubbling up.[30] Together, the two statements published under the title *Tribute to Freud*, with their slight changes of the nuances of certain incidents, the differences in emphasis, the alternative trajectories of development, the presence of more dreams in one, of more characters in one than the other, the wayward fragmentary shifts as opposed to (as related to) the pulsing elegance of hypotactic sentences, make the most astonishing and vital palimpsest H.D. ever produced in a career of intense concentration on that word about writing, that "form": the overwriting of one erased writing by another writing: semi (un)readable signs.[31]

The idea of inscribing, reinscribing, rescribing, new scribbling, is a tribute to Stein (there is no repetition, there is only insistence) as well as to Freud. ("I said that I wished I had asked an artist friend to sketch the series [of pictographs, the "writing on the wall"] for me, so that I could have shown it to him direct. He said that would have been no use. 'There would be value in the pictures only if you yourself drew them' ". [*TTF*, p. 173].) Not about relevation, but about representation. As much as H.D. believed in, fostered in herself the idea of relevation in order for her *to* represent.[32]

The question was in finding (what writes when the writer is a woman) the exact proportion and shiftings of reading and not-yet and yes, interpreting which would continue to generate writing precisely because such a proportion (a high degree of allegiance to the semiotic, to unreadable sign) also evoked listening, not speaking (not formulating the question but allowing the writing, the writer to "ask the question," language acquisition, language a question).

Forever read, forever beyond reading. Listening, listing, listeth, listed.

> with a debt to the presence and work of
> Beverly Dahlen, work called *A Reading*
>
> Swarthmore, PA–Nijmegen, The Netherlands
> Summer 1985–November 1985

"WHILE THESE LETTERS WERE A-READING"

An Essay on Beverly Dahlen's
A Reading

A Reading, *Oxford English Dictionary*

— the action of perusing written or printed matter, the practice of occupying oneself in this way
— the action of uttering aloud the words (reading a bill, reading Scripture, poetry reading)
— lecturing by offering commentary or gloss
— the act of expounding or interpreting
— being read (obs.) ("while these letters were a-reading")
— the actual words used in a particular passage (as opposed to variant readings)
— matter for reading (including light reading, and even lettering)
— the indications on a graduated instrument (reading a thermometer)
— an interpretation, as in the rendering of character by an actor, a piece of music by a performer.

In the middle of *Spring and All* (1923), William Carlos Williams makes two statements that certainly invent modern American poetry. His two principles of poetics (we have heard them henceforward many times, yet they still do not lack a tremendous generative power):

"Not to attempt, at that time, to set values on the word being used, according to presupposed measures, but to write down that which happens at that time . . ." and "To practice skill in recording the force moving. . . ."[1] In context and out, these statements provide a desire and an impetus not yet spent, for example, in the emphasis upon being in time, riding the crests and pulses of temporal motion. Such a statement is reheard, for instance, in parts of Olson's "Projective Verse."

And yet Williams' ruptures with convention (the rose is obsolete) and with "crude symbolism" as well as his break with "realism" ("not 'realism' but reality itself" [*I*, p. 117]) still leaves him with one of the

110

most static, iconic cultural statuary: an only partially examined set of gender symbols and gender conventions, at least a residue, and sometimes a full deck of old crude symbolism of the most prime variety. The radicalness of the poetics is matched by the almost unquestioned conservatism of the gender ideas. I am saying this about Williams (could say it about Eliot or Pound) and I am saying it grossly, baldly, without subtlety, in order to underline the problem in poetics (not outside of it) for a woman writing.

We follow him and leave him; we must both follow him and leave him. (O if this motion is choreographed wrong, it looks like the most obdurate paralysis—just to mention one kinetic problem in the double, in the split stance.) It is why one can begin with such a poetics, writing as women, and still have an enormous unmapped territory to explore. What does it mean when a woman writes down that which happens at that time (thus, say, Bernadette Mayer's *Midwinter Day* [1982]). What, indeed, can it be to follow the force moving, recording it, for what moves, what writes, when the writer is a woman.

Then there is another silent (less talked of) source, one herself not as prone as Williams and Pound to manifesto. This one a backwash; when, doing something, one sees one is doing what she did. She is there, suddenly, as if in déjà vu. Huh. But her enacted tactics and certain statements show the force moving in and by means of overlays of languages. H.D. has used a term from ancient scribal habits, palimpsest, to define this overwritten text. Such a text, made of at least two kinds of scribble at different times yet on the same parchment, is split between its wholeness as object or ground and its veering multiplicity as figure. It also takes a different tack (tact) towards time, suggesting a psychoanalytic sense of the persistence of earlier configurations, and residues which are volcanic, irruptive. Palimpsest is a surface erased, but imperfectly erased, with old words visible, perhaps readable and interpretable under the new ones. (And/Or perhaps old words just confusing the new.) Palimpsest, scratchings, incisions of memory and event, little traces and fleetings which may recede, may suddenly rear up as if the darkest letter. Palimpsest indicates the desire to manifest, by some verbal or textual gesture, the sense of presence, simultaneity, multiple pressures of one moment, yet at the same time the disjunct, the absolutely parallel and different, the obverse sensations of consciousness in reality.

The role of Beverly Dahlen's new work cannot be underestimated in entering these questions of poetics and the discourses of (on) writing at a very high and brilliant level. *A Reading* is a diaristic work, claiming no revision.[2] While this may not be fully true, it makes a commitment to "the force moving." On each section is noted the time and place it is undertaken, the time and place it is finished; the seven sections, each exactly located, make a writing practice of their own temporal immersion, suggesting Williams' proposal "to write down that which happens at that time." This apparently simple incentive, if followed scrupulously, and with no scruples, can produce a polyphony of effects—autobiography, documentation, interventions from music, film, news, associative spurts of the "stream of consciousness"—May Sinclair's 1918 phrase about Dorothy Richardson's novel *Pilgrimage*.[3] Varieties of bits of consciousness, dreams. Phrases of allusions (to Shakespeare, to Wordsworth, to Olson, to H.D., to Williams, to Freud). Chanty associations ("said who will help me, the little red hen. Rhode Island reds, Rock Island line. the sky falling, broken, broken into, what if that were god . . . [*R*, p. 24]; or "the theater and its double, the ego and its double" [*R*, p. 27]). Thus in *A Reading*, the irruption of combinations of what we know in words and out, phrases, expression, cullings, not treated with any form of ironic contempt (as in *Bouvard et Péchuchet*) or as a downfall from wholeness, but as part of the (language) materials of the mind at work. And this collection point is constructed from an underlying "Objectivist" ethics of "sincerity": specific fears, desires, pleasures, contradictions posed as they are experienced and lived.

Dahlen's *A Reading* is an articulation between lyric (the force moving) and documentary (record without judgment). And something else, this palimpsest where language (and thus social registers and discourses) constantly overwrites and whispers the otherness of half-seen, shadowy words. An "it," a space half-entered.

Lyric, documentary and palimpsest all express themselves in a continuous stream of metonymy which uncannily, the more it extends outward (writer as collector, as documentarian, as collagiste), the more it seems to layer itself over and over, a texture of singing through porous time and porous ego. Elusive. Fast moving. An impressionist surface of reflection and swift change.

To write metonymy is to write all margins, no page. Is to make some critique of the center such that the binary distinction between text and space disappears, and so that a work bleeds, as is said of a photograph printed to the edge. All is margin, all is center. And the once-compelling binaries like full, empty; frame, presence; absence, mark, become pluralized into voided markings, marked void.

Metonymy, sidling, sidelong creates the thing on the side, the thing to the side, the thing set aside, the desire repressed but palpable in its corrupted absence. Impossible to catch, the intense pressure of, pleasure of a gap: "*A Reading:*" says Dahlen, "beginning, as we always do begin, *in medias res:* 'before that and before that. everything in a line.' Invoking a metonymy which was already a metaphor, the word itself, any word, a representation, a replacement, a substitution for some thing, any thing, which was not there, naming backwards, following it forward, back and forth from nothing to nothing."[4]

Yet at the same time, by the very intensity of concentration, of commitment to lateral motion, to metonymy not as defense or substitution but as a path, a Way, such a writing turns the notion of time askance. Instead of narrative being the master form of forms, privileged above others, narrative must take its turn among an array of strategies. For instance, the phrasal pulse which is the major unit of composition in *A Reading*—its short unit of noticing without the demands of finished statement—undoes the hegemony of the sentence, and yet the period is used as a center of punctuation. This both/and strategy gathers up the closure of the sentence and the ongoingness of the phrase. It appears that Dahlen has an interesting commitment to multiplying closures in a texture of availability. In her words "finished never done."

Iris
meta-fars
pull tight

sticky
rainbows
of light

But entering
language pushing
language graffiti bare
as trees nuage
trick travelling must

wait waiting in

await

silent position

A person sits still in the middle of her life and writes herself something to read. She calls it *A Reading.* She is who she is, but also she is not.

She is not, because it is fiction; she is not because she has made up that many words into which

she is, but she is also, as she, read.

Read, represented, representing. She represents herself, a lawyer, cross-examines herself about her own defenses, thus not annulling them but postulating them as a source. She represents herself, in a written dailiness, a diarist without "character" and without "irony" and without "persona." We are in a fertile landscape, wary, longing, filled with the situations of consciousness (dreams, cant, obsessive scum of language, allusions, slips, memory, week-old dialogue, scraps of lust and scraps of theory).

Why is this writing called a reading?

Such a lateral postulating of further words in metonymy (not the reducing or condensing tactics of substitution in metaphor) can be viewed as a technique of reading, for it alone will offer for every new mark stroked a plethora of further paths and spoors. Because only metonymy guarantees the exasperating plenitude of signs, tones, registers, margins and pages alike, it encapsulates itself as reading. A reading—some procedure for writing so excessive and marginal that it may begin to say: woman.

How to unfilter grief, pain, political slaughter, the broken body of someone unrescued? How to pick up the trash. To register the daily turning of leaves. How to ungarble sunlight, how to read the dust on the windshield while driving due west at sunset.

at sunset.

to read markings. It is not the story of Kings, are we still
writing
the stories of Kings.

———————————

If a person sets out to write simply, that which comes, according, however, to a complex impulse, driven to flowering

> layered cloud culminating edges of
> liminal light already blown differently
> so that's what! violent conversable flux!

if a person sets out to write, as if every day, as if incorporating every thing encountered and associated, with the cunning illusion of imposing nothing, only of asking language and the mind up

> didn't have time to do a muslin, didn't
> fetishize pleasures, just any old day or street
> work, cut
> straight into the fabric
> tidal and slattern,
> the singing

she is surely replicating, reinterpreting the omnivorous ambition of certain modernist long poems (*The Cantos, Paterson*).

"I am preparing [says Dahlen] in the most banal way to say everything possible" (*R*, p. 18).

Child in arms, the mother looking away, puts her into a shopping cart. But o! the cart had moved! The child, amused, drops to the floor of the supermarket. The mother feels the rush of weight dropped down, and lost. She dropped her too far! The mother with guilty gaiety says "whoopsa poopsie." But no matter. The child, fallen past the sheltering space, was unhurt. So take heart.

Open anything anywhere. The Freudian secret H.D. knew too. Not to propose, but to have the work propose through her, her job being patience. Receptivity. Silence. Fearlessness. Permission. That is—her job is to claim a praxis. Not "writing" exactly, but transmissions, being a wire, being wired (we say) and making writing. Making marks to read. Hauled in, released, hauled in, released, when read, the release, a visceral pleasure, becomes extensive. Underground. Webbing, Veins. Caves with junctures joined. A beat, beat, beat like a heartbeat.

A person sits in the middle of her life. She is writing. It is a praxis. There was not enough to read, before. The self is produced by being written in just that way (this association fixes, that one loosens, each is produced). She sits allowing "the unconscious mind" and all the other minds to fill. She allows it. She allows all its, all it's, all itses and all of it.[5] It is the ever trailing chain of real associations in language, the free association of psychoanalytic technique pertinaciously pursued in and as the main rhetoric of the work. "It" is everything—everything out there and in here, so the pursuit of "it"—the tracking of this protean thing through the forests of our social, psychic, and linguistic existence is the purpose and meaning of this encyclopedic writing.

Reading "it"—the unknown, the unconscious, the past, the language, woman—by the endless invention of "it." Dahlen is both donor and recipient, writer and text, everything and nothing, mother and child in the nest of words that defines, protects, reveals, conceals and produces it. And drops it.

It speaks. It writes and it listens. It is the sum total of all pronouns, it is the foreignness and sense of distance in all, between language and thing, between thought and rationale, it is the space, it speaks

the space speaks, and some subtotal of that possible space is seeing (hearing) the speaking, can do and does a reading.

All the myths about reflection and the terror of the unmediated gaze may now enter. All the myths that mingle the necessity for representation—Medusa demands the mirror, with the terror (they say) and power (we say) of the flaring Medusa of the vulva. Therefore, "it goes on you can't look at it" (R, p. 54). The "it" that goes on is herself, HERself, she is the it, she cannot look at herself without a reading; you cannot look at women without a reading, she is you, you is she, she is her, her is she . . . She is hurt, you can't look at it. Castration is a cultural wound.

A Reading is an "interminable analysis," crossing the American— and the Wordsworthean—long poem with psychoanalytic theory in intensely fructifying ways. The epigram from George Steiner calls attention to Dahlen's literalizing of a Freudian challenge: to make a self-analysis, to make a total analysis, and to refuse termination of an analysis. If the end of analysis is "the strengthening of the patient's ego," a reasonable thought, still Freud qualifies until it is unlikely (in practical terms) that any permanent resolution can be achieved. Basically, Freud proposes certain practical conventions both for terminating an analysis and for controlling the challenge of "interminable"—

a radical word in the title of his essay that is barely glossed.[6] If there is "nothing in the unconscious which corresponds to no" (Freud, cited in *A Reading*, e.g. pp. 37, 43), then the closer one gets to the unconscious, the more nothing is refused (the less anything is refused). Hence "everything speaks" (*R*, p. 43), and the writer hears it.

Reads it, as in a reading of the signs. Someone (American, female, Dantesque) goes into a trackless woods and asks how to find "it." Which is the work. The words. The risk of working in this way, of working through. The risks of finding what is found. And "finding it, how know it" (*R*, p. 16). So she begins to set down words (spoor is the Dutch word for track, as in a train station) that track into, that trace into, trace out something. She leaves her own shining pebbles in the woods and then she comes to find them.

"the thing which was there is not a word but words track it"(*R*, p. 19) "everything possible." (*R*, p. 18)

And "the word in language is half someone else's" said Bakhtin; language "is populated—overpopulated— with the intentions of others."[7] Thus any word, in being set down is not in a condition of being written, but read—read in the state of (at least half) belonging to another, to others. "Discourse lives, as it were, on the boundary between its own context and another, alien, context" (Bakhtin, p. 284). All statements are dialogic; as a condition of their being they bridge at least two contexts, the one which must be construed before this so-called original use, the new use, the use by "me" and by "you" can be read. Hence reading precedes writing, inflects writing, saturates writing, is writing. Further, in "artistic prose" the "dialogic inter-orientation becomes, as it were, an event of discourse itself" (Bakhtin, p. 284).

A reading, even in the sense that there are too many words, and any writing must protect itself from the ennui of mimicking used-up gestures of language and structure. To write is impossible (it sometimes appears). One may only read—that is hear, register, interpret. The production of more (of that kind of thing, words) is made into a municipal version of the larger, world-encompassing activity, understanding voices, of others, of self, of the others in the self, that is, of living inside the social and psychic conditions of dialogue.

"A reading" is shorthand for a semiological work. Such a title evokes the multiplicity of sign systems that structure the world. These are read everywhere. As humans we are great readers, from the never-interpretable urgent, urging markings of "semiotic" (pre-oedipal) heterogeneity (in Kristeva's insistence on the mark as part of the earliest undifferentiated materials of the maternal *chora*) to the readable, social diversity of utterances which intersect with power—heteroglossia, in Bakhtin's social term.[8] *A Reading* is a semiological work, knowing that things can be read, must be read, whether the insistence comes from the necessities of social coordinates in constant motion or from the almost unverbalizable plastic mysteries of myth and psychoanalytic theories of origins. "It" therefore both exceeds and precedes. It is always full, fuller, fuller than can ever be read.

And in relation to the instances of major form in the American long poem? Robert Duncan is both eloquent and witty on the major form of his predecessors, for he does not think it possible to talk of their "plans" for long poems. For him the greater overriding necessity is flexibility: to reconsider, to "repropose" oneself.[9] In this one particular, there is some resemblance to George Oppen's situational poetics "out of poverty/ to begin//again."[10] To understand the major form you are immersed in as a poet, Duncan suggests only one tactic: a reading. Oppen, similarly, suggests in that "poverty," a scrutiny (a reading?) of the "substantial" meaning of some words: "*would with and*" so common as to be unread. For Duncan, Pound's problem in "losing track" of "things in *The Cantos*" involved his inability to read: "Pound just doesn't really read 'em ever, doesn't go into 'em" (*Sagetrieb* interview, pp. 102, 118). One sense in which Dahlen's writing is a reading is her confluence with the call for an heuristic establishment of form by the reading of those words she has "happened" to write.

A speaking in tongues, an approach to the condition of election whereupon speech flames above one, visibly, and out of fear, one gains the terror of parsing. A reading is the reading of, spelling out of such spontaneity, an ability to follow and engage with such welling until the writer, hearing herself, hears and renders palimpsests of words.

Beginning everywhere, beginning without opposition, beginning simultaneously.

reading is construing along a language line (writing goes in one direction "only"), made infinite and compounded by the setting down of any word, in a situation where all words are first words, last words, any word. Any word is a crossing of storied wonders of knowing, feeling, remembering, associating, deciding, desiring. Any one word, **A** word, deciphered into what it means will give rise to such clots and palimpsests of reading as make up the emotional and structural motions of Dahlen's *A Reading.*

(Someone could write an essay on the "A" in *A Reading.* "What I write is provisional. It depends" [*R*, p. 76]. "A" not "the" is one possibility; it has its head cocked to hear another possibility. Another word.)

———————

A selvedge, the edge of a self, something that will not ravel, only reveal, thus in the tissue/textual metaphor, a Penelopean work without absent Ulysses, rapacious suitors; to wit: it need never (? maybe) be unraveled because of the necessity of a woman to invent a cunning trick in the face of male power. So there is no more unraveling. "everything possible"

This work occurs through the probe of one (of "A" person not "the" person), with the individual self postulated, not only as an end (an impossible end) in wholeness but as a tool to collect, to associate and to invent the language materials that come coursing. There is a place— not the hypnagogic, for that is on the borders of sleep, there is a place, it seems, on the borders of wakefulness, in a wakeful trance, where association can flow and not be censored or invigilated.

The ball of the typewriter spinning jerkily, key by key the striking, second by second the clock or typewriter, "the force moving." And herein recorded as such, pure, "pure" and noisy marking ground, marking time: "tik tik tik tik" (and so on [*R*, p. 53]). The striking of place against time. Not the modernist strategy of swallowing up all time into space, history into myth, but some rocking on the cusp of time and place. Words.

> themselves,
> flake by flake will cover, will whiten
> fresh
> estrange
> our space (the lyric poem is dead said Marjorie
> Perloff)

Hence "the reading of the writing goes on" (*R*, p. 78), and like the poetics of H.D.'s *Tribute to Freud*, the slightest mark on the page could generate, in association and analysis, an eternity of writing. Of writing it which is reading it. The reading of what has happened in the poem, where one has been led, and under whose aegis, by what dark and unowning path has one been roused and discomfited—this, like Duncan's quest, occurs under the auspices of a Dionysiac Eros. But not only him.

In *Jimmy and Lucy's House of "K,"* in a letter about a selection from *A Reading* therein presented, Dahlen testily, charmingly lists a number of people, well-known and obscure, and other sources, like film and popular culture, which have found echoes in her work, whom and which she has knowingly cited, slid into, elided and slid under her work.[11] The writing can be "a reading" because of the enormous quantity of these allusions. No "writing" exists that is not in fact a reading of former writing, an anthology in part, an appropriation of prior texts. Pound's modern long poem was, after all, a version of an anthology, a new kind of *ABC of Reading*.

Further, the list Dahlen gives (and hypothetically, any such list will necessarily replicate this) contains a high proportion of male writers and cultural figures. The situation of a woman in some version of that-culture-in-which-we-all exist may be described as the desirous reader. She is the reader desiring something, some thing not yet there, perhaps partially there, fleetingly there, oppositionally there, reductively there; if there, perhaps unread, and unread is unseen, unheard. The desirous reader chases this woman, these women among words. She reads them in, she reads them out. To be woman is to read woman.

Is to read women. To read Woman. To read among men, to read the men through women. Wome/an.

Dahlen queries radically, outrageously, "For woman, perhaps, language as a second language?" ("Forbidden Knowledge," p. 13). There I think she means that the pulsing and unreadable chora is our first "tongue." And because it is unreadable, and lost, all language is a site of loss. The plenitude of Dahlen's writing, she claims in a Lacanian trope, is an endless substitution for that loss. (Although this nostalgia about a lost place is not foreign to me, plenitude seems to have a social and plural origin.) Her metaphor for women? We may be writers and translators from a language whose syntax, vocabularies, and registers we are also acquiring. A second language.

Yet in this sense all writers are "women." But if all are metaphorically "women," women writers in this claim end up preempted from the social and political space of their gendered identities. Must then hold on at once to double, triple, quadruple senses contained in "woman." As that item which is "not-man." ("the opposite," "the complement," but criss-crossed with competing claims to sameness). As a person, just like men ("the same," "human," but criss-crossed with competing claims to difference). As a marginalized and Othered cultural site ("the feminine" available to men, but from their gender position and inside their gender narratives). As a tempting array of decorations in our culture generally taboo to children (except as dress-ups) and to men (except as transvestite choices): face paints of all colors, garments which enclose, tighten, and reveal the skin, mechanisms which pull and re-arrange the flesh, shiny things hung all over, bright colors and patterns, exaggerated shapes, noisemakers (high heels, bell-like jewelry). (This too is "the feminine.") As an actual and effective set of activities and assertions now, a person undertaking the ambitious social agendas of critique ("the feminist"). As a set of once active taboos, necessities, struggles laminated into a historical sense of gender ("the female"). As persons, these gendered folk are also those in whom sexualities, social class, race, and identity choices mingle, jostle, in a poly-political com-pound. One does not acquire one language once. What writes when "a woman" writes?

In *A Reading* there is no fictional center of things; although sometimes there is *I*, *it* also occurs, and *you*, and *she* (and *she* is sometimes *me*). This occurs especially because "I" and "she" elide so greatly, both in terms of the psychoanalytic fusion of the pre-oedipal bond, and in terms of the cultural position of a female "I" which is accountable to a multiplex Imaginary which contains a pack of gestures and stances of she's and hers's. The "I" who is a woman cannot be a writer, must be a "reader" of these pronominal facts. She must write a reading.

A reading implies that all the signs and marks that are thrown up without the invigilator displace the writer. There is no longer a *writer*, or even A writer. There is something else, someone claiming that the •responsibility for making words is the responsibility for interpreting. There is no neutral reading, everything is the construction of meaning within de facto agendas. The work is a series of caucuses.

The linguistic, discursive, generic, tonal range of *A Reading* suggests that what Dahlen is really after is a profound critique of representation (of the means and tactics of presenting fictionally), including narrative, author, page, style. There is no more writing (endless mimesis of the same thing); must have a reading of what's there to reground representation in, at least, a critical reading of its formerly assumed and unquestioned mechanisms.

"forever a book that we loved, these were models of stories, likely to be repeated since the number of plots is only about seven, but we aren't interested in plots anymore, traps, let the light shine, through those holes, the negative space, the darkness through it. I said: it was the best demonstration of negative space I ever saw, it made waves of darkness. the light was diminished. created the darkness as if light were the ground and not the other way, you would have it, so he said let there be dark. it is all light anyway" (R, p. 101).

"It will look like that wherever you stand, where you stand will be a center with everything rushing away" (R, p. 73). In this universe which alludes to center but negates it, there are no promises, except "endlessly in that place" (R, p. 74) language will happen, without beginning, end, telos. As middle, Steinian, it can only be responsible to itself. As middle, feminist, it can only be responsible to its choral community. A reading must negotiate both light and dark, the spaces where there are no letters are luminous by the black ink richly spaced against it; it is the black ink that can make sense, the space is "only" there. Only there like the "ghostly whereness" (citation, where?) of women.

Nijmegen, 1985–Swarthmore, January 1986

"W H O W E"

On Susan Howe

A Drawing

The meaning of this is entirely and best to say the
mark, best to say it best to shown sudden places,
best to make bitter, best to make the length tall and
nothing broader, anything between the half.
                                        Gertrude Stein,
                                        Tender Buttons

Susan Howe takes the experimentalist desire for interrogation of the
mark and combines it with the populist mysteries of such oblique and
marginalized materials as folk tales and early American autobiography,
and fuses these under the complex and resonant sign of human femaleness. Her work with its minimalist elegance and economy of gesture
is also charged with social density, in her critical allusions to our
common culture (Swift, Yeats, Shakespeare), and in her austere judg-
ments of the shared political and ethical destructions of our experience:
the liquidation of Native Americans, of Jews in the Holocaust, the rack
of Ireland. She has felt the inflection of victor by loser, of other by
winner, and these subtle dialectics of power create her subtle political
diction. Her words, sometimes broken even into a magical "zaum"
tactic, can draw upon lost words or non-dominant languages (Gaelic,
Native American languages): her poems are repositories of the language
shards left in a battlefield over cultural power.[1]

Like much of Susan Howe's poetry, the early *Secret History of the
Dividing Line* (1979) is set at an intersection, as the title suggests, of
time and space in a particular emotional territory. It is formed by
probing uses of the meaning of Mark. Both N. and vb.

Mark — a written or printed symbol
     — a sign or visible trace
     — an inscription signifying ownership or origin
     — a sign of depth

— a brand imposed
— a grade
— an aim or target
— a boundary
— a tract of land held in common
— a kind of money
— to notice
— to make visible impressions
— to set off or separate
— to consider, study, observe

Howe chooses to have her making a mark bounded by two Marks to whom this book is dedicated: her father and her son. Inscriptions and depths. Perhaps the *secret* history of the dividing line is its situational quality, a boundary explored between groups whose differences seem marked, but whose fusions and mutual yearnings the poetry seems to enact: tribe to tribe; generation to generation (adult to child, father to daughter); male to female; dead to living.

Howe plays on a basic myth of the hero, or the father—something from which the searching daughter feels alien, something for which the searching daughter feels desire. Thus the air-grasping syllables, encoding the word *hero* in anguished slow motion:

> O
> where ere
> he He A
> ere I were
> wher
> father father
>
> (*SHDL*, p. 6)

Later, Howe proposes the debate between the woman as hero (subject) and as heroine (that O or object).

> Who
> whitewashed epoch
> her hand
> knocking her O
> hero
>
> (*SHDL*, p. 32)

These experiments with the ruptured vocables of experimentalist diction are often set in/against an elegant intellectual poetry, one of whose forebears is Wallace Stevens, while another is Emily Dickinson.

> Intellect idea and (Real) being
> Perpetual swipe of glaciers dividing
>
> pearl (empyrean ocean)
> Text of traces crossing   orient
>
> and occident   Penelope
> who is the image of philosophy
>
> (*PS*, Part II)

Howe makes works which seem to distill the quintessence of traditional lyric poetry, its luminous greeny white sap-filled songs. This essence she tests and recreates by projecting the lyric into the hardly populated vastness and silence of modern page space. She works in issues of transcendence—as possibility, but also as impossible political privilege. Of "feigning" and the sincerities of artifice. She works between abstract thought and precisions of image. She maintains a Woolfean admiration for the odd and quirky, the resistant and wayward.[2] And makes fruitful a subtle play between determinate meaning and indeterminacy: a woman—a person mainly gendered female—writing "feminine" discourses, knowing and rewriting "masculine" discourses, in the name of a feminist and critical cultural project which wants to transcend gender. This project colossal in its hybris. In its unsettling. Howe has pointed to the ambition in an interview. She reads a quotation from Aquinas: " 'Pythagoras said that all things were divisible into two genera, good and evil; in the genus of good things he classified all perfect things such as light, males, repose, and so forth, whereas in the genus of evil he classed darkness, females and so forth.' In reaction to that, I wrote 'Promethean aspiration: To be a Pythagorean and a woman.' "[3]

With "Pearl Harbor" (Part I of *Pythagorean Silence*) the reader receives simultaneously the historical reference of violence of disasters of war—of attacks and provocations, and an imagistic sense of billowy, nacreous, sheltering space and sound. Here, too, contradictions in the luminous vulnerability of the emotional terrain: a He and She whose perspectives differ as vastly as does judgment from mourning. The poet replays shadowy scenes, for "Only / what never stops hurting remains / in memory." She tries (in a maneuver reminiscent of many quest plots of many women writers) to come to terms with a "pure and severe" and absent male quester, later seen as "Possession my father," and a time when "midday or morrow / move motherless" (i.e., "Poverty my mother"). Can one construct "parents" adequate to female ambition from these raw materials? This is done in the plangent voice of the child, daughter or soul, working into voice until "biography blows away" and she has simply distilled the pure essence of some story (say: quest, knife, ivy; the hunt, the dream, the shadow, the spindle).

Building upon this psychological and familial work, all of Howe's writing also does spiritual and metaphysical work yet without the authoritarian or prophetic claims that often accompany this practice. For instance, Howe will produce a text which draws on the reading of deeply felt markings, signs seen under pressure, signs in the typological sense. With her interest in the anti-authoritarian mark, Howe's work can be seen as a fruitful juncture between H.D. and Oppen. That practice of H.D. which centers most noticeably in *Tribute to Freud* rests upon the uncloseable reading of signs; word, gesture, memory and dream are all glyphs for an infiniating practice of decoding. That practice of Oppen which speaks of the lengthy preliminary work done to find one word creating the small space to "stand on"; such poetic practice makes islands of clarity or necessity thrown, like the Whitmanic "filament, filament," into the surrounding mystery. As in Oppen, Howe's work can show little interest in the connectedness of syntax, and more in the spaces of silence, the electricities of awe. The syntactic mode Howe favors? "Paper anacoluthon and naked chalk"—anacoluthon being a lack of grammatical sequence or coherence. (*ASFT*, p. [50])

And one of many favorite genres (all Howe's genres exist in transparently matted palimpsests) is something like the ode which lifts things to limitlessness, whose main debate is between overwhelming boundlessness (like the sea of death in Lawrence's "Ship of Death") (like the "more happy love, more happy, happy love" with the verbal excess in Keats' "Ode on a Grecian Urn") and some vulnerable boundary which may compromise ultimates of song, of bliss, of void. In Howe one feels the loft, the heft, the debate of the ode, the apostrophes of power, of self-questioning. The persistent ground of "alterity, anonymity, darkness."[4] All concepts coded feminine. As the ode, as genre, may be—the ode, as the genre which symbolizes poetry in its ecstasy, its poetic diction, its excessive, overblown, portentious, mellifluous scale. The ode's appeal to the sublime, its sense of boundariless dissolutions, its febrile outcries are also coded feminine: hysteria, emotionalism, exaggeration, the sense of an ecstatic dance on the boundaries of the sensible. If there is a female practice of the ode (different from male writers) it may lie in the indirection needed to examine the site of female ecstasy from the peculiar perspective of the seeker and the sought—the desirous, orgasmic, ambitious mother and the "incestuous," ambitious writer who appropriates those visceral ambitions. And while much of Howe is ode-like, perhaps the most startling ode is her prose critical study *My Emily Dickinson*—her passionate and vital exploration of the history of literature and the political context of Dickinson as American woman writer. But all genres are plumbed by the scrupulous lead of Howe's mark. The protocols of genre fermented by her mapping, weeping eye.

A lyric "I" a "mind's eye" "walk[s] through valleys stray/ imagining myself free" (*PS.*, Part III). What impedes her? and who is she? She is the female speck in the history of texts. And she is the scout of its presence. The roaming vagrant one, the errancy, the "Thorow"— thrown like a die into the game of culture's chances, thrown out, but thorough and pertinacious. Evoked, claimed is Thoreau, the watcher, the condenser of phrases, the one who knows the mystery of what he sees. Stubborn—o she/o he is stubborn. She is as stubborn as quarry is stubborn, before the end, and she is stubborn for quarries disappeared. The knife may slay, one voice be quelled. But Howe is driven to hear the condensed and impacted operas of the Others, the ones about whom few orators speak, the ones few encyclopaedists commemorate, the ones massacred, the ones of smoke. Iphegenia. Ophelia. Flora. Psyche. Little "humanchild." Operas of rage could be made. What genre is adequate to this discovery—that there are holocausts of the destroyed? Should the page be black? How then is one "a writer"?

> O lightfoot
> No spread of your name
> no fabulous birth stories
> no nations taken by storm
> Moving in solitary symbols through shadowy
> surmises   ("Thorow")

From an interview: "Q: If you had to paint your writing, if you had one canvas on which to paint your writing, what might it look like?" Howe's answer: "Blank. It would be blank. It would be a white canvas. White."[5] To write: to be caught in hopeless joy between black and white, said and unsaid, between the overwritten and underwritten, between desire and obliteration. Divided in language, but speaking the language. How to draw these signs on whiteness, how to incise words formed in imbeddings, words with the fused detritus of all their imbeddings. Reading up and reading down, reading back and forth across.

The ground can never be cleared of the prior. It saturates us—political powers, social places, duties, infusions of norms, irruptions of protest. Thus the sign is never empty, it is never EMPTY; it is full, fused and jostling, an active "stage for struggle" (as Bakhtin says, somewhere). Howe's innovations on the page, her sculptural sketches of signs, make a poetics of her responsibility to and in this multiple struggle.

This "I" in the text is a wraithe seeking the wraithe sought; she is, Howe says, the "Scholiast." The Scholiast! strange word, which means annotator. Writer of notes on margins of canonized texts. An ancient commentator on an ancient author. "Some clue." A textual hunt uses the metaphors of fox and hound, victim and pursuer. The annotator flees through a forest of texts, filled with beautiful allusions to transfiguration, to lyric, to folk tale—"cherubim golden swallow" and "snow chastity berry-blood (secrecy)"—trying to find, to track, to catch, for an instant, the little ghosty-geist of otherness.

> through a forest glade
> > she fled
> hazel wand
> > a deer again
> no mother
> > but a gentle doe
> chased by white hands
> > across summer sands

> > (*PS*, part III)

Bits of the choros behind the choros. Hounded. Some monologue never before spoken, some attenuated distant voice that speaks to us in fragments. Bits of phrases. Half-gasps. Make a primal doubt of patriarchal relations, of "that 'happy king' " (*PS*, Part III). Treating a figure unrecorded, barely able to be brought into text, fleet of foot, running through the margins; no wonder the talk is of "clues," of "surmises," of evanescence. The text—all written history—is a wood. The gentle doe is fleeing; the gentle, ferocious writer is tracking through that tricky landscape, trying to

take them $\left. {in \atop at} \right\}$ their $\left\{ {wood. \atop word.} \right.$

As in a ballad, something has happened. Some fatedness that cannot be explained or stopped, no motives, no causes. Just the effects, an intense spotlight on details, the shadow on others. And like ballads, filled with murder, infanticide, rape, revenge, final entrapments, betrayals, violent love, violent death. In this scene, we know where we are, the beauties of the image phrases ("white hands"; "gentle doe") heighten the interplay of the powerful and powerless. The implacability of what (we imagine, we construct, we, culturally, know) can happen.

Hunting the wren.

(Once I ate pâté de grière. The bones were very small. I would not do that again.)

What does it mean to disperse these ballad materials around the page space, and evoke, also, word by word, epics, histories, orations, encyclopaedias, meditations, psalms, philosophies, elegies, masques? (Why is Howe at once subtle and prolix with genres?) In terms of the social territories evoked, ballads are the obverse of at least encyclopedias, epics, histories, orations. Possibly philosophies. And all texts have had strong bonds with power which means also with powerlessness: "Battles . . . fought . . . on paper." (PS, Part III) "pearl harbor" "white foolscap." To begin with, we are evoking the genre of the powerless and the genres of the educated—folk genres and literate genres. Intermingled, tangled, disentangled, claimed as a female textual ground. So to reanimate the genres, to claim major intertextual ties with classic works, and to watch, to follow the wraithe on the margins into her centers that are dispersed and profound, taken together as strategies show the depth and power of Howe's ambition, her omnivorous, intelligent allusiveness.

The song, the psalm, the fairy tale. Hamlet, Ophelia, Cordelia, Lear. What is female about this? Certainly some relational vulnerability, otherness proposed, the other side of stories. Ballad, "peerless poesy," meditation. The 23rd Psalm. Pilgrim's Progress. Arthurian legend. Spenser. Swift. Tristan and Iseult. A refusal to play the game of belatedness, a turning of loss to privilege. She is claiming both margin and page. Every textual space. Spine. Title. Dedication. Entitlement and dedication. The fox, the hounds, the doe. The father and mother. The foundling. The struggle against female erasure. Self-erasure and self-affirmation. A theatrical. A masque. A ritual for naming. For naming loss. For naming that one is what one is, in the manner of tragedy. For naming Liberty. Stepping outside of the gates of the city into the whispering woods. And stepping back inside the gates of the city unafraid of abstractions. Stepping and restepping across that line, that secret line where civilization meets mystery. To perfect oneself by the cunning of language. To admit one's greed (one's need) for inserting oneself into and transforming English lyric and Celtic story. "Our law"; what we were given of tradition is what we must break off, examine, fabricate. Making it ours, for it now has "ourself" in it.

> Little girl in your greed
> come down
>
> come down
>
> ivy and roses   ourself
> will be
>
> without defect
>
> without decay
>
> (*PS*, Part III)

Not only ballad, not only epic, not only genres affiliated with heavily gendered griefs, but

a feminist appropriation of

every genre large and small.

The note. The note! a feminist task of the Scholiast!—the annotation, condensing enormous cultural pressures into a tiny meaningful margin, tracking around the monumental, following traces; stepping beyond the woods (the words) into "volumes of secrets to teach / Socrates" (*DOP*, p. 21).

She is inside the book writing almost outside the book. She writes on the margins of the institution of "the Book." She is writing on "white foolscap"—the paper of dunces, of the seley, she is writing blank. And writing wily. For annotators do not take the process of textual making for granted; they intervene in the processes of signification, canonization, attention-making. They point. They undermine. They bear shards of almost irrelevant information. Clues. They keep certain names alive ("But crucial words outside the book / those words are bullets" [*DOP*, p. 93]). Bullets are the little marks between sections of text that enter the emptiness of the unlocated or unsaid, exist on the borders of text. Bullets are killing shots. The claim for the centrality of texts in the construction of culture is made politically enormous by the power of that literate gun. The "gun" of Dickinson—that kind of loaded Gun.

Whose driving intelligence gets into language as ferocity. This strange thing, the female writer—shoots that "imaginary" gun and its dramas of Eye, Thumb, fire, into the layered and resistant textures of man-made culture.

"How do I, choosing messages from the code of others in order to participate in the universal theme of Language, pull SHE from all the myriad symbols and sightings of HE" (*MED*, pp. 17–18).

"She [Dickinson] built a new poetic form from her fractured sense of being eternally on intellectual borders, where confident masculine voices buzzed an alluring and inaccessible discourse. . . . Pulling pieces of geometry, geology, alchemy, philosophy, politics, biography, biology, mythology, and philology from alien territory, a 'sheltered' woman audaciously invented a new grammar grounded in humility and hesitation" (*MED*, p. 21).

The impossible question posed in every crevice of this work is: How to make a culture that does not demand subjugation when "Culture representing form and order will always demand sacrifice and subjugation of one group by another" (*MED*, p. 93).

The page is not neutral. Not blank, and not neutral. It is a territory. Why does Howe erase or elide some words? *the isolation of a letter. the isolation of a syllable.* Why does she confound grammar? *a well with clefts, words as stones.* Why does she use syllable-sounds of semi-meaning? ("enend adamap blue wov thefthe") ("Thorow") *Crypto-grams, language always having "another" message.* Why and how vibrations of shadow words, as if visual afterimages, come in her *intri-cate split spell-ings:* "iris sh" (*SHDL*, p. 40) or "life la / nd friend / no lighthous / marin / ere" (*CG*, [p. 9])? Why does she make pages of cut-ups, of upside-downs, of palimpsests? Traces one can barely read, texts of physical beauty (in words) that enact their own destruction and dispersion. Mergings, as when words are almost double printed "humanchild humanchild" (*PS*, part III). Or whole shadow sounds, as if the harmonics of language in "Transcendent could be whis / buried" (*PS*,) where the whole weight of Indo-European consonant relations, not to speak of our culture's relations with the underwritten, undersaid, socially repressed, becomes the fulcrum for the line break, "whispered" to "buried." *And archaicism, the whole history of the language in one gesture* She wants to show the half-seen, the half-forgotten. Her work is filled with memories of abandonment; she represents the silence half-sounded of the powerless. Her work is filled with the rhetorics of

philosophy and theology, and represents the sounds of power in relation
to doubt and silence. She is suspicious of languages and discourses as
already made and inhabited things; she wants to enter and inhabit the
untoward crevices of language . . . archaic words, names that may no
longer have things, shadows of things and feelings difficult to name.

How deep and intransigent the nature and level of resistance to smoothness and "normalcy" of poetry: the deformations in (un)grammatical,
in (non)-word "play," in (mis)spellings, in investigation even unto the
syllable, unto and into the letter, the mark. And in form—line breaks,
page canvas, the use of space/silence/silencing/ the piercing of whiteness. Back and forth to move over the boundary line separating language
from sheer vocable, sheer babble. The knowing glossolalias of generic
intercuts. The polyvalent allusions to deeply imbedded classics.

Only every distortion is adequate.

To that level of resistance and despair. And desire. To that desire!
to attempt a cultural practice—an ethical and humane practice—that
does not demand "sacrifice and subjugation" to "form and order" in
order to write (MED, p. 93).

Identification with Cordelia. Sincerity. Unfitness. Muteness. Passivity.
Inadequacy. Poverty. Exile. Death. It is Cordelia's silent language
found!

Identification with Lear. Bluster, Power. Vulnerability. Hubris. Loneli-
ness. Madness. Tragedy. It is Lear's language anointed with his discoveries of otherness!

Bifocal. Trifocal. Manifold.
The isolation of a letter. w   The letter of question
who   why   whowe
is the rest of the word   rath (PS, Part III)? Is it "wrath"?

The recreant will recreate.

If there is a zero or nul space of "Woman," a "hole" in discourse, it
cannot always be filled by a mechanism of reversal, from zero to totality, from negative to positive, from anguish to affirmation. It must
recognize and acknowledge—must pull into textuality, and put into
culture the elements of its almost effaced stories in all their residual,
fragmentary quality. And claim the dynamism of the hegemonic stories

in their canonical splendor. "Rowed as never woman rowed / rowed as never woman rowed / through the whole history of her story" (*DOP,* p. 83). To be "Woman" is to be the site of such social practices: as soon as their traces are revealed, they are brought into regulation.[6] To be a woman (not a Woman) writer, is to efface regulation. By every means possible. Is to mark over the mark with the mark of the "marked marker."

An important, underutilized essay of Gertrude Stein argues implicitly that experimentalist writing occurs in opposition to "forensics," and in temptation by it. The mastery and the power.[7] That loaded word is also the title of her essay; it alludes to discourses of dominance. Forensics (defined conventionally as public argumentation, formal debate, presentations of law courts) is understood as the dialect, ideolect, or rhetorical mode of a specific group which holds and practices power ("they made all walk"), social replication ("forensics is a taught paragraph") and definition. For Stein, forensics is a system of normative definition, which, in the imposition of authoritative norms, trains one to patterns of assumptions (including those of gender). "Forensics establishes which is that they will rather than linger and so they establish" (p. 391). The writer of "Forensics," the *she* seems to be debating the value, if any, of forensics to her—forensics as disputation, as power, as definition, as "eloquence and reduction" (p. 386). Among other functions, this essay, therefore, is a debate between authority and the antiauthoritarian. It is clear enough that complicity, obedience, agreement, and renunciation of one's own bent are part of the system of forensics.[8] The question is "how to write" (to borrow the title of the whole book which this essay completes) when the writing space is colonized by forensics. How to gather authority without authoritarian power; how to indicate clarities without the limitation of certainties; how to give and receive pleasure without rhetorical or generic proscriptions; how to indicate one's volume without squatting hibernations of mass. *How to Write.* This, Gertrude Stein indicates, is her problem; this, Virginia Woolf indicates, is her problem; this, Marianne Moore indicates, is her problem; this, Susan Howe indicates, is her problem.

Howe bases her poetics on the evocation or proposition of "silence" or "a white canvas. White" as a trope for an anti-authoritarian practice. The foregrounding of otherness. The critique of centers, hierarchies, authorities. The suspicion of dominant meaning. The apprehension of power. The claim of power via critique. The seductions of dominant meaning scored with suspicion. And, often this has a gender valence. As in Howe's essay "The Captivity and Restoration of Mrs. Mary Rowlandson" in which Howe proposes a truth (specific, suffered, female) in opposition to Truth (official, a "masculine covenant" [p. 116]). Indeed, Howe uses this important essay to locate gender differences in both the production and the consumption of a text. She analyzes the duplicity of the female text ("each time an errant perception skids loose, she controls her lapse") which can at once "confirm orthodoxy" and "subvert" (p. 117).

As someone situated on borders between allegiances, as someone who eschews what she perceives as untempered affiliations, Howe has had sometimes provocative relations to varieties of contemporary feminism. For instance, she is notably unimpressed by the discussion of Dickinson in Gilbert and Gubar's *The Madwoman in the Attic* (cf. *MED*). In the 1986 interview, Howe spells out explicitly the analytic and cultural danger she sees in reiterating a paradigm of the semiconscious, mad woman artist: the end in breakdown, disability, death too easily acceptable as a script.[9] The Falon interview makes starkly clear what was at stake in this received paradigm (which *Madwoman* did not, of course, begin, and which, in my view it analyzed; but which, in Howe's view, it perpetuated). Howe speaks of her own fear of being an artist based on her apprehension that madness and breakdown were the retributive punishment for ambition. Tremendous psychic struggles are revealed in Howe's persistent linkage of "the bond between mad and made" (*ASFT*, p. [46]). The apparent insanity of other women artists blocked her from her own declarations; to struggle against such received interpretations of other women artists by analyses of their intellectual breadth was to struggle for one's own ambition and achievement, at once an act of cultural criticism and of personal necessity.

Fundamentally, Howe is mounting a critique of the tendency of *The Madwoman in the Attic* to a "victimization" hypothesis, which underplayed the agency of women. Yet despite this attack, Howe is notably feminist. Whowe? She is concerned with the unspoken stories, the unsung songs: "I wish I could tenderly lift from the dark side of history, voices that are anonymous, slighted—inarticulate."[10] She maintains the historical consciousness of the Creonesque politics of violence and self-justification; her response, quite similar to Woolf's: "Malice dominates the history of Power and Progress. History is the record of winners. Documents were written by the Masters. But fright is formed by what we see not by what they say."[11]

Howe maintains an uncompromising suspicion of power and a subversive response, subversive "of powers and control and order."[12] Like the

Woolfean paradoxes of women's writing articulated in *A Room of One's Own*, Howe offers the parallel analysis of a gendered writing beyond gender. A series of citations show the full arc of the paradox. "A poet is never just a woman or a man. Every poet is salted with fire" (*MED*, p. 7). "There's a *time* of poetry and a mastery about it that transcends chronological time and gender, and that . . . has its own time and its own gender" (Falcon interview, p. 28). "Yet gender difference does affect our use of language, and we constantly confront issues of difference, distance and absence, when we write" (*MED*, p. 13).

Importantly, she is a feminist by virtue of her rage, including her rage at the misappropriation (as she sees it) of a woman writer—in the case of Gilbert and Gubar, by women; in the case of the mis- editing of Emily Dickinson, by men.[13] The rage of Howe, the brilliant, lacerating indignation is a steely motive. In the 1986 interview, Howe speaks of being released to rage by virtue of an exemplary feminist text: the "tremendous effect" of the galvanic rage of Kate Millett's (1969) work *Sexual Politics*; Howe's reading of Millett led her to those changes in her paintings and environments (Howe was then a visual artist) which in turn quickly provoked her to a drastic almost interdicted change of medium—into words, into writing, into articulation of sound forms in time.

Howe appears to be on the cusp between two feminisms: the one analyzing female difference, the other "feminine" difference. For the latter, she is close to Julia Kristeva, who evokes marginality, subversion, dissidence as anti-patriarchal motives beyond all limits. Anything marginalized by patriarchal order is, thus "feminine"; the "feminine" position (which can be held by persons of both genders) is a privileged place from which to launch an anti-authoritarian struggle.[14] The female use of this "feminine" of marginality and the avant garde use of this "feminine" of marginality are mutually reinforcing in the work of some contemporary women: Lyn Hejinian, Kathleen Fraser, Beverly Dahlen and Howe. This mixed allegiance will naturally call into question varieties of flat-footed feminism. Just as Woolf continually proposes political and cultural feminism and the critical position of homosexuality, yet satirically portrays monomanical reformers and colonizers of otherness (suffragists and lesbians among them), so Howe continually proposes at least a feminism of cultural critique while declaring strong opposition whenever she suspects unitary (undialectical, uncritical) feminist enthusiasm. The only danger is that Howe's precise kind of feminism may be misread by a- or anti-feminist commentators.

Certainly *The Liberties* cannot be misunderstood in its approach to the question of women's representation in culture. This major work from 1980 (first published with, but unrelated to *The Defenestration of Prague*) begins with, and returns to the tie between Stella and Jon. Swift. Howe makes her own "liquidation"—payment of a debt, assessment of liabilities and assets—in analyzing Swift's "liquidation"—abolishing, metaphoric killing of Stella. Swift abolished things about his life-long companion, documents, artifacts, writings, for none of Stella's letters, few of her poems, and no portrait has survived. Stella is therefore taken by Howe as an absolute baseline of women's cultural condition: although she had a fairly bold life, she has been historically obliterated, liquidated. Although Howe has mentioned that the title *The Liberties* alludes to a particular neighborhood in Dublin rich with cultural layers, yet one might easily hear an echo of Swift's elegant epitaph, translated from Latin by Yeats. "He served human liberty." Male liberties are preserved and eloquently assembled; female liberties though equally forceful are with greater difficulty disentangled from guilt, pain, loss, obliteration. Howe's work is written against the grain of such liquidation, to examine and assess a Stella, a Cordelia, who, how: whowe.

This is a play, a masque in which Stella and Cordelia meet to piece together their stories and identify what they have in common. Obliteration. Their quest is a trek, and these events occur: memory, intelligibility, muteness, map-reading, ellipses, telling, explosive silences, interpreting traces, emphasis shifted. They dress in boy's clothing: to be safer? to neutralize their pain? to cross-dress into other subjectivities? at least to claim the liberty of boys. What does one do when one feels the electric power of language from the feminist margins of cultural credibility? Resistance, refusal, austere respect commingled with lacerating grief, resistance to the already-said of literature (to Swift, to Yeats, to Shakespeare), a sounding of dominance with the mark lines that have dredged the margins. Stella, Swift's friend and Cordelia from *King Lear* meet in the wild-woods of Howe's page space: a space devoted, consecrated to marginality, a page space that is a canvas of margins. Reading a book, they are examining what is inside the book, what is outside:

Howe has taken the responsibility of writing the book outside the book. Thus rewriting the books we assumed we knew, against the grain of the most precious canon: Shakespeare! Swift! Yeats! piecing together their story, piecing together what they have in common, trying to answer Cordelia's question "Did we survive at all." They have in common their vulnerability to the definitions of them by others' stories.

They have a consciousness of violence, done to them, around them; violence to the vulnerable is a repeated motif in Howe's work, and within her text, often the quarry speaks. They recall phrases associated with their story (Cordelia meditates upon "speak again"), but these are cited only to be assessed. Recited they become different, voiced critically. They have in common a female relation to dominant story, muted and trying a voice, storied but claiming their telling. They investigate. They spy. They scry. They wait.

"Whowe." Sometimes the characters seem to be whole, but their integrated knowledge, unstable, alternates with explosive silences, blackouts staged by Howe. They panic. They are self-possessed. The dangerous dialectic of claiming *made* from *mad/e* is a brilliant dramatic and intellectually compelling site in this work. "Surely [says Beverly Dahlen] she cannot simply enter the tradition, identifying with it as if she were male; she is, I think, in grave risk to do so. But what other identity is there? Surely, to ask that is to bring us to the heart of the matter: woman as absence and the consequent risks involved in the invention of our own traditions."[15] A female writer. A female writer faced with a complex (the tradition) more often inimical than welcoming, and filled to brim, with multiplex inscriptions of women and the female and the feminine. A female writer looking for a way to write. How, indeed, to write. Whowe to write. The path Howe chooses here, this examination of a fictional character, and a semi-fictionally available historically attested person, bridges a way to the definition of "our own traditions" to treat the palimpsested absence, filling it with our (with whower) annotations and firm marks. Yet they are already filled with what they establish; filled with taught paragraphs. Who we? Who? How? Who howe (who is any of us) to attempt this? And whooo-wee—the cheer, the whoop, the enormous, outrageous pleasure, the pride, of making this attempt. The pride in Howe occurs not so much in overt exclamations of joy, but in gestures towards election.

Left upon the stage at the end are versions of a community of seekers, versions of the whowe: a sojourner, a lonely bastard, and a fool. It is this kind of combination of marginals, fused into one, who becomes the center of *Articulation of Sound Forms in Time*. For that work can be read as an allegory of how the center, how major man—white, colonist, Protestant, male, minister, armed with God's word and courage and rectitude—how that man, entering almost accidentally some marginal space, goes from the straight and narrow to sheer errancy, sheer wanderings. Mr. Hope Atherton, militant new American, wanders on the margins of the colony at which he was a center. His oblique

vision and experience of the Other ("Indian") and himself as Other is
forever defining. Following from Howe's study of the margins as marginal (in *The Liberties*), *Articulation of Sound Forms in Time* offers a
vision of the center as marginal, marginalized, prone to a hopeless—
yet potentially saving—breakup of its most cherished paradigms.

The deepest effect of this experience of otherness is the dissolution of
language. This work again fervently enacts Howe's language strategies.
The isolation of letter. Of syllable. Phrasal constructions. Word squares
mingling Native American words and word parts with phonemes from
"our" language ("amonoosuck" and "ythian"), these macronics making
an "uncannunc" set of nonce formations (*ASFT*, [p. 16]). Words are
situational, meteoric, unrepeatable, impacting the whole history of
language in one gesture. There is word "play"—the pun as the intersection of personal revelation (condensation, distortion) and linguistic
possibility. And all these (words as if graffiti puns, macronics, words
scattered like a handful of jacks) (words effaced; words without space,
as in Roman inscriptions) the critical appropriation of all burlesque or
archaic language habits for high critical ends. The taxing struggle to
assemble and maintain a self-questioning (who? how?) cultural position: anti-authoritarian, yet authoritatively provoked by one's female
identity: Howe. We. WHOWE.

I have taken my pun on Howe's name from herself, to point up the rich
sense of self and of community (who we?) that must be sustained to
sustain this kind of feminist critique.[16] The end of *The Liberties* set a
proof to herself. It consists of a series of word squares alternating S and
C (for Stella and Cordelia, but also to herself: Susan, SEE!), followed by
a series of riddles whose answer becomes How: a question, a salutation,
a hold, a hole, a depression. Offering thereby an astonishing self-portrait
of an artist, a woman, trying to inherit herself, to work herself into her
own—"patrimony"? "anarchy"? No, into her own "liberty."

Taking liberties.

Hence a work of "howness: both concavity and depth" from a "howdie:
a midwife, origin obscure" who gave it life from the concavity and the
depth at once. "Across the Atlantic, I / inherit myself." During the
masque at the very end, a Sentry comes on stage to say "I am afraid,"
as who would not be, having written, seen, undertaken, dared and
proposed such a work. A work which pursues Shakespeare (the drama
like a mix of heath scene and Beckett), Swift, Yeats, and *must do so*, a

compulsion (deference deranged, damaged, exploded by feminist questions, by whowe) undertaken in fear and desire ("dare / / tangle").

To take such liberties. To take them at their word. To take their word. How to write. Whowe to write.

1984/1987/1989

O T H E R H O W

Poetry and Gender: some ideas

Possession of many of the elements that make poetry into poetry somehow depends on positioning women? Poetry gendered in a different way than fiction is? Sometimes it is possible to think so.[1] Love, Beauty, Nature, Seasonal Change, Beauty Raked by Time, Mediating Vision or Muse, the pastoral, the carpe diem motif, the satire—all these prime themes and genres from the history of poetry seem to have swirls of gender ideas and gender narrative blended like the marblized end papers of old books. It's so beautiful, so oily with color, who could want to pick it apart?

Knowing when to begin and end is knowing what to say between poems being part

of the poem.

Helping them write a report, they need silvery sky dusk lilac stars stars starry bibleots rosy as a local coral flouncing the poem is that the answer?

small folding arrangements?

Further, the centrality of the lyric voice (few characters in a poem little dialogue) means that one point of view is privileged. And the speaking subject is most often male.

'my female side' proudly
'my anima'

Overexposed post
card of the 50's sans one bitty cloud to darken
azure at the pectoral monument.
By implication or odd window, houses'

140

estranged effect
boasting seedy pleasure withered or perspicacity
deranged; what circle, what perimeter

to draw around such interlinear spannings.

If, in a bourgeois novel, the truth lies

in between, what "in"

is in "the bourgeois poem":

Now in the modern period, that lyric voice is ruptured, and poems can feature a controlled social array, as do novels. They may be "polyphonic," as novels. Even the masculine subject can be refused, interestingly, curiously, awkwardly, by a male poet, as by fiat or assertion—Tiresias in Eliot's notes to *The Waste Land*. And women writers speaking in a female, or a neutral-yet-gendered voice are not necessarily confessional of their lives, though still they may be "confessing" their throwing themselves wildly against, careening into conventions of representation. Into the terrible inadmissable congruence of poetry and gender. So all in all, even with exceptions, the institution of gendered poetry and the male-gendered poetic voice are embedded in the history of poetry.

As a woman writing, my language space, my cultural space is active with a concatenation of constructs—prior poems, prior poetics—a lot of which implicate women. But not often as speaker. As ideal. As sought. As a mediator towards others' speech. As object. As means. As a thing partially cannibalized. Neutralized.

"Avant-garde" or experimental poets cannot simply discount this past; they must consciously address the social and formal imbeddings of gender. Nothing changes by changing the structures or sequences only. Narrative "realist" poets, including feminists, cannot simply discount this past; they must consciously address the formal and social imbeddings of gender. Nothing changes by changing the content only.

A woman, while always a real, if muted or compromised, or bold and unheard, or admired but forgotten (etc.), speaker in her own work is most often a cultural artifact in any of the traditions of meaning on which she draws.

Poems Today

Many poems today look too much alike. They sometimes act and sound alike. They repeat. They repeat the relations and they repeat the exclusions. They repeat the satisfactions. Many a poem says the same kinds of things: these things are, or are called, poems. This is a tautology which protects nostalgias, sentimentalities, implicitly moralized short stories, domesticated mystery, and shallow transcendence. Protections may sometimes extend to banal fragmentation and shocking diction. Moreover, the iconicity of the text (the lyric icon on the page) seems deeply related to the beauty, inviolability, self-containment and iconicity of the Female Figure as object which the text denominates.

Alexei Kruchenykh (translated by Marjorie Perloff): "before us, the following things were demanded of language: clarity, purity, propriety, sonority, pleasure (sweetness for the ear), forceful expression (rounded, picturesque, tasty)," which, the Russian futurists noted, represented, in critical language, the grounding of poetry on Woman: "as a matter of fact: fair, pure (oh of course!), virtuous (hm! hm!), pleasant sounding, tender (exactly!), finally—tasty, picturesque, round . . . (who's there? come in!)."[2]

How, then, to disturb these long-imbedded pleasures? How, then, to invest in the possibilities of a critical language that ruptures deep (constitutive?) assumptions of poetry as a genre? "What language" (asks Phillipe Sollers) "would escape this insidious, incessant language which always seems to be there before we think of it?"[3]

Language and Gender

Writer? Becoming one on whom language plays and through whom language exacts poetic convention, etymology, terrible puns, vernacular turns, ugly gobbets, professional jargon, mindless babble, baby syllables, dialect renderings, nursery rhymes, old pop music, precious adjectives and dubious adjectives, connectives, newspaper information, disinformation, conjunctions, pronouns playing with the social space evoked ("he" "she" "it" "we" "they"), "little" words like *as* or *with*, like *the*.

"by" whom, beside whom and made by whom it may course or occur, declaring the destruction of uncontested rhetoric (but never the destruction of rhetoric).

Writer? A position to activate elements of language to join so that its activities enjoin the reader, you (to hear a sound to know a space that "never" was before).

> Comb the hairy
> language a vernac
> vert knack of saying what
> no one esp.
> desires
> hearing—how much it's the same.

But always prior inscriptions. Incessant marking. A writing whose condition is over writing. Want "in fact" a description of our language situation? Neither language use nor language acquisition are gender neutral, but are "imbued with our sex-inflected cultural values.' "[4] Talking. Eliding. Agreeing. Questioning. Completing. Insisting. Leaving no space for others to speak. A woman's silence is a "social silence." It is created by the praxis of "protecting others' speech."[5] How to depict the kinds and quantities of social silence at the core of works. Silence at the core, and silence inscribed in the absence of works. Banality. Pause. "Utterance . . . is constructed between [at least] two socially organized persons" even in the absence of an actual addressee. Thus social status, hierarchial status, gender status all matter: "there is no such thing as an abstract addressee, a man unto himself, so to speak."[6]

Foregrounded, this statement suggests the multifarious gender allusions or gender situations that can be called up just by language and its shifting, its tones, the social resonances of idiom, of the colloquial. The dialogic creation of meaning, the subtle capacities for cueing, status, power, and the interconnection of social and verbal realms are facts that have barely been self-consciously accounted for in the understanding of poetry.

> Still one could refind
> a taste for old beauty.
> Spillways of leaping
> abyss to azure
> extend thin ness ness ness
> that rusts rustle rond soft spectacle.

If language is "overpopulated with the intentions of others," it is teeming with, inter alia, gender ideas.[7] I mean, I'm not talking of the signifier/signified, but of palimpsests of (saturations of) signifying.

"Each word *tastes* of the context and contexts in which it has lived its socially charged life."[8] If each word has lived a socially charged life, each word has a "narrative" or two which it brings with it. What are the tactics which can either reaffirm the narrative(s) the word is telling or can try to break into by distorting or deforming, opening the storied words?

If literary language itself as the reasonably smooth formation of meaning cannot account for the sheer brutality of voicelessness — and if "giving voice to the voiceless"—what I used to say I was doing, an early feminist formulation—begins to sound both patronizing and unconscionable, then poetry has to be allowed to depoeticize itself and enact a rejection of the cultural character of its own idiom.

Depoeticize: reject normal claims of beauty. Smoothness. Finish. Fitness. Decoration. Moving sentiment. Uplift.

Want the poetry of shifters, a pronominal poetry, where discourses shift, times shift, tones shift, nothing is exclusive or uniform, the "whole" is susceptible to stretchings and displacements, the text marks itself, and there is no decorum. Anything can be said. Want the poetry of a raggedy, hewn, and situational character, with one criterion: that it has caused pleasure in the making. Pleasure in the writing and intransigence in the space for doing writing, and that is it. My only interest: in making objects that give me pleasures; they may also be interesting enough to sustain and renew whatever regard, look, or reflection is by chance cast upon them. That is it. Period.

Thinking about language in my poetry, I imagine a line below which is inarticulate speech, aphasia, stammer and above which is at least moderate, habitual fluency, certainly grammaticalness, and the potential for apt, witty images, perceptive, telling and therefore guaranted "poetic." That is, readable (reasonable) within intentions we assume. Since "Medusa" (finished in 1979) and again since "Crowbar" (finished 1983) my poetry wanders, vagrant, seeking to cross and recross that line: mistaking singular for plural, proposing stressed, exposed moments of genuine ungrammaticalness, neologisms, non-standard dialect, and non-normative forms. I struggle to break into the sentences that of course I am capable of writing smoothly. I want to distance. To rupture. Why? In part because of the gender contexts in which these words have lived, of which they taste.

Shadowy the sombre emission of light tawnies.
I read the paper naked
government atop me
sweet pea to myself.

A sense of missing the
important, redefining the minor the nothing the corner
turned and missed it

something mmmm say small
that's not "the same."

Rupture

To refuse the question as asked. To break through the languages of both question and answer. To activate all the elements of normal telling beyond normal telling.

Write the unwritten, paint the undepicted?

Must make a critical poetry, an analytic lyric, not a poetry that "decorates dominant culture" (to cite Michael Palmer) but one which questions the discourses. This situation makes of representation a site of struggle.

Recurrent Terms

delegitimate
deconstruct
decenter
destroy
dismantle
destabilize
displace
deform

explode

Rupturing Narrative Sequence

An especially convincing part of the early—mid-70's feminist aesthetic of sincerity, authenticity, uncovering unmediated truth is the idea that many stories culturally produced and maintained did not include female(s)' experiences. The "images" projected on my screen were not

constructed by me but only with a particular version of me in mind. I
went to those movies and—look—there "I" was! All stories interpret
experience, construct what we call experience. As a woman writing, I
had to seize some power over story as a social institution. Seize the
mask. Not carpe diem, the dominant injunction to me as delightful
object in one poetic romance, but carpe personam, the female injunction to myself as critical subject in a politics of narrative. Seize the
mask, the fictive, examine the instruments whereby writing "are"
fabricated.

An intense play between subject and object(ified) is created in the
invention of stories for the semi-silenced, or unheard female, or other
marginal characters in traditional tales (myths). This prevalent revisionary stance of female writers, happily now foregrounded by feminist
criticism, is incited when a writer receives, as Woolf said, "in imagination the pressure of dumbness, the accumulation of unrecorded life."[9]
The silent faces of the others, the extras in the story, the ones to whom
"it" is done, those who did not "get there" but always were there,
without their tales of causes and effects, reasons and fates leave the
impress of absence, gap or void. This hoarse whispering silence is especially hard to bear and especially generative.

Curiously the simple idea of writing the woman's voice or "side" into
a well-known tale (telling the same story from another side) creates an
internal dynamic of critique out of simple reversal or an apparently
contained point of view experiment. I found this in writing "Eurydice"
and "Medusa" in the 70's.[10] It is not enough to tell another story, for
such a story of the unreckoned is more than just one *more* tale; reckoned
in, it wrecks the "in." Intellectual and political assumptions are ruptured, narrative sequence, causality, resolution and possibly the meanings of words or apt language themselves are all brought into question.

Given the presence of rape in the Medusa myth, which I had intuited,
I made the rape not only sexual violation but cultural and epistemological violation—the creation from an inarticulate dumb creature of a
brilliant monster, colonized by the persistence and radiance of the
world view represented by Perseus. Him I cast as the rapist instead of
the savior of the menaced city. What is known everywhere as the
resolution of the myth—the killing of the monster Medusa by Perseus—
is, in my view, the story's beginning: in violation as colonization. What
the myth books tell us is cause (she turns people to stone) is in my
myth the effect, ascribed an ambiguous value. She has been hardened,
an unfortunate personal aftermath of rape, and this rigid, ungiving self

is at the same time a boundary stone that marks the necessary turn of a world view. That exemplary feature, the thing that persists even prior to story in iconography and fears—the snaky Medusa head with its lolling tongue—here is the only "proper and triumphant" emergence as resolution: the birth of a volcanic corona of resistant knowledge, resonant voice.

Rupturing Iconization—text as object

Because of the way canonical texts are culturally used especially by literary criticism, as objects, as if final or fixed, with no sense of historical movement (no sense of the way texts are continually reused and transformed, remade in a social conjuncture with readers), I wanted to invent works that would protest or resist this process, not protect it.

(No more poems, no more lyrics. Do I find I cannot sustain the lyric; it is no longer. Propose somehow a work, the work, a work, the work, a work otherhow of enormous dailiness and crossing. All the "tickets" and the writing. Poems "like" essays: situated, breathless, passionate, multiple, critical. A work of entering into the social force of language, the daily work done everywhere with language, the little flyer fallen to the ground, the corner of a comic, a murder, burning cars, the pouring of realization like a squall green amber squall rain; kiss Schwitters and begin)

While modernism has gone far in eroding linear telos and syntactic direction, it still iconizes texts by proposing them as sacred objects, poets as priests, their status sublime. Certainly this position occurs because of political desperation—which it is only sensible to feel, but it replicates the power relations that we know, substituting "poet" for "legislator" but a secret one, an "unacknowledged" one, a hermetic one. A party (even the Poundian self-justified party of one) out of power, but waiting in the wings.

Iconization seemed to be considerably abetted by text as one way street—ending in one place, repressing its drafts or choices, discounting in the poem events not-this-poem. The invitation to read once in one direction, start to finish, top to bottom, beginning to end seemed to symbolize iconization.

One way to disturb the "one way street" of the poem is to make a text run, like a musical piece, da capo al fine in a recursive structure that, by virtue of repeating the middle, drew attention to on-goingness, and impeded closure.

A second way, in an homage to Emily Dickinson, could draw upon her rhetorical strategy of indicating variants, to keep the poem open, perhaps; to indicate the enormous changes of meaning, even in a narrow compass, that could be achieved by a minute (in some cases) alteration of a word. I'd like to think that the variant words, lines, and, more rarely, stanzas which she invented constituted her protest against the iconization of a text, against ending as statement, climax, moral thought. Against the stasis of poetry.

In "Crowbar" (1983), the whole argument comes to a poised end in the doubling of two words: *hungry* and *angry* which grasp towards the odd *-ngry* ending they hold in common. *Hungry* meant complicit with the psychic cultural construction of beautiful, seductive and seduced women; *angry* meant critical of the same. The simultaneous over-voicing of the penultimate word in a very long poem means that ambivalence marks the end as it had the beginning. Explanation generates its own self-questioning.

Most recently, in a 28-section work called "Writing" (1984–85), I put words on the margin, try to break into the lyric center with many simultaneous writings occupying the same page space. I overwrite, or interleave typeset lines of writing with my own handwriting, not trying to obliterate, or to neutralize but to—to what? To erode some attitude toward reading and writing. I wanted simultaneous presence without authority. Wanted to make meanings that undid hierarchies of decidability. I wanted no right/correct sequences of feeling emblematic in right/correct sequences of reading, in order to state there is no center, just parallels: "everything is happening on the side." The desire to create something that is not a complete argument, or a poem with a climax, but where there are ends and beginnings all over the work. A working work. This is explicitly contrasted with lyric poetry and with novels.[11]

I was also rejecting that singular voice which "controls tone." The lyric voice. Controls tone? It hears the itch of, is in the center of languages. Voices are everywhere—the bureaucratic, the banal, the heightened, the friendly, the deadpan, the dreamy. Saturated with the multi-vocal, who can think of controlling tone? It is enough to collect them in one spot, and call that spot a poem.

Rupturing Poetry

Not incidentally, I am tired of "poetry"—that bike wheel mounted upside down thinking it is a real bike, forgetting it was undone by Duchamp. Tired of Hollywood poetry, like Hollywood cinema, endless discursive mimetic narration which only had different people in starring roles. And judging from their pictures in APR, the stars are pretty similar too.

There must be some way of reaching so deep into assumptions of and about poetry that this changes.

Write poetries. Write writings, write readings, write drafts. Write several selves to dissolve the bounded idea of the self

who is "I" who is "you"
who is "he" is "she"
fleeting shifts of position, social charges implying a
millenia of practice. To disturb the practice

by "itness" a floating referent, a bounding alone the
multiplex borders of marginality. An avoidance of
transcendence everywhere, including in the idea of the artist—
—no genius. no god. no prophet. no priest.

Rupturing the History of Poetry
by *The "History of Poetry"*

To read something new, something different from the production of the figures of women and men that reproduce gender relations, I felt I had to write something different. What then could be more (or less) different than an/other version of poems that have already been produced, the "same" poems but respoken, written from the position of marginality. My desire has led me to construct counter poems—counterfactual poems—postulating that there are many women poets throughout history (some real, some imagined) who have written poems uncannily positioned as having views aslant of dominant views of themselves in whatever era is being reentered.

The whole *"History of Poetry"* concerns my facing and being haunted by the Western lyric tradition, speaking as a woman poet. For "woman" has always been a central site and icon for that tradition as a specially stressed sign, rather more rich than a sheep or a daffodil. "Woman" has been constructed by that tradition as the permanent object of scrutiny, rather than as the speaking subject, even when, as we all know, there have always been a few women poets. A Corinna. A Praxilla. Indeed, our whole poetic tradition is made up in great proportion of lyrical/ social statements which produce women in various ways (semantically, linguistically, in image, in sequence, by allusion), produce them almost exclusively as the objects of regard. Women have been the signifieds with little or no literary control of signifiers.[12] And often then, when they make poems, critics (e.g., Zenobius) tell them that these poems are indecorous, unseemly, unconformable to standards even the most ill-equipped literary man knows. This special subject/object/scrutinized position creates a staggering and fascinating problem for the woman writer, who is presumably a speaking subject in her work while a cultural artifact or object in the thematic and critical traditions on which she, perforce, draws.

My aim is to refabricate—revamp, as you might say—Western lyric tradition. This particular revamping is done from the perspective of invented and real female poets who are looking at the classic texts, voices, meanings and cultural stances that make up the lyric, and who are "writing" poems that intersect with, but differ from, very well-known poems. So I call what I'm doing The "History of Poetry". This is because the very idea of a history of poetry is a fictional sequence formed by choices, exclusions, interests, silences,—a whole and contingent politics of discourse. We are schooled to see the history of poetry as a museum of discrete, highlighted intact sequential objects; we may as well see them as an imperially assembled and classified but random set of fragments. Surrounded by the unwritten. And the destroyed.

Sometimes, through the ages, a poet has written something "after," say, John Dowland. Although after everything, this sequence is really "after" nothing. It isn't "after" at all; it is simultaneously with and/or against John Dowland and everyone else.

Within The "History of Poetry" the tactic of citation implies deep, wounding and even malicious dialogue with already-written poems. Instead of invention, at that point, there is (in Craig Owens' term) "confiscation" of the already done.[13] In writing, the supposed female writer uses that precise set of words that signals an intersection between her poem and very well-known texts. By putting known phrases from "great poems" (i.e., already written, disseminated and absorbed poems) into a structure speaking differently, series of reverberating questions are set in motion that begin to dissolve or erode a former

world view; or one has evoked in all the oscillating bliss, two opposite
and alternative world views simultaneously. So at all times the critique
and distancing are filled with yearning and complicity.

At the center of the poem "Crowbar" occur these lines about a gesture
made by another woman poet, Karin Lessing, with whom I visited the
Fontaine de Vaucluse, site famous for Petrarch and Laura.

> 'Tis poem
> that around
> its words
>
> it's Words.

> The silver ring she threw away
> ringed by the fountain's silver ring.

The whole *"History of Poetry"* could be seen like the gesture of a
woman throwing a ring into the famous rock crevasse/fountain by
which she is completely surrounded. Is it homage or marriage? that is,
connection of the deepest kind. Or is it divorce, stripping oneself of any
affiliation to the fountain image of woman. All our words are ringed by
Words, all our rings are encircled by another powerful, fecund circle by
whose flux and outpourings we are at times seduced. The double position of being outside and inside, critical and complicit marks the sequence.

But if I write work, as above, critical of a lyric tradition, I am still fully
dependent upon that tradition for its effects. The "shell" is there, but
I am making another kind of "animal" live inside it. Yet a shell will
always define the animal in key ways. This strategy of refabrication is
binary—it meets its adversary at every turn. And somehow replicating
or mirroring its opposite. Suppose, then, I did not want to have any
"shell" at all, any "tradition" against which I made analytic lyrics or
any other claims. (This was Kate Stimpson's challenge, once, at a reading. It was utopian, unassimilable, and pivotal.)

This neutral or zero-space writing situation is a complete myth. The
page is never blank. It is (even if apparently white) already written with
conventions, discourses, prior texts, cultural ideas, reading practices.
But the gesture of turning away from poetry as already written, however
quixotic or impossible that task, by the repeated, stubborn, and self-
contradictory practice of postulating an elsewhere, an otherhow!

"Turning away from" is a tame and bland phrase: I could mean burn the library down (Woolf said burn the university down; Stein said burn forensics down; Williams said burn the library down).[14] But I do not mean burn the library down (Sappho, burnt . . .) I mean the concerted and endless practice of critical rupture. Instead of constructing an "anthology" or a new "poet" as alternatives to existing poetries, one might postulate another kind of textual space through which and onto which a plethora of "polygynous" practices teem.

Feminist Poetics, Modernism, the Avant-garde

The poetics this discusses of course draws on both modernism and the avant-garde. Both are powerful, richly developed practices, and consequently both may overshadow what I am saying, cause it to pale, turn, return invisible. Destabilizing language, form, narrative has historically been the task of both modernist and postmodern innovation. But there is a central problem with these two twentieth-century movements of linguistic and formal critique. The problem is Gender Politics. Modernism has a radical poetics and exemplary cultural ambition of diagnosis and reconstruction. But it is imbued with a nostalgia for center and order, for elitist or exclusive solutions, for transforming historical time into myth. This is symptomatically indicated by the incessant conservatism about gender evinced by male modernists—from Yeats on Maud Gonne's political activism to Pound on woman as Sargasso Sea, octopus, chaos. Male modernist texts work to transform women historical and plural into Woman, hysterical and singular, work to transform difference, distinction, and variousness into exoticism and romantic types, work to split the complexity of women's cultural practices into manageable binaries.

Modernism is associated with an attempt to take various permutations of "new women" and return them, assimilate them to the classic Western idea of woman as Other (angel or monster, Lady or Fresca). Otherness is a static, dichotomized, monolithic view of women. This view is necessitated by, interdependent upon the religious/spiritual transcendence also typical of modernist practice, its anti-secular resolutions, even in texts midden-filled with the unsorted detritus of the dig into our culture. The eyes in the tent for Pound, the Lady in "Ash Wednesday," the Beautiful Thing in *Paterson*. And a female modernist like H.D., who of necessity has struggled with the idea of Woman? She projects the icon out from herself (likes being the icon); she plays fruitfully with the matrisexual coincidence of being the goddess and loving the goddess. She interests because in making a place for herself, she has to restudy and cut athwart the position she is, grossly, assigned in poetry.

Because of the suspicion of the center in avant-garde practice, the desire to "displace the distinction between margin and center," because of the invention of a cultural practice that "would allow us constructively to question privileged explanations even as explanations as generated," drawing on avant-garde practice seems more fruitful for me.[15] Its idea of power and language seem more interesting: the resolute lack of synthesis, the non-organic poetics, the secular lens.[16] But while the "postmodern" dispensation of centerless heterogeneity of discourses seems to be more plausible as a position, one is thereafter shocked by the quietism and asocial turns of its duel poetics of immanence and textuality, at odds with historical responsibility to the political and functional contexts of language. And its degree of tolerance for and curiosity about a "feminine" position in discourse, if it is plausible to talk in those terms, is coupled with a bizarre distance from and even distaste for the historical situations created by gender and racial inequalities.[17]

And there are further questions which the avant-garde must answer. 1) Does it secretlylovingly to itself hold the idea of poet as priest, poem as icon, poet as unacknowledged legislator? Then turn yr. back on it. Or, not to tell you what to do, My back. 2) Is its idea of language social; or does it claim, by language practices, to avoid (transcend), arc out of the limits posed by the social to its writing practices? Dialogic reading means dialogic writing. 3) Where is/are its women: where in the poems, serving what function? where in its social matrices, with what functions? where in its ideologies? How does it create itself by positioning its women and its women writers?

And then: if the thought is turn yr. back, they will appropriate that back. Violin d'Anger.

Then one sees a moving and serious reconsideration of gender in feminist "humanist" poetries—combined with an attention to wholeness, healing, lyric transcendence, and affirmation that is not a uniformly plausible, though it is always a repetitively narratable, sequence. If one could retain that passionate, feeling ethics without the uniformities of telos . . . Is it possible?[18] Which way do I turn? what do I turn?

Writing—Marginalities?

"Also, there were notes, comments, scribbled over and across and on the margins of the original text, in red pencil. These, hard to decipher, were in themselves a different story or, at least, made of the original a different story." Doris Lessing.[19]

"What would be a word, not the word 'marginal' to describe this? Marginal is a word which asks for, demands, homage to center" (asked Jeanne Lance).

Not "otherness" in a binary system, but "otherhow" as the multiple possibilities of a praxis.

Even "margins" decisively written are another text. The margins must multiply. Woolf kept her first diary in the white quads between the printed lines of a book. Where did I read that? Midrash makes annotation keep perpetual dialogue, conflicting interpretations put next to each other. Did I read that? So write crossings, contradictions, the field of situations, the fields of "placelessness" and mobility. " 'Do what you can.' "[20]

Write through the page, unframed, a text that plays its affiliations. Strange croppings. Social densities of reference brought to the surface. A writing through the page from edge to edge. Evacuate the margins! A writing over the edge.

A writing over the edge! That's it. Satisfing one's sense of the excessive, indecorous, intense, crazed and desirous. She's over the edge! And the writing drives off the page, a variagated channel between me and you.

Being $\left\{ \begin{array}{l} \text{a woman} \\ \text{a writer} \end{array} \right\}$ is a $\left\{ \begin{array}{l} \text{political} \\ \text{poetical} \end{array} \right\}$ act.

Creolization

It is possible that we are already creolized. We "whites" are certainly gonna be among the last to know with our sly fibers of race privilege woven into the most elegant understandings. Culture is no where—no ONE where—but everywhere, and never perfect, neither in its (myth of) golden origins, nor in the heroic actors of realms of Otherness over whom we may still find ourselves sanctimoniously weeping, nor in its glorious telos of solution and balanced function. We live in a world of unintended consequences and we are all creolized. Creolization is not some process that has occurred to a pitied and gently condescended to "Them." The processes of appropriation, syncretism, fabrication from disparate, ungainly materials, adaptation, compromise between conflictual forms, and creative intersection are functions we already live as whomever we are.[21]

And the language? Nathaniel Mackey, the African-American writer has proposed, for his purposes, the term "calibanization," which he takes from the West Indian poet Edward Kamau Brathwaite and from a general analysis in Afro-American literary criticism.[22] I grab this to mean a resonant, self-conscious multi-linguality, choice of patois, dialect, neologisms, puns, technical jargon of certain specific work-based groups (teachers, dancers, mothers), all mingled in a kind of macaronic or pastiche—both of these terms reanimated with the most serious and aggressive concern, and losing their clownish, motley implications. I see a language broken into. One whose capacities to represent "transparently" can no longer be credited, but whose connotive, denotive, and textural powers must be engaged. This souped up calibanized language is visible in certain North American writers. Language is a situation where a multi-poly-mishuganah set of discourses is set into play to explore and enact our crossings. The language of poetry is the language of anything: taboo words, grunts, babytalk, "French."

French! *Et o ces voix d'enfants, chantant dans la coupole!* Is not *The Waste Land* the first great poem of creolization—and of a mortified and astonished resistance to its powers?

What Writes?

pigs as fingers, toes
hat tassel a "powder puff" tickle
tummy
doh doh doh doh

as transformation d——g d——g d——g,
long cadences ending maybe in yougurt.

pulling upon those wide winging blank labia
dat? dat?

Wandering stars and little mercies, space
so empty, notched each moment.

Tufted white nut rising who or which is
"I" is "yo" the parade feather tit
mouse, did she see her first real bird?

Made from hearing the deep insides of language, language inside the
language; made from pick-scabbing the odd natural wounds of language
outside, unspecial dump of language everywhere here.

"Paradoxically the only way to position oneself outside of
that hegemonic discourse is to displace oneself within it— to
refuse the question as formulated, or to answer deviously
(though in its words), even to quote (but against the
grain)."[23]
my father said my mother never had any talent
how to acknowledge alterity the marginality and speak from
its
historically, personally wounding presence without
so that she never did anything; implied, they had discussed
it
come to the conclusion, some people just have it some don't.
how to acknowledge anonymous (ourselves) but compel the
structures and tones, the social ocean of language to babble
burble, to speak
real talent, he said, would have found a way, this
conversation does not go on too long, shifts to "blacks"
of course.
The sung-half song.

If poems are posies what is this?
To whom?
And who am I, then, if it matters?

I am a GEN $\left\{ \begin{array}{l} \text{der} \\ \text{re} \end{array} \right.$ made by the writing; I am a GEN $\left\{ \begin{array}{l} \text{re} \\ \text{der} \end{array} \right.$
read in the writing.

Jan. 1985/June 1985/Aug. 1985/June 1989

*A poetics gives permission to
continue.*

THE PINK GUITAR

1. The torso, the turban, the turned-away face of Ingres' 1808 painting called *La Baigneuse de Valpinçon* or *The Large Bather* reappear, amid some clutter of bodies, in his later orientalized paintings: the *Harem Interior* (1828) and the *Turkish Bath* (1863).[1] The *Turkish Bath* has, in its great circle, over 20 female figures, two black, two brown, all nudes, most erotic in conventional gesture, some overtly sexual: playful, lubricious, languid, narcissistic, preening, posturing for the viewer, fiddling with themselves. Whatever all those words mean. That foregrounded back-turned torso, the hidden, inward face of *The Large Bather* were clearly iconic for Ingres, and mysteriously so, for in its interiorized, non-frontal "purity" it withdraws as much as is exposed in the tarted-up meat-markets of the later works. In his final use of this image, in *The Turkish Bath*, Ingres has given the female something to do. She is playing a hidden instrument, perhaps a mandolin. Her mandolin as hidden as her face.

These well-known images by Ingres, themselves palimpsests of each other, were further over-written in Man Ray's tampered photo (1924) of Kiki of Montparnasse (a.k.a. a woman artist, Alice Prin).[2] Ray posed his model to evoke the Ingres and drew knowingly upon the progressively more overt orientalizing Ingres proposed for the torso, for Kiki is marked with her turban, her gypsy-like earrings, and the exotic silk on which she sits, wide-hipped, a great shadow where her buttocks crack at the base of the spine. Her enfolded arms are hidden, her agency thereby removed. Her solid, curved, lush back has, imposed upon it, brilliantly placed sound holes, black f-openings (f-openings!) which recall the *f* for function in mathematical symbol, force in physics, forte in music, and the abbreviation both for female, and for feminine gender in grammar. She is thereby made sonorous with cultural meanings. Once by Ingres, she becomes, by Man Ray, the *Violin d'Ingres*, the hobby-horse which plays with the representation of women and sexuality without altering the fundamental relations of power, proprietorship, and possession so succinctly evoked.

Homme-age. I. ngres. These wry and salomesque swirls of veils of other texts. Man. Ray. I am dressed therein. I drape them, they drape over me, they are some of that thru which I see.

Violon d'Ingres. Violin d'anger. Vial in danger.

It "just means hobby in French"   it "just means that women are his hobby"   "you see, Ingres was really a painter, but he also played the violin"   "sort of like our saying 'Sunday painter,' meaning they weren't really serious about"

I am deadly serious.

                    It is
I pick up this guitar.   ↓ ↑   a woman! I say
                    I am

For when I pick it up, how do I "play" the women whom I have been culturally given?[3]

And find that the languages, the words, the drives, the genres, the keyboards, the frets, the strings, the holes, the sounding boards, the stops, the sonorities have been filled with representations that depend, in their deepest satisfactions, on gender and sexual trajectories that make claims upon me (and could compromise what I do).

My pink guitar has gender in its very grain. Its strings are already vibrating with gender representations. That means unpick everything. But how to unpick everything and still "pick up" an instrument one "picks," or plucks. How to unpick everything, and still make it "formal," "lyric," "coherent," "beautiful," "satisfying," when these are some of the things that must be unpicked. (Kristeva used the term "the impossible dialectic."[4]) The writing therefore becomes unpalatable, difficult, opaque, shifty, irresponsible, suspect, and subject to many accusations.

And could I change the instrument (restring, refret, rekey, retool, rehole)

Invent
new sonorities
new probes
new combinations
new instruments

I struggle for a tread. Everything must be reexamined, re-seen, rebuilt. From the beginning, and now. And yet I am playing, I am playing. I am playing

with a stringed lever.

2. How much insomnia can any one person stand?

It was an unbreakable drama of silence, to protect his obsessive and incessant speaking. By tag finishings. Polite uninterruptions. No rage. No, or little, spontaneous laughter. No puncture. The seriousness of his obsession and its vulnerability were patent. I had been commissioned with the unspoken responsibility of guardianship. If I had really "had it," I walked away. But that communicated, as it happened, nothing. Or very little. As far as I know. This whole thing was undiscussable, although it occurred for many years. My silence and little spurts of pleasant sound became a canvas, a terrain, a geography he could enter with his words. Irrespective of me. There was no me as me, the only "me" was a necessary, even crucial, occasion ("The Listener"). I certainly was not "attentive," except on the surface of my face. What, then, was "listening"? and what relation had it to really hearing? By which, and thru which repeated events much was damaged, and much was destroyed. And much was learned.

But most cannot be said.

They speak of bi-focal. Or the metaphor of "bi-lingual" for the multiple negotiations into the different cultural practices in which we are constituted. I am bi-silent, tri-silent, am made of dual/duel, trebled/troubled, base/bass and impacted silences. Which test, temper, distort, and suspect fluencies. This blankness is social (silence is social as speech is social; silence, says Cora Kaplan,[5] silence protects others' speech); it is gendered (or in relation to hierarchies of power).

It is like the ground of the page. The blankness already filled with words thru which one negotiates. The page paradoxically both open and filled. These rhythms—of start and stop, the praxis of randomness, the choices of motion over, under, through, small tunnelings and explosive rejections are a socially grounded set of structures. These structures or plots of feeling, and the feeling patently evoked (that I want to evoke) correspond to something, some outline of emotions and practices in the social and familial world—the shapes of the social structures in relation to the shapes of the art.[6]

" 'Tell me, given the options, where would your anger have taken you—
where has it taken you?' "[7]

3. titles   dog food   telephone   trash bags   bath powder (harried
mother)   decaffeinated coffee   dog food   network   cold
medicine   toothbrushes   hemorrhoids   (the rh for
redness)   toys   skin moisturizer   women's
laxative   network   local department store   tomatoes   cookies   -
sauces   drain opener   coffee   stockings   toys   bacon   cough
medicine   sales   batteries (for toys)   air freshener   credits[8]

To enter from the shifting ground of interstices "between the acts"

I wanted not catharsis but engorgement, not mimesis but uncovering,
not mastery but plurality, not a "form" but a method—of montage, of
interruption . . .[9]

then ate, walked around, and left my light burning.

4. The man, he said, plays a transformative blue guitar. He bespeaks
his difference in a flat, factual, and informative tone. "Things as they
are / Are changed upon the blue guitar." The doubling of "are,"
by its very awkwardness, bolsters the authoritative apothegem. The
balance of the situation as Wallace Stevens constructs it: he and them;
artist and curious onlookers; a unique one and a group from which he
is quite distinct. But still there is a fittedness between them and him,
many and one, audience and Man of Imagination. The pleasant sing-
song aphorisms harness a nursery rhyme or folk melody to the depiction
of modernist claims. This makes an endorsement of those claims. However, there is one distinction. The crowd says "A blue guitar." The man
says "the blue guitar." The crowd allows for numerous like-colored
instruments; the particular artist claims his is the one, perhaps a temporary myth that enables the writing, perhaps a more intellectually aggressive erasure of any other practitioners.

Into this scene gallumphs the female artist, hauling a different colored
"lyre, guitar, or mandolin." You want difference! she says, heehawing
into all that elegance and ideological balance. I'll give you difference!

A pink guitar upsets a lot of balances. Including, and first of all, mine.

A rosy writing space, a rose colored instrument, a new kind of pinko,
which I hold and, by my play, try: to hear its sounds, to read its marks.

5. A woman writer is a *marked marker.* She is marked by the cultural attributes of Woman, gender, sexuality, the feminine, a whole bolus of contradictory representations which are as much her cultural inscription as ours. She is marked by being variously distinguished—defined, singled out—by her gender. Others may note it even if she does not, or claims not to. She is marked by some unevenly effective traditions of both "unspeaking" and "unspeakable" female self, and by some also uneven set of incentives to cultural production, although she makes many many things. She—any woman—is culturally represented and interpreted (in all forms of representation from pop song to prayer, from B-movies to modern paintings). The works and the workings of these representations, in picture and text, in ideologies and discourses, mark or inflect precise configurations of her personal markings. Her own marks on a page — writing, drawing, composing; her capacity to make those marks; and what she can, or may, mark (or notice) will bear some marks of this matted circumstance of gender. Many possibilities for gender valences of a woman and her artworks are suggested by my remarks. As a *marked marker* a woman writer may not, or need not be circumscribed or limited by gender, but she will be affected. Marks of these gender narratives can be made legible in feminist readings.[10]

For any woman, and especially for a cultural producer, a vital question is how to imagine herself, and how to imagine women, gender, sexualities, men and her own interests when the world of images and, indeed, basic structures of thought have been filled to overflowing with representations of her, and displacements of any "her" by the representations others make. Thus: how to create an adequate work Of and About women (but never exclusively of or about women), while being By a woman, when strata of previous images of women, some quite culturally precious, suffuse and define culture, consciousness, and individual imaginations.

6. "If we *had* a non-patriarchal symbolic order, what would the language be in that situation? What would the non-patriarchal 'word' be?"[11]

7. What is entering this page space, and who is in charge here? what singing cometh, and who's singing what song? and is this "autobiography"? And so on. As very hungry herself, hungry, mostly open and thirsty. Given their thirst they step so lightly, O all right, Holstein, hard not to be sentimental. Once I wrote "giving birth to myself" sincerely. Yet I was never giving birth to myself, but to a labor: cultural critique. "Birth" was always an odd metaphor, because what comes out at birth still enters into—already was entered into—nettings of social materials, is not formed in and of itself. Enters and is joined into

multiple praxes. It is the newness of the child, the promise of something different, the child as utopian moment. . . . The cows line up, jump, heave their silly weight up. They hunch. Many bones, skin, nouns, many stomachs and no memory, and the turmoil of regurgitations. Black muck. The stench of the manure pile, the flies against her flank. Soooo Bos. Whose bossy head was second in all the alphabets. In London, 1964, I tore a label (beer: Courage and Barclay) until the word that was thereby isolated in a broken circle is the rip of "RAGE." Make that a collage! The history and relationships, the memories associated with, the meanings, the linkages, the fissures among, the differentials, the fallow and the shunned, if I were to pick up every item and associate across the bondage of memory (I have covered about 20 inches of space, and, honest enough, have already been singularly selective). . . . Stepping into the same diary twice. So pour the milk back over the cow. This fleisch is milchig. Cows not to convert. Cows not to channel. Cows not to instruct. Only the silky, and o they are milky.

8. Are the facts of my life (like "my best selling novel." "my face staring from . . . " my rose-colored living room, with "its dramatic ochre entry." my feet tucked up under. "my casual yet my elegant." my half-finished cup of cold coffee.) here? I'd rather eat myself than be consumed. RAVISH myself. "I'm ravished." A slip for "I'm famished." Bad enough, but in front of my uncle?

It is a voice, it is, in fact, voices—and from where. If I said "midrash," it would have some cultural charm, although Hebrew was Greek to me, and Greek was a botch, and it did have something to do with "my father." But by midrash I mean the possibility of continuous chains of interpretation, thinking into

9. the relations of things. It's like when you open a catch-all drawer and everything there including your hand, and your gesture, means something, has some history, of its making, and of its being there. A focused catch-all. Where the production of meanings is, if not continuous, so interconnected that one has the sense of, the illusion of, the "whole" of life being activated, and raised to realizations and power. Thru language.

The today, the practice of thought   as the practice of writing. A pressure   a vision   a set of interactions   feeling curious   sometimes feeling despised.

the neon bleakness of desire in the mall. The blank page (or screen), the open silent space, and the words well up, as from a conduit. What writes?

"For it is against itself (and against the world as discourse) that the essay struggles. It drifts, it wanders in order to trace a map of its own questionings. . . . "[12]

So that my "fig newtons" stand for your "diaper pins" and it looks as if I am getting all of it, in. When the all is not whole (in the globular sense) but not fragmented (in the painful sense), but just slowly in pieces and together, wandering across the page, lunch boxes of violence rejected yet yearned for, night images right at the borders of sense and pleasure, red ribbons invested with symbolic intent, me in contradictory and "uneven development," and the one good Phillips head screwdriver in the house, where is it! It is not women only who live this way, but the sliding up and down the scales of importance, the destruction of scales of importance, the indomitable horizontality of structures, the insistence of non-transcendent heights, and material depths—

ARE

galloping and gulping, elusive, hybristic, subversive

the essay.

"as if hearing *an 'other*
meaning' always in the ·
process of weaving itself, of embracing
itself with
words, but also of getting rid of words
in order
not to become fixed, congealed in them"
(L. Irigaray)
"constructivist writing" (C. Bernstein)
"Semiotic/symbolic" writing (J. Kristeva)
multi-discursive, interrogative, polyvocal, heterogeneous
interactive
recognizing "subjectivity" (S. Griffin)
no more "confines of relevance" (B.
Dahlen citing G. Steiner)
"moments of linguistic transgression"
(M. Jacobus)

associative, critical
                    "to question the apparatuses" (G. C.
                    Spivak)
                    "make it impossible for a while to
                    predict whence,
                    whither, when, how, why . . . " (L.
                    Irigaray)
a motion captured in motion
                    "vatic bisexuality" (H. Cixous)
hysterical, site-specific
an interested meditation
                    "atopical or hypertopical mobility of the
                    narrative voice" (J. Derrida)
                    "washed by heteroglot waves from all
                    sides" (M. Bakhtin)

the site of many centers
a non-transparent textuality
                    "form as an activity" (L. Hejinian)
contradictory
its multifariousness AS resistance

It is a Way: of talking, of listening; the intense calm of everything
connected, everything ruptured; the pleasure of a babble of

10. Touch on any part, on any sight, a sock, a hole, a wall, pictures, a
resistance to museums, yet pictures always on the wall, and defining
eras by those pictures. Wander looking for the odd lots, stop in front of
something smallish, a little unofficial, by someone who did the best he
could. That's all. Or a self portrait by a woman no one ever hears of.
She. Sincere, intransigent. Or a few squares floating, by an escapee. One
or two lines on a page. That's all I need . . .

the entrance into this otherness is fraught   discourses come through us
and we choose and are chosen by them. But "Otherness" is a dangerous
metaphor. Some "I" am very much here, working in a set of spaces and
practices. So never writing in the illusion that this play is only textual.[13]
This is serious; in many ways its play is a measure of its grief. The
material figure of the writer-gendered-female stands, in her political,
visceral need

for the $\left\{ \begin{array}{l} \text{writing} \\ \text{reading} \end{array} \right.$ of this $\left\{ \begin{array}{l} \text{reading} \\ \text{writing} \end{array} \right.$

"Otherness" is a cultural construct like "the feminine," against which and through which I struggles. It is sometimes attractive and confirming that these textual practices are called "feminine," but the argument draws sub rosa on the power of those binary formations that it would reject and overturn. The feminine is where I am colonized. The feminine is the dream of an elsewhere, a someplace uncolonized. The feminine is orange/blush/pink/peach/vibrant red "in" this year. The feminine is a short blue one, or a long plaid one, but never a short plaid one or a long blue one. It is that kind of knowledge.

But to intermingle the utopian "feminine" space (of religious and a-social aura, of "ultimates") with an attracted loathing for the blush/red etc. feminine with a rooted feminist lust for material social justice in the quirky voice of a person mainly gendered female—well, this is approximately the practice. Have I "undone the binary"? Was it in my power? I did make trinaries, quadrinaries. I have made permanent quandaries.

11. The practice of anguage. The anguish of language. The anger of language. "A 68er" said Meridith Tax: and this is what it means to this work.[14] Inchoate in the 60's, coming to focus abruptly in 1968, the idea that culture was a political instrument, that language, hegemony, discourse, form, canon, wrongness, allowable and taboo were always historically formed, and were notions constantly debated, reaffirmed and disallowed. That culture was an arena of struggle.[15] And furthermore, to see from where I was standing meant to see with a specifically formed kind of female eyes. Cross-eyed; cock-eyed. Funny evocations. (It was the female that was the most startling to think about, since it was that around which the most intense contradictions of affirmation and denial occurred.) If one sees inside one's gender, class, race, sexuality, nationality, and these from and engaged with one's time, then culture is a process of rereading and rewriting, a practice. Soon after, by 1969–70, I had seen in a startled and famished (ravished) flash the necessity of the feminist cultural project. No less than the reseeing of every text, every author, every canonical work, every thing written, every world view, every discourse, every image, everything unwritten, from a gender perspective.

This is a major cultural project, intimately linked to the practice of questioning powers of all sorts, to the uses of culture in all arenas, to the nature, or definition of culture. And this is a central project of our generations (of women), this feminist cultural practice.

12. June 1979. Some anger. That is what is framing and saturating this writing. There is an anger and about what? about my life, and how to be female at this moment, the challenge of creating a new self which I am failing. ███████████████████████████████████

██████████████████████████████ the problem of masculine and feminine ██

████████ paralyzing conflict. Cut off, burned out ███████████

██

██

██

██████████ the defenses which are the only thing I nurture.

But how can I insist on anger? ████████████████████████████████

██████████████████████████████ Even in these "essays" there must be some decorum! ██████████████████████ The reader does not need to be informed of the despair of the writer, a despair compounded by (of) the very difficulty of writing at all, a kind of self-hatred, existing in proportion to the fascination of this writing which I am driven to use while also saying, and hearing others say, it is "too easy" and therefore suspect.

("I have a sense of the writer drunk on her own shrill voice") ("confessional") ("repeatedly questioned the integrity") ("not authentic") ("too experiential") ("healthy self-doubt nonexistent") ("garish") ("untransmuted, not art") ("personal") ("narcissistic")

and therefore suspect.

Don't apologize and too trite and too personal and too busy and too hard and too easy. You get the picture? being no dope and "reader, it was not to have ended here."[16]

13. Therefore the metaphor of quest. A trek. A climb. A struggle toward—the transfigured. Probably the largest shift in this writing, between the late 70's of its beginning, and the continuations of the mid-80's was a muting of the visionary sense of transfiguration. What substituted was something closer in, closer to the ground, examining what I really felt, no matter the contradictions—as in Duchamp. If sincerity

led to unresolvable contradiction, the very datum became pivotal. The loss of the quest for (what was essentially personal) "wholeness" was no loss. But what that quest said by using that term remains vital. And what was that? Was it a desire for justice? Was it hope? (Pretend these terms have been properly "deconstructed," yet still, though battered, can be sustained or understood.)

So, quest. (butterfly, spinning sac, threads, cocoons) like an earthworm changing into an airplane. Pupa, chrysalid, butterfly; silkworm weaving the silkword "metamorphosis." Psyche. Haunted by psyche, and hounded by the glories of that telos: Monarch! Swallowtail! Mourning Cloak!

That "psyche" image bound for glory fueled my ambitions and is reflected in certain essays of the 1970's; it also appears in the work of H.D. But there was something about quest narratives that I became uncomfortable practicing. That modified my practice, or drove it underground. The plots and triumphs were too given, and they drew for their appeal on structures of feeling (apotheosis, climax, ending, transcendence) of which I was agnostic, suspicious, and would no longer take for granted. Did quest end? Was there triumph? fulfillment? synthesis? I began to think of these as religious structures, but worse, of the writing that might practice them as "sermon." Sermon, as opposed to essay. They did not narrate the ongoingness and mixed struggles of the writing of rupture and critique: that practice.

My butterflies change. A cabbage white is plain enough: persistent, ubiquitous, almost the mosquito of butterflies, and as textual as a little page with its shimmering black spots. Though not to make "textual" the new sentimentality.

And "textual" heras: Arachne, challenging even the goddess with her weaving which depicts the rapes of women by gods. Philomel, muted, mutilated, weaving the depiction of her rape and mutilation; Procne, the reader. Penelope, buying time for personal loyalties and choices with the studied, strategic destruction and remaking of her weaving. Names, identified as constructive agents, figures who make and unmake texts, or, to use an old-fashioned word, works. Who are workers in "writing."

Their strategies of resistent representation.[17] The emphasis to fall on the struggle to make the works. The career of that struggle. But/and the utopian project is not ended.

14. 23 November 1981. "I" cannot be displaced   I cannot   I just got
here!   feminists the last humanists, yet I have become decentered.   I
am a walking margin   the first decentered creature   in the sunny
depths   harsh crisp color and a triangular shape blurred. Yes. Where
there is looking. So hard to compare. But always "I" or I, know.
For when I say "I," I hear voices,
I want to say I (and also some other pronouns),
some me itted,
or she me'd,
yet when I say I
I mean I,
and yet is only a smallest part of I that I can use.
And when I say I what might be meant is
"i"
meaning a quarter I or an eighth,
to measure it,
maybe with a little round heart on top to dot it,
to dot the 12-year-old self,
in turquoise ink or a round blank circle of the wide-eyed girl

what I   indeed.

So when I say I
what
I mean is an i
which is it   speaking
it speaks as I speak,
(and Creeley knew it and Rimbaud)
squeaked speaked.

At doing the I as she,
the I as me,
a her, a we, a they, a them,
doing the I as he . . . as you
anarchic, wayward, flaw-ridden, maddening
As much no-me as me.

Deployed in playful anguage.

There is no I when I "speak"
but places of gridded and bubbling social voice
a tone   a humming thru a "G" perhaps
or a "B flat"

girl and boy
a sol fa la, a solfeggio moment of the resonant throat
no I no "I" no i
just an mmmmmmm trying to figure justice.

15. I start writing. "January 1982. To honor the plurality, porousness,
and mobility of discourses; to combine personal and analytic; to reveal
thinking as a heart-felt activity; to bring 'subjective' and 'objective'
into dialectical exchange and mutual translation; to name the interests
creating interpretation; to reveal the revealer; to fabricate the text as
an instance of social and ideological need . . ."

To multiply the tones, the positions; to saturate oneself inside the
existing heterogeneity of speaking

To account for the different textures and discourses of life, to include
the angry whine of a child, to bring decorums, pleasures, and taboos
into fructifying mixtures (and a great deal is left out; a whole, different
set of options; they are, in part, censored by the writer).

And "I don't write fiction." ("You're kidding!")

Fighter bombers patrol the borders, cruising along a line drawn in the
sky, and it is a low line, 300 meters, they say. Accidents happen. F-16s.
Why is it necessary to "train" pilots to fly that low? Below radar, it is
said. Is there a prediction that they will be someday flying somewhere,
some place so obscure and miserable that it does not have radar, some
"them" underneath the rumbling machine? Perhaps they are really
showing "us," those in whose name this occurs regularly. The job of
these planes is control of their own nation and its neighbors by a
banalized terror. The terror is the teasing half-memory, half-visualiza-
tion of what is possible from those planes, what is carried inside those
planes, and who is, with serious casualness, flying them.

But I am writing. A deliberate intermingled generative. Some voice
which thinks, thinking, the process of picking and unpicking, returning
to a generative body of work. A voice which accumulates the pressures
of its situation and spurts it in allusions to genres: poems, essays,
narratives, epigrams, autobiographies, anthologies, handbills, marginalia, glossolalia, wire services

writing in the interstices of texts, boring thru the white between the
lines, scribbling on the margins

rhythms (of responding   of ceasing   of picking up again)

converging and dispersing sightlines

not finished not caring

16. Her body was more or less her own—she could experience some of its feelings, but as she gridded those feelings or sensations with words, she participated in a cultural knowing in which female bodies have been variously type-cast. Her body was traversed with these ideas, sometimes they were "water off a duck's back," sometimes "they stuck like leeches." Her body, her mind, while they remained private possessions of a named person, were certainly saturated with, brimming with concepts, dunked in the culture, stained with it, the little vascicles, fascicles of "self." All cells are cultural cells.

What body, then, is speaking? Does her body speak? Is it a body of words? Of cultural ideas? A body of language? A body of words inflected with its female body? A body of pulses, impulses, fissured, hopeful and afraid inside of and dyed with a complex of rich and contradictory readings of the female body? A body to whom things have happened AS a female body, rape, for instance, and other tragedies still. Does this statement immediately color things (do you see red; have I willfully made you see red)? If this language appears defenseless, unguarded, if it mentions certain blood, if it strips itself and waits for impulsive behaviors to strike, waits for the play of association, if it provokes feelings of bemused recognition at quotidean interruptions

then what? From what is she writing?

Does simply saying "female writer" reduce her to gynecology, when, by the same token, there is no way to take her as anything but a female body speaking words inflected by her being constructed female. In awe. A body speaking words in awe, marginality and resistance.

I would not erase or discount her (or anyone's) experiences $\left\{ \begin{array}{c} \text{in a} \\ \text{as a} \end{array} \right\}$ body.

I would not discount male experiences in a body. How do we know "things" except mediated? Is not the "body" part of this mediation? An African-American writer "writes the body" when he speaks of the multiplicity of experiences that follow from his melanin-laden skin.

But one wants, by the same token, no one reduced to body. Isn't isolating "the body" conceptually still an unhelpful gesture from a long-criticized, though apparently inexaustible, mind/body split that should immediately be declared moot? I am admiring the quality and extent of my own uncertainty. But, yet, do women (do men) write from the body? Does that question remain important? Why was that question posed in that way?

If the effect of this question is to make female writing "natural," downplaying agency and artistic choice, if the question freezes "body" as if there were just one giant Female Body effectively present throughout time and in representation. . . . then? If the effect of this question is to free taboos, accept the unacceptable, and promote knowledge that female writing, female emphasis may differ . . . then? If the question allows for the variety and play of that potential difference, but does not penalize if it is "absent". . . then?

And/But the body is not the body. It is language, it is writing, it is inscription, it is representation, it is hungry, it is sick, it is in political networks of care or rejection, it is mediated, it is not purer, more primal

than what?

One cannot write "the body" for there is no one spot where she can satisfactorily denominate "the body," although it would be folly to go to the other extreme and deny the specificity of her body. One can write bodies, languages of body, languages embodying positions. One can write of bodies criss-crossed, scarred and striated with their matter, their material situations, their embodiments. The body? I think the question occurred that way as a stage on a way to saying "socially and culturally embodied practices."

but then what?

17. Women's shoes.

"Dear Parent: Your daughter's name was referred to us as possibly being an excellent candidate for the 1989 LITTLE MISS PHILADELPHIA GLAMOUR GIRL PAGEANT. . . . Because of her beauty, poise and appearance I am VERY interested in learning more about her. If you feel she would like to gain some Modeling Experience, Portfolio's, and Talent Scholarships, all you need to do is fill out the enclosed information sheet and submit that along with a recent snapshot of her.

. . . There is NO PERFORMING TALENT in this pageant. Judging will reflect Beauty, Photogenticity, and Poise. . . . Our winner's will reign over Philadelphia, Pennsylvania as the 1989 LITTLE MISS PHILADEL-PHIA GLAMOUR GIRL, and will be making guest appearances at her convenience. We feel this opportunity will open doors for every little girl involved as our judges are all highly respected and well known in their fields of beauty, modeling and theatrical activities."

Information sheet question: "Does she enjoy having her photograph taken and posing for them?"

Questions: What is "photogenticity"? And who is them?

I am also interested in the possessive's being confused with the plural.

18. I am not writing the personal. The odd and somewhat debased notion of having a voice, or finding a voice, of establishing a consumable personality complete with pix, of engaging in self-revelation, even of engaging in autobiography is precisely the opposite of my deepest feelings about this work. I am not finding a voice, I am losing one.

When I write, I am not writing for myself, or even (grosso modo) as myself. I am writing the voice, a voice, one bricolaging, teasing voice of a working. A raw exhilaration. At ruptures. At relativizing the "universal." At creolizing the "metropole." At writing a feminist-feminine-female bolus of scrapping and loving orts into existence. Writing not as personality, writing as praxis. For writing is a *practice*—a practice in which the author disappears into a process, into a community, into discontinuities, into a desire for discovery.

Pluralist
discontinuous
interplays
of *interference*[18]

not just "language" but "pursuit"[19]

shrill, hysterical, sentimental, washing up then dirtying, obtuse, querulous, unsuccessful, critical, synthetic, ruining

"In other words, in the realm of thought, imprudence is a method."[20]
"Art should expose, not remove contradictions."[21]

I am doing work, and what kind of work is it? for whom am I working? and what am I bringing into being?[22]

19. I am not a writer, as such. I am a marker, maybe that is a way to say it. All the signs that emerge on the page (I put them here, they came here through me) (some were already there, in the weave of the paper, no tabula rasa)

demand my reading. The responsibility for making words is the responsibility for reading. The practice of writing is already a reading,   of the writing already written,   of the saturated page,

smitten with that already-written, in

language, anguage   I am some character in a little folk tale, call me "a-reading-a-writing."

20. A desire to change the authority relations to the text and possibly to language

A practice of interference, or trying to stop a normal, normative, coherent, flowing and consumable practice.

I am not even writing essays. I am writing, to take seriously this typo, essaus. Essaus. They are hairy and ungainly things, coming a little too late, and earnestly with their little savory stew, and not thinking quickly or slickly. My birthright? A kind of confusion about what happened. About tricks and tests. A rachel goes backward into her generations, writes essaus: Some justice there.

The struggle on the page is not decorative.

I am writing a kind of reverie, a textual practice of feminist leverage, a counter TO culture as it exists, a sincere artifice that raises

21. Say imprecision (I cannot know what I need to know)   say grief (I can barely mourn and yet I am filled with mourning for the lost, for the costs, for the dead of incomplete revolutions)   say repressed arousal (the shards of injustice around us, we stumble on, pierced by)   say longing (for another kind of identity, another kind of nation, other sets of social relations)   say inarticulation   from blinding sun to blinding rain   scotoma, scotamata   dizzy, dizzy, dark areas or gaps in the field of vision, those things that float across

the eyes, like fast scudding clouds. Is that what we want? what we can barely see?

Wo and Woe. wie wee que qui ween queen wean. A mental image of myself strumming tunelessly unstopping, at the same time weeping wee and quee. I stop it and resist it. I stop. But I have written some of it.

August 1989,
from materials
as early as 1979.

N O T E S

For the Etruscans

With special thanks to Carol Ascher, Frances Jaffer, Sara Lennox, Jo Ann McNamara, Lou Roberts, Mira Schor, and Louise Yelin for their own letters and notes on Workshop 9, not all of which are retained in this version of the essay. My source of inspiration for this kind of writing was Robert Duncan's *H.D. Book* (chapters scattered in little magazines through the past decades), Virginia Woolf's essays, and my own letters. But (and) many people have reinvented the essay.

1. Ellen Macnamara, *Everyday Life of the Etruscans* (London: B. T. Batsford, 1973), p. 181.

2. Virginia Woolf, "Professions for Women," *The Death of the Moth and Other Essays* (1942; reprint ed., New York: Harcourt Brace Jovanovich, 1974), p. 240.

3. James Wellard, *The Search for the Etruscans* (New York: Saturday Review Press, 1973), p. 192.

4. The second task of Psyche. See Erich Neumann, *Amor and Psyche: The Psychic Development of the Feminine: A Commentary on the Tale by Apuleius*, trans. Ralph Manheim (1952; reprint ed., Princeton, N.J.: Princeton University Press, 1971). See also Rachel Blau DuPlessis, "Psyche, or Wholeness," *Massachusetts Review* 20 (Spring 1979): 77–96.

5. Sources for this summary include Gayle Rubin, "The Traffic in Women: Notes on the 'Political Economy' of Sex," in *Toward an Anthropology of Women*, ed. Rayna [Rapp] Reiter (New York: Monthly Review Press, 1975), pp. 157–210; Nancy Chodorow, *The Reproduction of Mothering: Psychoanalysis and the Sociology of Gender* (Berkeley: University of California Press, 1978); Dorothy Dinnerstein, *The Mermaid and the Minotaur: Sexual Arrangements and Human Malaise* (New York: Harper & Row, 1976); Juliet Mitchell, *Psychoanalysis and Feminism: Freud, Reich, Laing, and Women* (New York: Vintage Books, 1975).

6. Frances Jaffer, "Procedures for Having Lunch," unpublished manuscript.

7. Sigmund Freud, *New Introductory Lectures on Psycho-Analysis*, trans. W. J. H. Sprott (New York: W. W. Norton, 1933), pp. 154–55.

8. Aimé Césaire, *Une tempête, Adaptation de "La Tempête" de Shakespeare pour un théâtre nègre* (Paris: Editions du Seuil, 1969), p. 88.

9. Virginia Woolf, *Orlando* (1928; reprint ed., New York: New American Library, 1960), p. 204.

10. Virginia Woolf, "Mrs. Thrale," *The Moment and Other Essays* (1949; reprint ed., New York: Harcourt Brace Jovanovich, 1974), p. 52.

175

11. B. Ruby Rich, "The Films of Yvonne Rainer," *Chrysalis: A Magazine of Women's Culture* 2 (1977):115–27.

12. Anaïs Nin, *The Diary of Anaïs Nin*, vol. 1, *1931–1934*, ed. Gunther Stuhlmann (New York: Swallow Press and Harcourt, Brace & World, 1966), p. 34.

13. Julia Penelope Stanley and Susan J. Wolfe (Robbins), "Toward a Feminist Aesthetic," *Chrysalis* 6 (1978): 68.

14. Anita Barrows, "Form and Fragment," typescript, pp. 7– 8, in Lynda Koolish, "A Whole New Poetry Beginning Here" (Ph.D. dissertation, Stanford University, 1981), pp. 7–8.

15. Deena Metzger, "In Her Image,"*Heresies* 1 (May 1977): 2.

16. Jean Baker Miller, *Toward a New Psychology of Women* (Boston: Beacon Press, 1976), p. 51; Carol Gilligan, *In a Different Voice: Psychological Theory and Women's Development* (Cambridge: Harvard University Press, 1982), p. 22.

17. Dorothy Richardson, "Leadership in Marriage," *New Adelphi*, 2nd ser. 2 (June–August 1929): 247.

18. Doris Lessing, "Dialogue," *A Man and Two Women* (New York: Popular Library, 1958).

19. Julia Kristeva, *About Chinese Women*, trans. Anita Barrows (1974: New York: Urizen Books, 1977), p. 38.

20. Sheila de Bretteville, cited in Metzger, "In Her Image," p. 5.

21. Combining two citations from Jaffer, the second from a letter in response to Workshop 9, the first, from a review of *Literary Women*, by Ellen Moers, *Chrysalis* 1 (1977): 136.

22. Metzger, "In Her Image," p. 7.

23. Virginia Woolf, *A Writer's Diary*, ed. Leonard Woolf (New York: Harcourt, Brace, 1953), p. 13 (dated 1919).

24. At this point in the original essay, I discussed the mother-daughter relations and the imbedded fictional artwork in *Kunstlerromane* by women such as Lessing, Woolf, Gilman, Olsen, Stead. The argument was based on a (then unpublished) chapter of my *Writing Beyond the Ending: Narrative Strategies of Twentieth-Century Women Writers* (Bloomington: Indiana University Press, 1985); it can best be consulted there.

25. Virginia Woolf, "Women Novelists," *Contemporary Writers* (New York: Harcourt Brace & World, 1965), p. 27. Review dates from 1918.

26. Joanna Russ, "What Can a Heroine Do? Or Why Women Can't Write," in *Images of Women in Fiction: Feminist Perspectives*, ed. Susan Koppelman Cornillon (Bowling Green, Ohio: Bowling Green University Popular Press, 1972), p. 14.

27. Analysis of "Essentialism" as a philosophic concept made by Sybil Cohen to the Delaware Valley Women's Studies Consortium, April 1984.

28. Lucy Lippard, *From the Center: Feminist Essays on Women's Art* (New York: E. P. Dutton, 1976), p. 92.

29. Confirmation of these strategies in Barbara Currier Bell and Carol Ohmann, "Virginia Woolf's Criticism: A Polemical Preface," in *Feminist Literary Criticism: Explorations in Theory*, ed. Josephine Donovan (Lexington: University Press of Kentucky, 1975): 48–60; and in Melissa Meyer and Miriam Schapiro, "Waste Not/ Want Not: Femmage," *Heresies* 4 (1978): 66–69.

30. Roman Jakobson, "Linguistics and Poetics," in *Style in Language*, ed. Thomas A. Sebeok (Cambridge, Mass.: MIT Press, 1960): 350–77.

31. Because locating just one set of strategies, my description is, necessarily, completely incomplete. It does not deal with an absolutely parallel, but aesthetically opposite use of the oracular, gnarled, compressed tactics, suggesting the difficulty of articulation, not its fluidity: Emily Dickinson. Marianne Moore. Laura Riding. Mina Loy. As Jeanne Kammer has said: "There emerges a complex psychology of linguistic parsimony related to a professional identity. Haunted by the specter of the sweet-singing 'poetess,' the woman poet may have come to the 'modern' style of the early decades of the twentieth century by a very different route than her male counterparts" ("The Art of Silence and the Forms of Women's Poetry," in *Shakespeare's Sisters: Feminist Essays on Women Poets*, ed. Sandra Gilbert and Susan Gubar [Bloomington: Indiana University Press, 1979], p. 156).

32. Raymond Williams, "Base and Superstructure in Marxist Cultural Theory," *New Left Review* 82 (November–December 1973): 9.

33. Ibid.

34. Raymond Williams, *Marxism and Literature* (Oxford: Oxford University Press, 1977), p. 112.

35. Ibid., p. 124.

36. Virginia Woolf, *A Room of One's Own* (New York: Harcourt, Brace, 1929), p. 101. Compare Richard Wright's observation in 1956: "First of all, my position is a split one. I'm black. I'm a man of the West. These hard facts condition, to some degree, my outlook. I see and understand the West; but I also see and understand the non- or anti-Western point of view. . . . This contradiction of being both Western and a man of color creates a distance, so to speak, between me and my environment. . . . Me and my environment are one, but that oneness has in it, at its very heart, a schism." In *Présence Africaine*, no. 8—9—10 (November 1956), the proceedings of the First International Conference of Negro Writers and Artists, cited in *The Black Writer in Africa and the Americas*, ed. Lloyd W. Brown (Los Angeles: Hennessey & Ingalls, 1973), p. 27

37. Russ, "What Can a Heroine Do?" in Cornillon, pp. 14–15.

38. Léopold Sédar Senghor, *Liberté* I, cited in *Selected Poems/Poésies Choisies*, trans. and intro. C. Williamson (London: Rex Collings, 1976), pp. 12–13. *Négritude* (a black aesthetic) is a controversial concept: distinguished writers and critics oppose it (Wole Soyinka, Ralph Ellison) and embrace it (James Baldwin, Senghor).

39. Susan Griffin, *Woman and Nature: The Roaring Inside Her* (New York: Harper & Row, 1978); Judy Chicago, *The Dinner Party: A Symbol of Our Heritage* (Garden City, N.Y.: Anchor Press, 1979); Tillie Olsen, *Silences* (New York: Delacorte Press, 1978); Mary Daly, *Gyn/Ecology: The Metaethics of Radical Feminism* (Boston: Beacon Press, 1978).

Family, Sexes, Psyche

1. H. D., *End to Torment* (New York: New Directions, 1979), p. 35. The memoir was written in 1958.

2. Ezra Pound appears in *End to Torment* and, as Odysseus, in "Winter Love," *Hermetic Definition* (New York: New Directions, 1972). Richard Aldington and D. H. Law-

rence appear in *Bid Me To Live (A Madrigal)* (New York: Grove Press, 1960). Lord
Dowding appears as Achilles in *Helen in Egypt* (New York: New Directions, 1961).

3. *End to Torment*, p. 7. I retain the capitalization of the typescript, Hilda Doolittle,
Norman Holmes Pearson Collection, Collection of American Literature, Beinecke
Rare Book and Manuscript Library, Yale University. With thanks to Mr. Donald
Gallup, former Curator of the Collection of American Literature, and with gratitude
to Perdita Schaffner, for her generous permission to consult and cite from this and
other H. D. material.

4. Olive Schreiner, *The Letters of Olive Schreiner, 1876–1920*, ed. S. C. Conwright-
Schreiner (Boston: Little, Brown 1924), p. 36.

5. *Bid Me To Live*, pp. 54 and 56.

6. Ibid., p. 54.

7. Ibid., p. 88.

8. H. D., "Narthex," *The [Second] American Caravan: A Yearbook of American
Literature*, eds. Alfred Kreymborg, Lewis Mumford, and Paul Rosenfeld (New York:
Macaulay, 1928), p. 234.

9. H. D., *HERmione* (1927; New York: New Directions, 1981), p. 9. H. D.'s title is
HER.

10. Ibid., p. 118.

11. H. D., "Winter Love," p. 105.

12. H. D., *HERmione*, p. 170.

13. H. D., *Helen in Egypt*, p. 166.

14. Ezra Pound, *The Selected Letters of Ezra Pound, 1907–1941*, ed. D. D. Paige (New
York: Harcourt, Brace & World, 1950), p. 272. The letter dates from 1935 and was
addressed to T. S. Eliot. Frances Jaffer called my attention to this letter with her
poem "Triptych," published in *Feminist Studies* 4, 2 (February 1978): 134–36. Three
Jaffer words have come into this essay: *noisy, half-assed* and *nasty*, with thanks to
their psychic source.

15. H. D., *Palimpsest* (1926; Carbondale: Southern Illinois University Press, 1968), p.
149.

16. H. D., *Trilogy* (New York: New Directions, 1973), p. 11.

17. H. D., *Tribute to Freud* (1956; Boston: David R. Godine, 1974), p. 31.

18. This dark, large bronze is in the Rodin Museum in Philadelphia.

19. H. D., "H. D. by *Delia Alton*" [Notes on Recent Writing], *The Iowa Review* 16, 3
(1986): 184. Written 1949–1950.

20. H. D., *End to Torment*, pp. 18–19.

21. Compare this citation from Virginia Woolf: "What a curious relation is mine with
Roger at this moment—I who have given him a kind of shape after his death. Was
he like that? I feel very much in his presence at the moment; as if I were intimately
connected with him: as if we together had given birth to this vision of him: a child
born of us. Yet he had no power to alter it. And yet for some years it will represent
him." *A Writer's Diary* (New York: Harcourt, Brace and Company, 1953), pp. 326–
27. Woolf is referring to her *Roger Fry: A Biography* (1940). Just as that book is the
child of their relationship, so *End to Torment* is the child of H. D.'s relation with
Pound.

22. H. D., *Tribute to Freud*, pp. 36–37.

23. H. D., *Helen in Egypt*, p. 187.

24. H. D. says that Pound understood and identified with the dilemma of the woman artist: " . . . he wanted to make them, he did not want to break them, in a sense, he identified himself with them and their art." *End to Torment*, New Directions typescript, p. 52. But I am stating here that this is not so in all of Pound's guises.

25. H. D., *Helen in Egypt*, p. 170.

Pater-daughter

1. Paraphrased from Lawrence Lipking, *The Life of the Poet: Beginning and Ending Poetic Careers* (Chicago: University of Chicago Press, 1981), pp. 139 and 145.

2. William Carlos Williams, *Spring and All* (1923) in *Imaginations*, ed. Webster Schott (New York: New Directions, 1970), p. 151. Henceforth cited in text as S&A. *Paterson* (London: MacGibbon and Kee, 1964) will be cited in the text as *P*.

3. Ezra Pound, *The Pisan Cantos*, p. 108, in *The Cantos* (New York: New Directions, 1948). Henceforth cited as *PC* in text.

4. Teresa de Lauretis, *Alice Doesn't: Feminism, Semiotics, Cinema* (Bloomington: Indiana University Press, 1984) makes the vital distinction between historically situated female-gendered persons (women) and various summations of Woman in the history of ideas.

5. Represented as hallucinations, even when identifiable. By using clues of distinctive eye color, Wendy Stallard Flory has identified three pairs of "eyes" appearing at a climactic moment in *The Pisan Cantos*, with three women in Pound's life: his wife, Dorothy Pound; his other companion, Olga Rudge; and Bride Scratton. *Ezra Pound and The Cantos: A Record of Struggle* (New Haven: Yale University Press, 1980), p. 217.

6. "Political unconscious" is the highly useful and succinct phrase of Fredric Jameson, *The Political Unconscious: Narrative as a Socially Symbolic Act* (Ithaca: Cornell University Press, 1981).

7. *The New Freewoman*, December 15, 1913, p. 244. They asked her to consider "adopting another title which will mark the character of your paper as an organ of individualists of both sexes, and of the individualist principle in every department of life." Another account of this "shift from feminism to individualism" in Gillian Hanscombe and Virginia L. Smyers, *Writing for Their Lives: The Modernist Women 1910–1940* (Boston: Northeastern University Press, 1987), pp. 165–70.

8. *New Freewoman*, December 15, 1913, p. 244.

9. Written in 1915, published in 1917 in *Poetry* respectively, as follows. "Canto I," *Poetry* 10, 3 (June 1917): 113–121; "Canto II," *Poetry* 10, 4 (July 1917): 180–188; "Canto III," *Poetry* 10, 5 (August 1917): 248–254. This citation p. 113. They are reprinted in Ronald Bush, *The Genesis of Ezra Pound's Cantos* (Princeton: Princeton University Press, 1976), pp. 53–73.

10. Interview with Daniel Cory, "Ezra Pound," *Encounter* 30, 5 (May 1968): 38.

11. "Canto I," *Poetry* 10, 3 (June 1917), p. 117.

12. See Griselda Pollock and Deborah Cherry's brilliant reconstruction of the loss of Elizabeth Siddall as an artist by the pressure exerted ideologically by her position

as muse for Dante Gabriel Rossetti. Pollock, *Vision and Difference: Femininity, Feminism and the Histories of Art* (London: Routledge, 1988), pp. 91–114.

13. Georges Poulet, *Exploding Poetry, Baudelaire Rimbaud* (Chicago: University of Chicago Press, 1984) p. 49.

14. Williams, *The Autobiography of William Carlos Williams* (New York: New Directions, 1951), p. 229.

15. I have been citing from *The Waste Land Facsimile and Transcript of the Original Drafts*, ed. Valerie Eliot (New York: Harcourt Brace Jovanovich, 1971), pp. 23, 27. There is a much higher proportion of scurrilous parody in the original drafts than in the version which we have. Indeed, Vivien Eliot used Eliot's Fresca lines (rewritten—by him, or perhaps by her?) in one of her pseudonymous writings (from 1924); it functions there as a parody of *The Waste Land. Facsimile*, p. 127. Later, I use a line or two from "Sweeney Among the Nightingales," and modify "Burbank with a Baedeker: Bleistein with a Cigar."

16. *Facsimile*, p. 127. Eliot said this to Valerie Eliot. The "pure Ellen Kellond" phrase is his own. It is better known that Vivien Eliot contributed two lines to *The Waste Land*—both within Kellond's monologue, and possibly both based on her words: "If you don't like it, you can get on with it" and "What you get married for if you don't want children."

17. Sally Mitchell sent me this wording of a late Victorian ad for "female" pills; made of lead or mercury, they would poison (at least) the fetus and cause a miscarriage.

18. Margaret Homans, "Keats Reading Women, Women Reading Keats," typescript. "But one can know very little about, for example, Fanny Brawne's apparent dislike of [Keats'] dwelling on her Beauty, because Keats destroyed all her letters to him." (later) "[Fanny Brawne] has attempted a critique of his writing—indeed of the central tenet of his creed in his worship of Beauty—and he responds by declaring her reading invalid. And then by further effacing her critique by burning it."

19. Pausanius, on one of the five victories of Corinna over Pindar. "In my opinion, her victory may be attributed first to her dialect, because she did not sing like Pindar in Doric, but in a dialect which Aeolians would understand, and secondly because, if one may really judge from a portrait, she was at that time a remarkably good-looking woman." *Lyra Graecae*, ed. and trans., John Maxwell Edmonds, (London: W. Heinemann, 1922–17) 3: 9.

20. Aelian: "When the poet Pindar competed at Thebes he happened on ignorant judges, and was defeated five times by Corinna. By way of exposing their lack of good taste, he called Corinna a sow." *Lyra Graecae*, 3: 9. I hereby second Joanna Russ's scintillating study *How to Suppress Women's Writing* (Austin: University of Texas Press, 1983).

21. *Imaginations*, p. 169.

22. *The Collected Poems of William Carlos Williams*, volume I, ed. A. Walton Litz and Christopher MacGowan (New York: New Directions, 1986), p. 40. Poem dates from 1914.

23. Who is an actual person— Marcia Nardi—a minor poet and reviewer. Her career and her relationship with Williams have been traced in two excellent articles, both contemporaneous with the original writing of *"Pater*-daughter"': Theodora Rapp Graham, " 'Her Heigh Compleynte': The Cress Letters of William Carlos Williams' *Paterson*," in *Ezra Pound and William Carlos Williams: The University of Pennsylvania Conference Papers*, ed. Daniel Hoffman (Philadelphia: University of Pennsyl-

vania Press, 1983), pp. 169–93; Sandra M. Gilbert, "Purloined Letters: William Carlos Williams and 'Cress'," *William Carlos Williams Review*, 11, 2 (Fall 1985):5–15. Graham establishes that Williams subtly revised Nardi's letters to make her seem more stereotypically feminine than her original letters—more whining, more vascillating, more self-indulgent.

24. Here is a clue as to how, or whether. Note that the woman has no name, and note marginalities/femininities of her concerns. Since she is nameless, it is hard to gather data from this about her survival, but this is itself a datum. William Stafford remembers a set of powerful men from his (Iowa) graduate student days in the 1950's—Donald Justice, James B. Hall, Bill Belvin, Don Petersen, and Leonard Woolf. "And there was a girl whose talent gained Workshop respect—she confided to me during one time when the Romantics were getting their usual demolition, 'But I *like* Shelley.' No one else heard her, and she throve. Later, when Penn Warren visited, she was so excited that she spent her grad assistant pay for a dress to wear to class." *Writing the Australian Crawl: Views on the Writer's Vocation* (Ann Arbor: University of Michigan Press, 1978), p. 159.

25. Henry M. Sayre has proposed that the use of the letters question Williams' authority as an author, since he is the object of Cress's writing. I do not myself think his use creates that critical a rupture. *The Visual Text of William Carlos Williams* (Urbana: University of Illinois Press, 1983), p. 104.

26. Stephen Heath, "Difference," *Screen* 19, 3 (Autumn 1978): 73.

27. Loy, "Gertrude Stein," *The Last Lunar Baedeker* (Highlands: The Jargon Society, 1982), p. 26.

28. "Neutral" is a strongly sympathetic position about "equality" which nonetheless erases the possibility of the "sexing" or "gendering" of a woman's mind in the complicated ways a man can "sex" or "gender" his own.

29. Julia Kristeva, "The Novel as Polylogue," *Desire in Language: A Semiotic Approach to Literature and Art* (New York: Columbia University Press, 1980), p. 175.

30. Nancy Vickers, "Diana Described: Scattered Woman and Scattered Rhyme," in *Writing and Sexual Difference*, ed. Elizabeth Abel (Chicago: University of Chicago Press, 1982), p. 109.

31. *Imaginations*, p. 285.

32. Virginia Woolf, *A Writer's Diary* (New York: Harcourt, Brace, 1954), p. 324. C. R. means her Common Reader essays.

33. Margaret Homans, *Bearing the Word: Language and Female Experience in Nineteenth-Century Women's Writing* (Chicago: University of Chicago Press, 1986), p. 13.

34. Notley, *Dr. Williams' Heiresses* (Tuumba 28, Tuumba Press, 1980), p. [4].

35. James Breslin, *William Carlos Williams: An American Artist* (New York: Oxford University Press, 1970), p. 190.

36. A reading by Aaron Shurin, June 1989, Painted Bride Arts Center, Philadelphia: the evident ease and pleasure he had in constructing, as one of his "positions," himself as "little girl." I was struck by the asymmetries and historical meanings of gender once again. A (gay) male writer as little girl is not the parallel/opposite of a feminist writer as little boy. "Hetero-gyneity" of course not on the model of "heterosexuality" but "heterogeneity." "Poly-gyny" is a term unfortunately "taken" or colonized

as meaning the practice of having more than one wife or female mate at a time. But one could take it back.

37. *I Wanted to Write a Poem: The Autobiography of the Works of a Poet,* reported to Edith Heal (Boston: Beacon Press, 1958), pp. 94–95. He was speaking about reading the Coda to "Asphodel."

38. Semiotic and symbolic from Kristeva, "The Ethics of Linguistics" and "From One Identity to An Other," *Desire in Language: A Semiotic Approach to Literature and Art,* p. 28 and pp. 132–147. Also, Margaret Homans' proposal of the "bilinguality" of women: a possibility of drawing upon both "symbolic" and "literal or presymbolic language" which is not repressed at the time of female oedipalization. *Bearing the Word,* p. 13. Again, social polylinguality is the metaphor I crave, without gainsaying the power of this structure.

Sub Rrosa

1. The occasion for this essay was the centennial retrospective, *A Propos of Duchamp, 1887–1987,* the Philadelphia Museum of Art, Sept.–Dec. 1987. Useful commentary in Anne d'Harnoncourt and Kynaston McShine, eds., *Marcel Duchamp* (New York and Philadelphia: the Museum of Modern Art and the Philadelphia Museum of Art, 1973); Joseph Masheck, ed., *Marcel Duchamp in Perspective* (Englewood Cliffs, New Jersey: Prentice-Hall, 1975); Octavio Paz, *Marcel Duchamp: Appearance Stripped Bare* (New York: Viking Press, 1978).

2. In this piece, I am eliding the question how *Etant Donnés* . . . relates to other of Duchamp's artworks: his massive intextextuality with himself (so that doors, hinges, windows have told stories in his oeuvre as a whole; so that this piece evokes ready-mades), and the reasonable claim (by William Copley, in Masheck, ed., *Duchamp*) that this work summarizes motifs from his whole career.

3. Generally in art books one has seen only a bland reproduction of the door, or reproductions of nude studies for *Etant Donnés* . . . , which have a very different character. In 1987, the Philadelphia Museum published a replica of Duchamp's *Manual of Instructions for "Etant Donnés . . ."* which contains a small reproduction. Important early commentary in Anne d'Harnoncourt and Walter Hopps, " 'Etant Donnés . . .': Reflections on a New Work by Marcel Duchamp," *Bulletin of the Philadelphia Museum of Art,* 64, 299–300 (1969): 1–58.

4. "Retinal" is a term used with a piercing probity by Duchamp to characterize pre-cisely what he rejected, what he seceded from in art: painterly sensuousness consid-ered as the most valid expression in the history of art. Early on (1913 with the first diagrammatic *Chocolate Grinder*), "I began to think I could avoid all contact with traditional pictorial painting." ". . . Too great an importance is given to the retinal. Since Courbet, it's been believed that painting is addressed to the retina. That was everyone's error. The retinal shudder! Before, painting had other functions: it could be religious, philosophical, moral." In Pierre Cabanne, *Dialogues with Marcel Du-champ,* trans. Ron Padgett, (New York: Viking Press, 1971), pp. 37, 43. The inter-views were conducted in 1966. I have used *marked marker* to indicate the presence of a marked (hardly neutral) spectator. Of course, no viewer is neutral. But some pretend to be, and our culture is complicit with that practice. The formula "where I have put: **, read marked marker" is, of course, indebted to Duchamp's *The,* 1915, with its instruction "remplacer chaque [star] par le mot: *the.*" Certainly *marked marker* indicates a female spectator, but it could mean any spectator bringing his/

her various "markednesses" or social determinants in cultural acts up to the level of revelatory scrutiny.

5. Sub Rosa: in secret, privately, confidentially. Latin "under the rose," from the practice of hanging a rose over a meeting as a symbol of secrecy, from the legend that Cupid once gave Harpocrates, the god of silence, a rose to make him keep the secrets of Venus. In my title, the allusion is to Rrose Sélavy, Duchamp's "female" or "transvestite" pseudonym.

6. There is an important argument in feminist film criticism on the gaze as male, and then an appreciative critique and brilliant tracing of ways beyond binary reversals by the same author. See Laura Mulvey, "Visual Pleasure and Narrative Cinema," *Screen* 16, 3 (Autumn 1975); and Mulvey, "Changes: Thoughts on Myth, Narrative and Historical Experience," *History Workshop* 23 (Spring 1987).

7. Aside from desperate rhetorical flourishes about genre, one might calmly say that the work situates itself among: an anthropological or zoological diorama, a stage set, a shop window, a sculpture, a pornographic peep show, an essay.

8. Paz, *Duchamp* p. 96. My sense of the agendas of the female reader has been enhanced by Patrocinio P. Schweickart, "Reading Ourselves: Toward a Feminist Theory of Reading," in *Gender and Reading: Essays on Readers, Texts, and Contexts,* ed. Schweickart and Elizabeth Flynn (Baltimore: Johns Hopkins University Press, 1986). Duchamp, too, made a bland but rich statement that the spectator "brings the work in contact with the external world by deciphering and interpreting its inner qualifications and thus adds his [**] contribution to the creative act." "The Creative Act (1957)," in *Marcel Duchamp,* ed. Robert Lebel (New York: Grove Press, 1959), p. 78.

9. Fetterley's pioneering study is *The Resisting Reader: A Feminist Approach to American Fiction* (Bloomington: Indiana University Press, 1978), p. xx. Fetterley would "exorcise" the male mind "implanted" in her (p. xxii); I find it more pertinent now (armed with the power of an already existing feminist criticism) to explore the dialectics of reading from varieties of marked positions.

10. Mary Poovey: "All women may currently occupy the position 'woman,' for example, but they do not occupy it in the same way." "Feminism and Deconstruction," *Feminist Studies* 14, 1, (Spring 1988): 58–59. She also speaks of "multiple determinants."

11. "Signifyin(g)": a trickster mastery of ironic figures and contextual nuance. See Henry Louis Gates, Jr., *The Signifying Monkey: Theories of Afro-American Literary Criticism* (New York: Oxford University Press, 1988).

12. John Berger, *Ways of Seeing* (New York: Viking Press, 1972), p. 46. Mary Ann Caws has eloquently posed this issue in an essay which was a strong inspiration to this one: "To talk, again, about complications: insofar as it is a question of women's bodies, the female onlooker is—willing or not, partially or wholly—identified with the body under observation and under the rule of art." "Ladies Shot and Painted: Female Embodiment in Surrealist Art," in Susan Suleiman, ed., *The Female Body in Western Culture: Contemporary Perspectives* (Cambridge: Harvard University Press, 1986), p. 263.

13. Mary Ann Doane, "The 'Women's Film': Possession and Address," in *Revision: Essays in Feminist Film Criticism,* ed. Doane, Patricia Mellencamp, and Linda Williams, (Frederick, Md.: University Publications of America, 1984), p. 79.

14. A concept from Nancy K. Miller, *Subject to Change: Reading Feminist Writing* (New York: Columbia University Press, 1988), especially in "Arachnologies: The Woman, the Text, and the Critic."

15. Sandra Harding, *The Science Question in Feminism*, (Ithaca: Cornell University Press, 1986), p. 145.

16. As, d'Harnoncourt and Hopps, "Reflections," p. 21.

17. Duchamp, in Cabanne, *Dialogues*, p. 88.

18. John Golding, *Marcel Duchamp: The Bride Stripped Bare by her Bachelors, Even* (New York: Viking Press, 1972), p. 96.

19. Robert Pincus-Witten, "Theater of the Conceptual: Autobiography and Myth," in Masheck, ed., *Duchamp*, p. 164.

20. Paz, *Duchamp* pp. 158, 172.

21. Some people imply that this is a one-man erotic fantasy; in the smug words of Masheck, "a senile hobby, altogether private in its psychological functions" (Masheck, ed., *Duchamp*, p. 23).

22. This essay contains a thoughtful set of multiple responses to *Etant Donnés . . .*: disappointment, laughter, wincing, identification, subtle horror. Perhaps the most astonishing thing about the multiplicity is that (as he says on p. 108), he has never seen the piece *in situ*. When I wrote my original "Sub Rrosa," I had not yet read *Why Duchamp*. Gianfranco Baruchello & Henry Martin, *Why Duchamp: An Essay on Aesthetic Impact* (New Paltz: McPherson, 1985), p. 112.

23. This description is, naturally, not neutral; it is fully inflected with my position as a *marked marker*.

24. A reprise of Robert Pincus-Witten, in Masheck, ed., *Duchamp*, p. 164.

25. "The clitoris escapes reproductive framing. In legally defining woman as object of exchange, passage, or posession in terms of reproduction, it is not only the womb that is literally 'appropriated'; it is the clitoris as the signifier of the sexed subject that is effaced." Later in the essay, Spivak points to "varieties of the effacement of the clitoris" in legal and political-economic definitions of women; it seems appropriate to extend this to cultural representations. "French Feminism in an International Frame," *Yale French Studies* 62 (1981): 181. The essay is now collected in Spivak's *In Other Worlds* (New York: Methuen, 1987).

26. David Antin, "duchamp and language" (1972), in *Duchamp*, ed. d'Harnoncourt and McShine. "duchamps relation to art has been an endless series of stratagems stratagems involving complete systems that he puts into some degree of disarray," (p. 101). "it is not a visual space its a conceptual space in which vision is a prop (p. 107).

27. Cabanne, *Dialogues*, p. 38.

28. It may be relevant to note that the triplex of allusions (vulval, anal, clitoral) is unique to this piece. None of the three studies in the Philadelphia exhibition has any clitoral indication.

29. Naomi Schor wittily proposes that "the clitoris is coextensive with the detail. The clitoral school of feminist criticism might then be identified by its practice of a hermeneutics focused on the detail, which is to say on those details of the female anatomy which have been generally ignored by male critics and which significantly influence our reading of the texts in which they appear." "Female Paranoia: The Case for Psychoanalytic Feminist Criticism," *Yale French Studies* 62 (1981): 216.

Now collected in *Reading in Detail* (New York: Methuen, 1987). My sense of the ** is that any kind of female reading will reopen what is seen, what is foregrounded, what priorities are assessed, and what is thought.

Language Acquisition

1. H. D., *HERmione* (1927; New York: New Directions, 1981), p. 224. Given the title *Her* by H. D., which shall be used here. Henceforth *HER* in the text.

2. Julia Kristeva, "Place Names," in *Desire in Language: A Semiotic Approach to Literature and Art* (New York: Columbia University Press, 1980), p. 291.

3. "It is frequently noted in observations on the linguistic development of the child that intonation or sentence melody is one of the earliest linguistic features acquired by a child." This necessitates "a discussion of prosody which follows. Under prosody, we include intonation, pauses and stress." Ruth Hirsch Weir, *Language in the Crib* (The Hague: Mouton, 1962), p. 28.

4. Kristeva, "From One Identity to An Other," in *Desire in Language*, pp. 133–34.

5. H. D., *Tribute to Freud* (containing "Writing on the Wall" and "Advent") (1956; Boston: David R. Godine, 1974, p. 66. Henceforth *TTF* in the text.

6. Kristeva, *About Chinese Women*, trans. Anita Barrows (New York: Urizen Books, 1977), pp. 29–30.

7. This "relational definition" emphasizes that Kristeva offers "a theory of marginality, subversion, and dissidence" which intersects with notions of the female, seen "in terms of *positionality* rather than of essences." Toril Moi, *Sexual/Textual Politics: Feminist Literary Theory* (London: Methuen, 1985), pp. 166, 164, 166.

8. In "Stabat Mater" (1977) Kristeva offers, by parallel intertexts, each marginal, each central, a way of structurally representing the relationship of analysis and speculation. Recently translated in *Poetics Today*, 6, 1–2 (1985):133–52.

9. Kristeva, *Revolution in Poetic Language*, trans. Margaret Waller (New York: Columbia University Press, 1984), p. 50.

10. Kristeva, "From 'Oscillation du "pouvoir" au "refus," ' " *New French Feminisms*, ed. Elaine Marks and Isabelle de Courtivron (Amherst: University of Massachusetts Press, 1980), p. 167.

11. Kristeva, *New French Feminisms*, p. 166.

12. Ibid.

13. H. D., Letter to May Sarton, May 6 [1941]. Henry W. and Albert A. Berg Collection, New York Public Library, Astor, Lenox, and Tilden foundations. A look at the index to *Virginia Woolf's Reading Notebooks* also tells us what we could suspect: Woolf did not read H. D. (Brenda R. Silver, *Virginia Woolf's Reading Notebooks* [Princeton: Princeton University Press, 1983]). And the only "Aldington" who appears quite briefly in Woolf's world in the early 1920s is Richard. Interestingly, Aldington's brief appearance leads Woolf to some dour comments about "young men" who make their way in the world and to an annunciation of her feminist project. "All young men do it. No young women; or in women it is trounced; in men forgiven. It's these reflections I want to enmesh, in writing; or these are among them." (Entry of December 21, 1924), *The Diary of Virginia Woolf, Volume II, 1920–1924*, ed. Anne Olivier Bell and Andrew McNeillie (New York: Harcourt Brace Jovanovich, 1978), p. 326.

186   Notes

14. For a brief exploration of the essay's anti-Cartesian poetics of critique, see DuPlessis, *H. D.: The Career of That Struggle* (Bloomington: Indiana University Press, 1986), pp. 84–86.

15. Virginia Woolf, *Moments of Being: Unpublished Autobiographical Writings*, ed. Jean Schulkind (Sussex: University Press, 1976), p. 65.

16. Woolf, *To the Lighthouse* (1927; London: Hogarth Press, 1967), p. 83. Henceforth *TTL*, in text.

17. H. D., *The Gift*, abridged by Griselda Ohanessian (New York: New Directions, 1982), p. 83.

18. H. D., *Palimpsest* (1926; Carbondale: Southern Illinois University Press, 1968), p. 211.

19. Woolf, *Moments of Being*, p. 66.

20. Kristeva, "From One Identity to An Other," *Desire in Language*, p. 136. Theoretically, if one has access to the presymbolic mother, this "incest" would be true for both male writers and female writers. Kristeva's examples again come exclusively from male writers: de Sade, Artaud, Joyce, Céline. So again gender questions are aroused: since when a woman writes, a person constituted and represented as an "exchange object" who is, at the same time, the potential object of the presymbolic longings of others and who is constituted to be that, must "appropriate to itself this archaic, instinctual, maternal territory."

21. Alan H. Gardiner, *Egyptian Grammar: Being an Introduction to the Study of Hiero-glyphs* (Oxford: Clarendon Press, 1927), p. 8.

22. As reported in Quentin Bell, *Virginia Woolf: A Biography* (London: Hogarth Press, 1972), 2:129.

23. Adalaide Morris, "The Concept of Projection: H. D.'s Visionary Powers," *Contemporary Literature* 25, 4 (1984):411–36, also discusses the "Writing on the Wall" in conjunction with other, repeated events of vision and projection which defined H. D.'s work.

24. For an elaboration of this moment in the analysis see DuPlessis and Susan Stanford Friedman, " 'Woman is Perfect': H. D.'s Debate with Freud," *Feminist Studies* 7, 3 (Fall 1981):417–30.

25. H. D., *Compassionate Friendship* (1955), unpublished typescript, Collection of American Literature, Beinecke Rare Book and Manuscript Library, Yale University, p. 62.

26. See the excellent work by Adalaide Morris, analyzing the gift-exchange as a primary structure of H. D.'s psychic life, with readings in biography, in history of ideas, in the religious culture from which H. D. sprung. "A Relay of Power and of Peace: H. D. and the Spirit of the Gift," *Contemporary Literature* 27, 4 (1986):493–524.

27. In point of fact, the brilliance of the analysis leaves a shiver, as well as the brilliance of the rendering. The confrontation " 'I am an old man—*you do not think it worth your while to love me*' " is followed by a blankness "I simply felt nothing at all. I said nothing" (*TTF*, p. 16). Compare Woolf, *Moments of Being*: "I remember very clearly how even as I was taken to the bedside I noticed that one nurse was sobbing, and a desire to laugh came over me, and I said to myself as I have often done at moments of crisis since, 'I feel nothing whatever.' Then I stooped and kissed my mother's face. It was still warm. She [had] only died a moment before. Then we went upstairs into the day nursery" (p. 92). H. D. traces out her resistance ("but why

take up time going into all that, anyway?" TTF, p. 17) precisely around the issue of an association with a warm stove in Freud's room, reminding her of "a book that my mother had liked." "I could not remember a single incident of the book and would not take the time to go through all the intricacies of explaining to the Professor . . . ," etc. The release, the success of the analysis, suggests part of the poetics of the essay: exactly to "take up time going into all that." The poetics of continuance. Of association. Of flooding text. (The text floods into the "notes.") H. D.'s mother had died in 1927; *HER* took the first measure; her grief, it seems clear, repressed, at her mother's death is obliquely fixed, in *Tribute to Freud*, as one of the reasons for seeking this analysis.

28. Alice Walker. It is appropriate that I cannot locate this statement.

29. Kristeva, "Motherhood According to Giovanni Bellini," in *Desire in Language*, p. 237.

30. I have interpreted all this as if the main relationship explored (by one light) were not H. D.-Freud but rather H. D.- writing (her writing, her "writing on the wall," and so on). For this to have had any possibility of being written depends upon the major elucidation by Susan Friedman of the feminist and cultural meanings of the H. D.-Freud encounter, a work presupposed in the study made here. See *Psyche Reborn: The Emergence of H. D.* (Bloomington: Indiana University Press, 1981).

31. This idea of the palimpsest of *Tribute to Freud* and of the plenitude of the sign was written without consulting Deborah Kelly Kloepfer's essay "Fishing the Murex Up: Sense and Resonance in H. D.'s *Palimpsest*," but it should probably not be read without an acknowledgement to that work. *Contemporary Literature* 27, 4 (1986):533–73.

32. Gertrude Stein on repetition and insistence occurs for a few pages of "Portraits and Repetition," in *Lectures in America* (1935; Boston: Beacon Press, 1985, pp. 166–69.

While These Letters Were A-reading

1. William Carlos Williams, *Spring and All* (1923) in *Imaginations* (New York: New Directions, 1970), p. 120. Henceforth cited as *I*.

2. Beverly Dahlen, *A Reading 1–7* (San Francisco: Momo's Press, 1985). Henceforth cited as *R*.

3. "There is no drama, no situation, no set scene. Nothing happens. It is just life going on and on. It is Miriam Henderson's stream of consciousness going on and on." May Sinclair, "The Novels of Dorothy Richardson," *The Egoist* 5 (April 1918):57–58.

4. Beverly Dahlen, "Forbidden Knowledge" (1982) *Poetics Journal* 4 (May 1984), special Women & Language issue, p. 17. Hereafter cited in the text.

5. Phrases with the word "it" in them recur throughout *A Reading*; see p. 51, for example.

6. Sigmund Freud, "Analysis Terminable and Interminable," in *The Standard Edition of the Complete Psychological Works of Sigmund Freud*, trans. James Strachey, 23(1937–1939), (London: The Hogarth Press and the Institute of Psycho-Analysis, 1964): 220.

7. M. M. Bakhtin, *The Dialogic Imagination*, trans. Caryl Emerson and Michael Holquist (Austin: University of Texas Press, 1981), pp. 293, 294. Hereafter cited in the text.

8. The Kriteva to which Dahlen alludes is *Desire in Language.*

9. Robert Duncan, "Interview" conducted by Michael André Bernstein and Burton Hatlen, *Sagetrieb* 4, 2–3 (Fall and Winter (1985):120. Hereafter cited in the text.

10. George Oppen, *The Collected Poems of George Oppen* (New York: New Directions, 1975), p. 213.

11. Beverly Dahlen, "Notes from a Letter, September 1, 1985," *Jimmy and Lucy's House of "K,"* 5 (November 1985):26–27.

Whowe

1. Susan Howe's books include *Pythagorean Silence* [PS in the text, Part numbers] (New York: Montemora Foundation, 1982), *The Defenestration of Prague [DOP]* (New York: Kulchur, 1983; including *The Liberties,* first published in 1980), the earlier *Secret History of the Dividing Line [SHDL]* (New York: Telephone, 1979), and *Cabbage Gardens [CG]* (Chicago: Fathom Press, 1979). *The Europe of Trusts* (expected 1990, from Sun & Moon Press) is a collection of Howe's work consisting of *The Liberties, Pythagorean Silence,* and *The Defenestration of Prague.* Howe has also written *Articulation of Sound Forms in Time [ASFT]* (Windsor, Vt.: Awede, 1987). Other of Howe's works to be discussed or mentioned are: "The Captivity and Restoration of Mrs. Mary Rowlandson," *Temblor* 2 (1985):113–21; "Women and Their Effect in the Distance," *Ironwood* 28 (Fall 1986):58–91; *My Emily Dickinson [MED]* (Berkeley: North Atlantic Books, 1985); "Thorow," *Temblor* 6 (1987):3–21.

2. See Woolf's *Common Reader* in Howe's *Cabbage Gardens* with its collage from Sam Johnson to Beatrix Potter.

3. *"The Difficulties* Interview," conducted between Susan Howe and Tom Beckett, *The Difficulties* 3, 2 (1989), the Susan Howe Issue, p. 18.

4. The key phrase is cited from "Captivity and Restoration," p. 113. The summary of the ode is partially indebted to Mary Jacobus, "Apostrophe and Lyric Voice in *The Prelude,"* in *Lyric Poetry— Beyond New Criticism,* ed. Chaviva Hošek and Patricia Parker (Ithaca: Cornell University Press, 1985); Paul Fry, *The Poet's Calling in the English Ode* (New Haven: Yale University Press, 1980); and Jonathan Culler, *The Pursuit of Signs: Semiotics, Literature, Deconstruction* (Ithaca: Cornell University Press, 1981).

5. "Speaking with Susan Howe," interview conducted by Janet Ruth Falon (December 1986), *The Difficulties* 3, 2 (1989): 42.

6. From Howe's "Thorow": "Agreseror/ / Bearer law my fathers/ / Revealing traces/ Regulating traces," p. 6.

7. Gertrude Stein, "Forensics" (1928?/1931?) in *How to Write* (1931; New York: Dover Publications, 1975). Those two citations appear on pp. 385 and 386. Also of interest: "Forensics are a plan by which they will never pardon. They will call butter yellow. Which it is. He is. They will call birds attractive. Which they are. They are. They will also oblige girls to be women that is a round is a kind of hovering for instance" (p. 385). The overt social comment about gender may have a sexual discourse appended, since the word *butter* as used in *Tender Buttons* is a metaphor for transudate; indeed the title may involve the metonymic exchange button/butter, among other allusions and connections.

8. Compare the following: "I agreed to everything. This was not my business. And yet I am not puzzled. Because I was obedient. Now think of forensics" (p. 386).

9. Of course this spirited position is one kind of feminist attitude; look at Adrienne Rich's eulogy for Anne Sexton which grimly says there shall be no more suicides, as if Rich—and this too is typical and interesting—could make this occur by sheer force of will.

10. Howe, "Statement for the New Poetics Colloquium, Vancouver, 1985," *Jimmy and Lucy's House of 'K'*; 5 (November 1985):17.

11. Ibid. p. 15.

12. Falon interview, "Speaking with Howe," p. 35.

13. Howe, "Women and Their Effect in the Distance," an essay on Dickinson subsequent to *My Emily Dickinson*, in *Ironwood* 28 (Fall 1986):58–91. (This issue also has an essay by Dahlen on Dickinson.) In this essay, Howe examines the facsimile of Dickinson's fascicles and presents her conclusion: that Dickinson continues to be mis-edited by having her line breaks regularized and normalized visually to traditional common meter when Dickinson's visual text and page presentation of her poems in holograph are much more experimental, hesitant, anti-authoritarian and work across, while alluding to, the quatrain stanza.

14. For an elaboration of these points, see Toril Moi, *Sexual/Textual Politics*, (New York: Methuen, 1985). Despite the "feminine" being open to persons of both genders— still, there are persons who are *women. Female*, mostly. Their use of this "feminine" is bound to be inflected with their social and political experience of gender.

15. Beverly Dahlen "[Response to Rasula]," *HOW(ever)* 1, 4 (May 1984):14. The "she" is not Howe but contains a generalized portrait of the struggle of the female cultural worker.

16. The "whowe" of the title occurs in the "White Foolscap" section of *The Liberties*, *DOP*, p. 88.

Otherhow

1. Nancy Vickers, "Diana Described: Scattered Women and Scattered Rhyme," in *Writing and Sexual Difference*, ed. Elizabeth Abel (Chicago: University of Chicago Press, 1982).

2. Marjorie Perloff, *The Futurist Moment: Avant-Garde, Avant Guerre, and the Language of Rupture* (Chicago: University of Chicago Press, 1986), p. 125, n. 258.

3. Philippe Sollers, "The Novel and the Experience of Limits," in *Surfiction: Fiction Now and Tomorrow*, ed. Raymond Federman (Chicago: Swallow Press, 1981), p. 61.

4. Annette Kolodny (citing Nelly Furman), "Dancing Through the Minefield: Some Observations on the Theory, Practice, and Politics of a Feminist Literary Criticism," in *The New Feminist Criticism: Essays on Women, Literature and Theory*, ed. Elaine Showalter (New York: Pantheon Books, 1985), p. 148.

5. Cora Kaplan, *Sea Changes: Culture and Feminism* (London: Verso, 1986), p. 79.

6. Valentin Volosinov / M. Bakhtin, *Marxism and the Philosophy of Language* (1930), (New York: Seminar Press, 1973), p. 85.

7. Mikhail Bakhtin, *The Dialogic Imagination* (Austin: University of Texas Press, 1981), p. 294.

8. Ibid., p. 293.

9. Virginia Woolf, *A Room of One's Own* (1929; New York: Harcourt, Brace and World, 1957), p. 93.

10. Two long poems, "Medusa" and "Eurydice," appear in DuPlessis, *Wells* (New York: Montemora Foundation, 1980).

11. "Crowbar," and "Writing"—two long poems—appear in DuPlessis, *Tabula Rosa* (Elmwood, Conn.: Potes & Poets Press, 1987). The Emily Dickinson poem "Oil" appears in *Wells* and is repeated in *Tabula Rosa*. "The 'History of Poetry' " is one of two sections of that second book.

12. An echo of Laura Mulvey's phrase "bearer of meaning, not maker of meaning." "Visual Pleasure and Narrative Cinema," *Screen* 16, 3 (Autumn 1975):7.

13. Craig Owens, "The Allegorical Impulse: Toward a Theory of Postmodernism," *October* 12 (Spring 1980):69.

14. Respectively in *Three Guineas*, in "Forensics," *How to Write*, and in *Paterson*.

15. Gayatri Spivak, "Explanation and Culture: Marginalia," *Humanities in Society* 2, 3 (Summer 1979):206.

16. Ideas from Adorno in Peter Bürger, *Theory of the Avant-Garde* (Minneapolis: University of Minnesota Press, 1984), pp. 79–82.

17. Marianne DeKoven has commented that feminist critics should "acknowledge the antipatriarchal potential of form in historical, male-signed avant-garde writing, but at the same time acknowledge the self-canceling counter-move of that writing toward male supremacism and misogyny." "Male Signature, Female Aesthetic," in *Breaking the Sequence: Women's Experimental Fiction*, ed. Ellen Friedman and Miriam Fuchs (Princeton: Princeton University Press, 1989), p. 78.

18. A question now focused by Nancy Miller, "Changing the Subject": "I would now say that we must think carefully about the reading effects that derive from a poetics of transparence—writing directly from one's own experience, especially when doubled by an ethics of wholeness—joining the fragments." *Subject to Change: Reading Feminist Writing* (New York: Columbia University Press, 1988), p. 111. To which one can add—considerations that language is transparent, a container of thoughts, rather than a malleable medium or praxis.

19. In *Landlocked* (1958; New York: New American Library, 1970), p. 269. Martha Quest prepares a typescript with doubled and palimpsested pages.

20. Huston Baker, *Blues, Ideology, and Afro-American Literature* (Chicago: University of Chicago Press, 1984), p. 202 (the conclusion):

    Fixity is a function of power. Those who maintain place, who decide what takes place and dictate what has taken place, are power brokers of the traditional. The "placeless," by contrast, are translators of the nontraditional. . . . Their appropriate sign is a crossing sign at the junction.

    The crossing sign is the antithesis of a place marker. It signifies, always, change, motion, transience, process. To adept adherents of wandering, a crossing sign is equivalent to a challenge thrown out in brash, sassy tones by a locomotive blowing by: "Do what you can," it demands. "Do what you can— right here— on this placeless-place, this spotless-spot. . . .

    When I read that, it seemed completely apposite to "Otherhow."

21. I am generally indebted to the ethnographer James Clifford.

22. Nathaniel Mackey, "Review of Brathwaite's *Sun Poem,*" *Sulfur* 11 (1984):200–205. "Caliban" as a metaphor still draws upon a representation of the "male." However.

23. Teresa de Lauretis, *Alice Doesn't: Feminism, Semiotics, Cinema* (Bloomington: Indiana University Press, 1984), p. 7.

The Pink Guitar

1. "Orientalized" with reference to Edward Said, *Orientalism* (New York: Pantheon Books, 1978). The overlayering of representations and ideologies of the "Oriental" onto the "female" produces intense motifs of otherness from a "Western" perspective: "threatening excess," "insinuating danger," "unlimited sensuality," and a degenerate seductiveness. Citations from Said, pp. 56–57, 207. Linda Nochlin discusses aspects of Western ideologies in nineteenth-century "Orientalized" art, including the Orient's function as a "fantasy space" for the ideological projection of absolute erotic possession, in "The Imaginary Orient," *Art in America* 71 (May 1983):118–31, 186–91.

2. Or perhaps "a.u.a."—also unknown as. Shari Benstock, in *Women of the Left Bank, Paris, 1900–1940,* makes this identification in her Janet Flanner chapter (Austin: University of Texas Press, 1986), p. 109. She is used as a marker in a poem about the sexual fulfillments possible—or impossible—at home; see Williams, poem IX in *Spring and All* (1923).

3. I do not mean by my trope of "pink" to efface the brown that is usually the color of guitars, and thus the brown skin that is the marker of other cultural experiences.

4. Kristeva, *About Chinese Women,* trans. Anita Barrows (New York: Urizen Press, 1977), p. 38.

5. Cora Kaplan in *Sea Changes: Culture and Feminism* (London: Verso, 1986), pp. 79–80.

6. It is useful to think of the psycho-social situations in being female as setting up a specific possibility of a writing practice. Thus Luce Irigaray connects "self-affection" (women's bodies auto-erotic *in situ*) with the practice of openness and plurality in writing, or the rejection of analytic strategies of reversal which repeat hierarchies as generating textual tactics of border crossing, disruption, and rupture. These analyses in *This Sex Which Is Not One,* trans. Catherine Porter with Carolyn Burke (Ithaca: Cornell University Press, 1985), pp. 68, 78, 122, 222. These motifs of "disruptive excess" (p. 78) will answer all theories which conceptualize the feminine as lack or deficiency (a task also undertaken by Cixous). But it is also clear that tactics of a non-hegemonic practice of writing (as I argued in "Etruscans") may be strategically selected, for a variety of situational reasons, by any who find that the only plausible praxis within hegemony is a writing as critique especially of the deepest mechanisms of meaning. Thus the rupture of language, syntax, sequence, order, structures, and genres in what has been called avant-garde writing is absolutely parallel and interlocked with such feminist practices as are effervescently called forth by Irigaray in a manifesto-like passage in *Speculum of the Other Woman,* trans. Gillian C. Gill (Ithaca: Cornell University Press, 1985), p. 142. What then distinguishes a feminist practice of writing from any vangarde use is the infusion of these rhetorical practices with urgent and continuous confrontations with the political and representational oppression of wome/an, with an eye to enacting their end. So there is telos after all.

7. Robert Glück, *Jack the Modernist*, (New York: Gay Presses of New York, 1985). As cited by Aaron Shurin in a talk called "Narrativity," Painted Bride Arts Center, Philadelphia.

8. Slightly selected and modified list of the commercial sequences, taken from Louise Spence, "Life's Little Problems . . . and Pleasures," *Quarterly Review of Film Studies* (Fall 1984): 307–8; her appendix catalogued an episode of "The Young and the Restless" in November 1981.

9. Echoes of Walter Benjamin on epic theater and Jane Gallop on Lacan.

10. It is not women's poetry only which is gendered. Men's poetry, what is called "poetry," is saturated with gender, can hardly make a move, make an image, build a poem, make a climzx, without a she. Even the most innovative and experimental works cannot move forward, past a certain point in their unrolling, cannot write themselves without a traditional positioning of women. We are just beginning to be able to see male writing as, despite its claims, partial, marked, not gender neutral, not universal. The intellectual implications are terrific. As Elaine Showalter remarks: "The defamiliarization, or problematization, of masculinity is one of the most important tasks facing feminist criticism in the next decade. It is still a tacit assumption in literary studies that gender is significant for one sex only, indeed, that it is a kind of sophisticated, postfeminist code word for *women*. While *femininity* is now accepted as a construct with relevance to literary analysis, *masculinity* is treated as natural, transparent, and unproblematic. . . . From the perspective of a poststructuralist feminist critique, such blindness and lack of self-reflection is itself a sign of phallocentrism." "The Other Bostonians: Gender and Literary Study," *The Yale Journal of Criticism* 1, 2 (Spring 1988):182.

11. Peter Wollen/ Laura Mulvey, *"Penthesilea, Queen of the Amazons:* Interview," *Screen* 15, 3 (Autumn 1974), p. 128.

12. Laurent Mailhot, "The Writing of the Essay," a study of the essay form as used by Québécois writers, *Yale French Studies* 65, The Language of Difference: Writing in QUEBEC(ois) (1983):76.

13. This said with strong reference to Nancy Miller, "Arachnologies: The Woman, the Text, and the Critic," *Subject to Change: Reading Feminist Writing* (New York: Columbia University Press, 1988). Also in an intersection with Elizabeth Meese's brilliant and emboldening observations on "differance" and "deconstruction" in their uses for feminist theory: "We will need to speak of * * * in place of 'woman'— that something the meaning or nonmeaning of which our phallocentric structure will not allow us to say. And this unimaginable, imaginary something, this understanding of * * *, this «feminism(s)»—the effects of freedom/utopia itself—are not so different from what appears to be deconstruction's utopic project as it asserts its motion toward the unthinkable, unknowable point(s) beyond the system it deconstructs." *Crossing the Double-Cross: The Practice of Feminist Criticism* (Durham: University of North Carolina Press, 1986), p. 87.

14. In *In These Times* (Summer 1989).

15. These ideas then were focused by the work of Raymond Williams, especially *Marxism and Literature* (Oxford: Oxford University Press, 1977).

16. The final line, from Tillie Olson's *Yonnondio;* the writing was made by me in 1982, reflecting the psychological struggles of the mid- to late-70s, myself wary and struggling with a writing mode that was being rejected by others, whose voices appear here.

17.   Really a triple homage to critics N. Miller, Marcus, and Friedman here. Nancy Miller in her devastating unraveling of Barthes and J. Hillis Miller's denial of agency and authorship in her "Archnologies: which resists the erasure of "gendered subjectivity" as author. Jane Marcus who proposes the sororal relation of Philomel and Procne as a model for empathetic reading of female texts. In response I have political questions about casting only the Procne figure, of these two, as "the voice which demands justice"; "Marcus," Still Practice, A/Wrested Alphabet: Toward a Feminist Aesthetic," in *Feminist Issues in Literary Scholarship*, ed. Shari Benstock, (Bloomington: Indiana University Press, 1987). And Susan Stanford Friedman, "The Return of the Repressed in Women's Narratives," *The Journal of Narrative Technique* 19, 1 (Winter 1989): 141–56, proposes "Penelope's web"—a theory about the meaning of drafts and serial texts which offers an approach to the "textual unconscious," to repressed materials, to censorship, and thereby "integrates considerations of the author, the text, and history" (p. 156).

18.   "A counter-practice of interference"—counter to the studied holding apart of politics and the humanities/arts. Defined by Edward Said as at least including a breaking of academic field boundaries; an insistence on the political meaning of all acts and choices within the humanities; the denial of the "subjective and powerless" role of literature; a use of representation to "tell other stories than the official sequential or ideological ones produced by institutions of power." The praxis of interference is, as Hal Foster pinpoints, more than a subversive gesture; it is a "practice of resistance." Edward Said, "Opponents, Audiences, Constituencies and Community," in *The Anti-Aesthetic: Essays on Postmodern Culture*, ed. Hal Foster (Port Townsend, Wash.: Bay Press, 1983). Citations are on pp. xiv, 155, 157, xv–vi.

19.   James Hillman about Eshleman, *Temblor* 6 (1987):100.

20.   Said, citing Bachelard, using Tzara, *Beginnings: Intention and Method* (New York: Basic Books, 1975), p. 40.

21.   Brecht, somewhere.

22.   I am echoing Meaghan Morris here, *The Pirate's Fiancée: Feminism, Reading, Postmodernism* (London: Verso, 1988), e.g. pp. 7, 111–12; but I might as well be echoing Charles Bernstein, *Content's Dream: Essays 1973–84* (Los Angeles: Sun & Moon Press, 1986); or Gail Scott, *Spaces Like Stairs: Essays* (Toronto: Women's Press, 1989). Scott: "the job of imagining what I now think of as a 'writing subject' in-the-feminine. Not the 'self' as a (feminist or otherwise) predetermined figure, but a complex tissue of texts, experience, evolving in the very act of writing" (p. 11). Or Kathleen Fraser, *Each Next: Narratives* (Berkeley: The Figures, 1980): "Walking up to a new edge, I discovered in myself an old mute. But I stayed, allowing my curiosity to teethe on the silence. A hope for mutation? A belief in mutability" (p. 54).

Index

"(ambiguously) nonhegemonic," 7, 14, 15
African-Americans, representations of, 44, 63
Ascher, Carol, 12–13
Bakhtin, Mikhail, 117–118, 128, 143–44, 164
Brathwaite, Edward Kamau, 155

Césaire, Aimé, 4
Cixous, Hélène, 164
"Cress" (Marcia Nardi), 55–59

Dahlen, Beverly, 109, 110–122 passim, 163
Dickinson, Emily, 1, 125, 127, 130–131, 134, 135, 148
doubled position (of women), 6–8, 15, 141, 150–151
Duchamp, Marcel, 68–82 passim, 149, 166
Duncan, Robert, 118

essay mode, 6, 13, 59, 61, 66–67, 90, 102, 147, 154, 159–160, 162–164, 166–167, 169, 173
Eliot, T. S., 17, 39, 49–51, 53, 141, 152, 155
Etruscans, 1, 2, 3, 4, 7

"female aesthetic," 1, 3, 5, 8, 10, 11, 12, 13; objections to, 11; non-exclusivity of, 14
"feminine," 54, 121, 165, 171–172. See also "Woman," idea of
feminist cultural projects, 52, 59–61, 64, 67, 74, 81–82, 107, 109, 118, 125, 127–130, 133, 165. See also poetics of critique; Women writers, strategies of
Freud, Sigmund, 3–4, 32, 37, 38, 91, 95, 98–99, 102–103, 104, 106–107, 115, 116–117

gender and lyric poetry, 140, 147, 149–151

genitalia (female), representation of, 70, 73, 76, 77–81
Griffin, Susan, 5, 17

H.D., 17, 20–40 passim, 42, 43, 83–109 passim, 111, 115, 119–120, 126, 152, 167
hegemony, cultural, 3, 14, 24, 28, 52, 140, 142, 150. See also Women writers, problematic of
heterosexuality, cultural implications of, 20–23, 33, 39, 48–49, 62
Heydt, Erich, 31, 37
Holsteins, 3, 8, 161–162
homosexuality, representations of, 49, 62
hope, 19, 167, 173, 191
Howe, Susan, 123–139 passim
hunger, 7, 12, 46

Ingres, 157–158
innovative stylistics, 52–53, 59–61, 131–132, 138, 142, 144, 155
insomnia, 29, 159
Irigaray, Luce, 163–164

Jaffer, Frances, 3, 8–9
Joyce, James, 88

Keats, John, 24
Kellond, Ellen, 50–51
Komarovsky, Mirra, 13
Kristeva, Julia, 7, 59, 64, 83, 84–88, 93, 99, 106, 118, 135, 158

language acquisition, 90, 99, 105
Lennox, Sara, 17–19
Lessing, Doris, 2, 5, 10, 17, 33, 154
Loy, Mina, 48, 58

McNamara, Jo Ann, 14–15
"marked marker." See spectator, female

195

maternal imagery, 90–93, 106, 115
men writers, muse of, 42–44, 57
men writers, strategies of, 54–55, 62, 87.
    See also Eliot, T.S.; Pound, Ezra; Wil-
    liams, William Carlos
metonymy, 112–114
modernism, 16–17, 39, 42–44, 46, 62, 81,
    115, 147, 152–153
Mulvey, Laura, 36, 161
myths: Medusa 146–147

Négritude, 16
New Freewoman, 44–46
Nin, Anais, 1, 5, 10
Notley, Alice, 61

ode, 126–127
Oppen, George, 38, 118, 126

"palimpsest," 86, 111, 118
"personal life," 1, 4, 41, 47, 52, 53–54, 60,
    67, 83–84, 90, 99–100, 103–104, 115,
    156, 162, 172
"pink guitar," 61, 158, 160
poetics of critique, 16, 81, 121–122, 123,
    132, 133–135, 142, 144–145, 149, 152,
    167. See also Women writers, strategies
    of
"polygyny," 65, 74, 121, 149, 152, 156, 168,
    181–182
post-colonial strategies, 4, 154
postmodernism, 17, 153
Pound, Ezra, 9, 17, 22–23, 26–27, 31, 32–
    34, 39, 42–44, 46–47, 118, 120

rape, 49, 62–66, 152
Ray, Man, 157
reading and (as) writing, 5–6, 47, 86, 88, 94,
    97, 113–114, 115–116, 121–122, 156,
    164, 173
Richardson, Dorothy, 6, 12, 95, 112

Roberts, Lou, 13–14
Rodin, Auguste, 29–30, 35 (illus.), 39–40
"romantic thralldom," 20, 31

Schor, Mira, 13
sexual difference (male/female polarized),
    6, 59
social determinants, 15, 61, 72, 121
spectator, female, 69, 71–72, 73–75, 182–
    183
Stein, Gertrude, 17, 58, 80, 88, 109, 122,
    123, 133, 152
Stevens, Wallace, 17, 53, 125, 160
subject positions (female). See "polygyny"

universities, women and, 1, 2, 14–15

Williams, William Carlos, 9, 41–42, 48, 49,
    54–60, 61–64, 65–66, 110–111, 112, 152
Wittig, Monique, 8
"Woman," idea of, 42, 48, 57, 76, 80, 88
women, erasure of, 42–43, 52, 127, 129, 132
women, representation of, 4–5, 41–43, 44,
    48, 50, 74–77, 81, 116, 121, 124, 158
women writers, muse of, 21, 23, 25, 32 (dia-
    gram), 34, 36–37
woman writers, problematic of, 4–5, 12, 22,
    27–30, 52, 57–58, 64, 127, 136–137, 141,
    143, 161, 164
women writers, strategies of, 5–11, 24–27,
    29, 36, 39–40, 48, 55, 57, 60–61, 66, 96,
    100–101, 109, 116–117, 119–120, 122,
    125, 128–130, 132–133, 145–148, 153,
    158–159, 172–173
"writing from the body," 1, 2–3, 8–9, 170–
    171
Woolf, Virginia, 1, 4, 5, 7, 9, 11, 12, 15, 17,
    33, 37, 57, 60, 88–90, 91, 93–94, 98, 125,
    134–135, 146, 152, 154

Yeats, W. B., 17, 39, 42, 152